*Wounds of Returning*

# Wounds *of* Returning

RACE, MEMORY, *and* PROPERTY
*on the* POSTSLAVERY PLANTATION

Jessica Adams

The University of
North Carolina Press
Chapel Hill

Designed by Michelle Coppedge
Set in Bulmer types by Keystone Typesetting, Inc.
Manufactured in the United States of America

This book was published with the assistance of the Anniversary
Endowment Fund of the University of North Carolina Press.

The paper in this book meets the guidelines for permanence and
durability of the Committee on Production Guidelines for Book
Longevity of the Council on Library Resources.

Library of Congress Cataloging-in-Publication Data
Adams, Jessica, 1970–
Wounds of returning : race, memory, and property on the postslavery plantation /
Jessica Adams.
p. cm. — (New directions in southern studies)
Includes bibliographical references and index.
ISBN 978-0-8078-3104-5 (cloth: alk. paper)
ISBN 978-0-8078-5801-1 (pbk.: alk. paper)
1. African Americans in popular culture. 2. Racism in popular culture—United
States. 3. Capitalism—Social aspects—United States. 4. Property—Social
aspects—United States. 5. Memory—Social aspects—United States. 6. United
States—Race relations. 7. Slaves—Emancipation—United States. 8. Slavery—
Southern States—History. 9. Plantation life—Southern States—History.
10. Southern States—Race relations. I. Title.
E185.6.A24   2007
307.72089'96073075—dc22      2006036295

Chapter 2 was previously published in somewhat different form as "Local Color:
The Southern Plantation in Popular Culture," Cultural Critique 43 (Spring
1999): 163–87; copyright 1999 Regents of the University of Minnesota. Chapter 5
was previously published in somewhat different form as " 'The Wildest Show in
the South': Tourism and Incarceration at Angola," TDR/The Drama Review 45,
no. 2 (Summer [T170], 2001): 94–108; © 2001 by New York University and the
Massachusetts Institute of Technology. Both are reprinted here with permission.

cloth   11  10  09  08  07   5  4  3  2  1
paper   11  10  09  08  07   5  4  3  2  1

# Contents

# Illustrations

# Acknowledgments

On my journeys through New Orleans, walking or driving with the windows rolled down because my air conditioning was always broken, the city seemed to murmur things—messages, questions—that I sensed were urgent and profound. I needed to try to decode them, though I knew these mysteries must be infinite. At Tulane, Supriya Nair helped ground my flights of fancy in scholarly rigor, and her kindness has been a still point throughout graduate school and beyond. Rebecca Mark revealed expanses of creative possibility and sponsored their exploration. Felipe Smith offered an oasis of calm, blues and jazz floating from his office like a smoky haze; down the hall, Molly Travis was always ready with a warm welcome and an ideal teaching assignment. Joseph Roach introduced me to the antidiscipline of performance studies, and his embrace of the poignancy of history showed me that scholarly work could be poetry. Katy Coyle and Alecia Long took the time to share their unmatched knowledge of Storyville with both me and my students at Tulane. Wilbert Rideau and Ashanti Witherspoon, two extraordinary men, shed light on life inside Angola. At the University of Michigan, Patricia Yaeger generously read and commented on early drafts of this work, lending her brilliance to help me see my way through it. Charles Reagan Wilson at the University of Mississippi was a source of unwavering support for the project, for which I can never thank him enough. When I met him in Oxford, I immediately recognized a fellow connoisseur of the wild and strange in southern popular culture, and I have been incredibly fortunate to have him as an editor. The book benefited immensely from the comprehensive critiques of Russ Castronovo and an anonymous reader for the University of North Carolina Press. David Perry encouraged its completion across the varied landscapes of Georgia,

Arizona, Louisiana, and California after hurricane Katrina. Friends and family—Margaret and Tom Rasmussen, Richard Stone, and Katie Snyder and Tim Culvahouse—opened their doors and made it possible to think straight. Thanks to Michael Bibler's invaluable scholarly eye and rare friendship, my work is so much better, and my life so much more fun. Cécile Accilien has given boundlessly of her insights into southern and Caribbean society, and of her goodwill, creating a sense of community wherever we have found ourselves. Brandy Brown Walker's inimitable sense of humor and perspective helped make graduate school one of the best things I ever did; she and Robert Walker have always provided a safe port in a storm. Sitting with Elizabeth Lewis on her balcony in the Marigny, I gained a deeper understanding of life in general, and Tennessee Williams in particular. Neighbors, dinner companions, and inspirations Felicia McCarren, Ali Laichi, and Julie Kreuger made Bayou St. John home. Uptown, Ruth Harman and Jack Holdridge created an environment for laughter and meditation, as well as a context in which to learn about the inner workings of Louisiana's legal system. With elegance, a love of kitsch, and a knack for spotting delightful madness, Shelby Richardson Lovell shared uniquely New Orleanian experiences. In Ann Arbor, Tricia McElroy dispensed sanity with a southern accent. My family—Adamses, Rasmussens, Rankins, Tartaglias, Stones, Petruskas, and Rosens—have served as sounding boards and accompanied me in the flesh or in spirit on my travels across the South, sometimes helping to carry large boxes of books. Adam Stone, kindred spirit and darling companion, taught me to sail and gave me the world.

# Prologue

The Dutch colonial government of St. Eustatius in the Windward Islands was the first to acknowledge the independence of the American colonies, for which it paid with the destruction of its teeming wharves by an angry Admiral Rodney. Statia is now an obscure destination for all but its few residents and the giant oil tankers that refuel and unload cargo into the crater of an extinct volcano. Some of these ships are larger than any allowed into U.S. waters, municipalities unto themselves, behemoths trudging across the seas carrying one of the world's most vital commodities to and from the former free port that sold people alongside bolts of cloth, sugar, weapons, and silver plate in the protected curve of its harbor.

The American Revolution was underwritten by sugar produced not so much in Statia, small as it was, but on plantations in other parts of the Caribbean. As molasses, sugar made its way to New England; Rhode Island was famous for its rum, which ships transported to West Africa, where they emptied their holds and filled them again with slaves. Meanwhile, Dutch merchants in Statia supplied arms to the rebels. For trading abroad, the Dutch used blue glass beads. Beads could be transformed into slaves, and if slaves themselves could somehow earn enough beads, they could buy their own bodies (set up like a board game played for the highest of stakes). It is said that when Emancipation came, they hurled thousands of beads from the cliffs. The currency that had defined them sank in the indigo swells. How could something as simple and intrinsically worthless as glass beads have come to determine human worth? Yet the beads did not go far; they wash back to these shores with the storms. Today, they circulate as a defining motif of the island—given as gifts, coveted as souvenirs. Few things ever really vanish into the economies that have followed slavery.

*Wounds of Returning*

#  Introduction

Times don't change, just the merchandise.
*Sarah Graves, Federal Writers' Project Slave Narrative*

---

O
n a sunny summer day early in the twenty-first century, trains on the Norfolk Southern line rattle from the freight yards above St. Claude Avenue down Press Street toward the river. Along the levee, the New Orleans Public Belt Railroad runs between oil tankers and warehouses, passing the front porch of the meticulously restored Lombard Plantation—"one of the best-preserved West Indian–style Creole residences in the state"—featured in an 1882 *Scribner's* article by Lafcadio Hearn on the scenes of George Washington Cable's "romances."[1] The Desire streetcar line has come and gone, the sweep of its tracks still visible in the asphalt. The fields where sugarcane grew in the 1700s and 1800s have been replaced by shotgun houses, bars, Catholic churches, and public schools that saw bitter struggles over desegregation when *Plessy* was reversed in 1954. In 1960, white students marched down St. Claude bearing the Confederate flag, singing "Glory, Glory Segregation" to the tune of the Battle Hymn of the Republic to protest the integration of what was the all-white Francis T. Nicholls High (named for a Confederate soldier), which became the almost all-black Frederick Douglass.[2]

Cruise ship passengers standing at the rails of their gleaming vessels gaze out across the city blocks spread below them. As they travel slowly toward Caribbean destinations, they get a glimpse of the Chalmette Battlefield, a scene from the War of 1812, fought against a backdrop of cane fields, slave cabins, and big houses with carefully landscaped gardens.[3] Today, the site is marked by an imposing stone obelisk. A cemetery containing the graves of

Buffalo Soldiers and other military dead extends along the edge of the commemorative park, between the Murphy Oil Company and the grassy stretches where American and British soldiers once bayoneted each other. The Malus-Beauregard House, built in the 1830s, sits serenely empty between war memorials and the Mississippi. Perhaps, as the cruise ships move downriver, the blazing refinery stacks and the rust-covered hulk of the Domino sugar plant make its antebellum architecture look quaint.

On 7 June 1892, Homer Plessy made his way from his home near the French Quarter to the East Louisiana Railway Depot at the foot of Press Street. He heard the rattle of freight trains along the river. The fruit in the warehouses was slowly ripening in the summer heat.

When he bought a first-class ticket to Covington, Louisiana, on the other side of Lake Pontchartrain, Plessy knew he would never get that far. His object was simply to perform whiteness—but to perform it imperfectly. Arranged between the Comité des Citoyens, an activist group of Creoles of color associated with the French-English newspaper *The Crusader*, the arresting detective, and the railroad—which was finding the new "equal but separate" regulations mandated by the state's 1890 Separate Car Act expensive (and just how expensive they were would become evident over the next fifty years)—Plessy's act of civil disobedience challenged increasing racial segregation in Louisiana by pointing out that the basis of segregation itself was flawed.[4] Homer Plessy was seven-eighths white, and his intention to ride in the Whites Only car went unchallenged. By prior arrangement, someone pointed out that Plessy was "black" and therefore in violation of the law.[5] The conductor told him to move to the Colored car. He refused and was arrested and charged; the facts of the case that would eventually reach the Supreme Court were in place. Plessy's arrest presents, with few actors and on a stage set with remarkable economy, the problematic that remained after the end of chattel slavery.[6] Its violence is absent. But simply the fact of the Separate Car Act—a law regulating travel by train—and the Comité's choice of a light-skinned man who could pass to challenge it suggest that the regulation of both modes of transportation and metaphors of mobility was at stake, that the property being adjudicated was both human and otherwise, and that racial identity can be a slippery, signifying thing.

"Every man has a *Property* in his own *Person*," argued John Locke; "this nobody has any right to but himself. The labour of his body, and the work of his hands, we may say, are properly his."[7] Following this theory, liberal democracy, C. B. MacPherson writes, rests on a "conception of the individual as essentially the proprietor of his own person and capacities, owing nothing to society for them. . . . The individual, it was thought, is free inasmuch as he (specifically he) is proprietor of his person and capacities. The human essence is freedom from dependence on the wills of others, and freedom is a function of possession."[8] There are obvious incompatibilities between the idea that freedom involves self-ownership (the self as free because self-owned property); the existence of slavery (bonded because owned by another); and the fact that the slave, never just an item of movable property, was necessary to define the personhood of the owner (one type of human property shaping the identity of another type of human property, with the border between them in need of constant reinforcement).[9] In the *Plessy* case, the clash between self-ownership and being owned— passive versus active property status—is clearly the essence of racial difference. Before the court, former "carpetbagger" judge and popular novelist Albion Tourgée argued that by being forced to travel in the Colored car, Plessy, his name gesturing back toward some dead Frenchman, was deprived of his white property in himself. Presumably the white part of Plessy owned the colored part, as if reinscribing slavery as auto-possession. Perhaps Tourgée imagined a holistic individual beyond race, regarding his own parts as more and less valuable, a positive to a negative. Blackness disconnected from slavery existed outside the bounds of private property—because white society understood blackness as lacking value, there was no conceptual space in which to imagine blacks owning themselves and thus fulfilling the terms of what society recognized as personhood. The crucial idea in Tourgée's defense lay in his implication that the state of Louisiana had effectively legalized human theft. The one-drop rule that declared Plessy black, and the Separate Car Act that segregated him among people of color, had taken his white blood: not only a body-snatcher but a vampire state, selectively sucking the blood of its mulatto citizens, thus depriving them of any property in themselves and, therefore, protection under the law. Ownership and property are revealed as eerie, disturbed by phantoms, unsafe in the dark—and, I will argue, the anxieties they contain continue to affect life on the postslavery plantation.

As epicenter and emblem of slavery in the Americas and a primal scene in the emergence of the United States (Washington and Jefferson, dreaming of freedom at Mount Vernon and Monticello), the plantation has always signified an irreducible social strain, and the many plantations that are rumored to be haunted—and so attractive to tourists as a result—probably are. It is confounding to imagine John Quincy Adams saying, "I don't know why we should blush to confess that molasses was an essential ingredient in American independence"—by which he meant molasses produced by slaves on West Indian plantations.[10] But it is easy to imagine that his words would have consequences and that the plantation, echoing with such historical revisions and haunted by them as by the dead, would come to exert a force difficult to escape.

The landscape of Plessy's performance is the site of a functional evolution: first chattel slavery, then the industrial exuberance of railroad lines—the year after Plessy's short ride on the local East Louisiana Railway, the Southern Pacific railroad arrived in New Orleans, connecting it with the limits of the western frontier, along the Sunset line to Los Angeles—and gradually the encroachment of the city. How does slavery signify in postslavery geographies? This project takes landscape as palimpsest and, consequently, metaphor. It has grown out of my suspicions about what lingers on the plantation, and it argues that in order to understand the multivalent effects of slavery, we need to look very carefully at place. When Avery Gordon suggests that "haunting is a constituent element of modern social life," she refers in part to the "compulsions and forces that all of us inevitably experience in the face of slavery's having even once existed in our nation."[11] And as I point out, the strange and contradictory possibilities that slavery released into the realm of the normal still shape social spaces, including the reimagined plantation. The forcible yoking of bodies with property that was the most essential characteristic of chattel slavery left scars that remain visible: one night I close a book on the history of Reconstruction and awake to news reports of a man who has seen the ghost of Frederick Douglass in his living room in Rochester, New York, and of the details of Edgar Ray Killen's trial in the deaths of James Chaney, Michael Schwerner, and Andrew Goodman during the Freedom Summer of 1964.[12] "Wounds of returning" is the literal translation of "nostalgia," a word that, John Frow writes, was "originally defined in the seventeenth century in terms of a set of physical symptoms associated with acute homesickness" and later "came to be closely connected with the 'specific depression of intellectuals', melancholia. By the nineteenth century it had been extended to describe a general condition of estrangement, a state of ontological homelessness that became one of the period's key metaphors for the condition of modernity."[13] In everyday usage, nostalgia has come to signify the longing to return to a past that probably never existed and to places that have changed irrevocably. But "wounds of returning" suggests something more complicated—that the past itself may return, inflicting new wounds and reopening old ones. Frederick Douglass still has work to do in this world; the killers of Chaney, Schwerner, and Goodman must be brought to justice; and so many other raw abrasions await relief, among them the persistence of the plantation as a site of forgetting.

With the end of slavery, the plantation was (and is) still functioning as an agricultural entity.[14] But new technologies and the rise of new economic forces and cultural forms caused it to evolve in terms of what it could do and what it meant. After Reconstruction, a combination of expanding railroads and the emerging rapprochement between northern and southern whites structured by a shared nostalgia for the "Old South," along with warmer temperatures, made the postwar South a popular destination with northerners. Tourism was becoming more common as it became more affordable, and southern resorts were, ironically, popular destinations in a climate of concern over the perils of nervous exhaustion.[15] In an age of "machines, rapid urbanization, and labor unrest," a "pre-War, exotic South" that was "all but 'lost'" could satisfy a desire for a past now perceived as simpler.[16] In addition, the southern landscape offered "the chance to experience something unique and very different," something like "an up-close encounter with the ruins of an old plantation, a run-down former slave cabin, or an old Confederate soldier."[17] By the end of the nineteenth century, the development of mass culture caused images of plantation life to circulate far more rapidly and widely than they ever could have before. The Old South as a site of whites' leisured longing was evident in the enthusiastic reception of southern local color writing published in northern periodicals; white northerners and southerners collaborated in an "uncritical celebration of southern heroism," as Barbara Ewell and Pamela Glenn Menke note, "particularly in the popular press."[18] Black poverty became a "picturesque" sight on the itineraries of white northern tourists. And as black people became became picturesque, became spectacle, they were alienated by whites, cast as "foreigners," strangers at home.[19] At the same time, interregional white courtship and marriage symbolized the reunion between North and South, recalculating the meaning of the slave South as "romantic." The violence with which whites enforced segregation went along with a powerful desire for slavery times. At least Aunt Jemima and Rastus were still for sale.[20] By 1915, tributes to the "faithful slave" and the Ku Klux Klan were arriving at the offices of the United Daughters of the Confederacy from as far as Seattle and Los Angeles; Washington state had its own branch of the UDC, as did other nonsouthern cities like Chicago and New York.[21]

The twisted romanticism was grounded in fear that the borders separating races were vulnerable. This fear becomes apparent in the hysteria over "white slavery," or the forced prostitution of white women, which accompanied the dual rise of urban life and consumer culture and the attendant renegotiation of women's roles in society. Hysterical concern over enslaved whiteness actually makes sense when we consider the nature of antebellum relationships between master and slave and how they shaped racial relationships in general. Walter Johnson writes,

Before they entered the slave market or inspected a slave, many slaveholders had well-developed ideas about what they would find there. These ideas had less to do with the real people they would meet in the market, however, than they did with the slaveholders themselves, about the type of people they could become by buying slaves. . . . They dreamed of people arrayed in meaningful order by their value as property, of fields full of productive hands and a slave quarter that reproduced itself, of well-ordered households and of mansions where service was swift and polished. They dreamed of beating and healing and sleeping with slaves; sometimes they even dreamed that their slaves would love them. They imagined who they could be by thinking about whom they could buy.[22]

Slaves exerted a special power to transform the whiteness of their owners into property. Johnson continues,

At a very high price, whiteness was doubly sold in the slave market. . . . The hybrid whiteness of the [mulatto] slaves was being packaged and measured by the traders and imagined into meaning by the buyers: into delicacy and modesty, interiority and intelligence, beauty, bearing, and vulnerability. . . . Descriptions of light-skinned slaves were projections of slaveholders' own dreamy interpretations of the meaningfulness of their skin color. Indeed . . . it was the buyers' own whiteness that was being bought. In buying these imagined slaves, they were buying for themselves ever more detailed fantasies about mastery and race.[23]

In a sense, whites were buying the ability to trespass upon whiteness itself. The complicated thrill of owning a white-appearing slave came partly from the chance it conferred to savor white property in otherwise unavailable ways.

As Johnson's account suggests, it was the nature of chattel slavery to make everyone involved, whether directly or indirectly, into something saleable. The concept of personhood itself (as in "white people") had already been linked to property through Locke's influential notion of capitalist exchange, but the distinction between personhood as property and chattel slaves as property was porous; thus the general white panic over regulating contact between whites and blacks after Emancipation. Black people's bodies had a quantifiable value under the law during slavery, and the concept of whiteness, taking shape in this context of evaluated bodies for sale and the associated idea of racial difference, accrued "a cash value," as George Lipsitz notes.[24] Africans in Charleston during the early days of the slave trade had their shoulders branded with the letters RACE, which stood for Royal African Company of England, but which also made explicit the role that black bodies would be forced to play in the emerging nation: the body as object as commodity as symbol of the future.[25] In concert with slavery, whiteness in the United States became legally defined as a thing that could be owned. Cheryl Harris writes that during slavery, "because whites could not be enslaved or held as slaves, the racial line between white and black was extremely critical; it became a line of protection and demarcation from the potential threat of commodification, and it determined the allocation of benefits and burdens of this form of property." And as Harris describes, after slavery ended, whiteness continued to exist as a form of property.[26] But while whiteness (which long escaped a specific identification with "race," it being "normal" and therefore invisible in the mainstream white imaginary) may have a cash value, it is not supposed to have a price. The essence of whiteness is that, though it can be owned as property, it cannot be sold. The widespread conviction that white women were in fact becoming objects of monetary transactions is so interesting not because it was based in large part on prejudice and panic, but because it reflected something that really was happening. According to Karl Marx, capitalism has the ability to enslave,[27] and as contemporary reports on the white slave issue pointed out, consumer culture has the capacity to commodify everything.

Stephen Best observes that "slavery is not simply an antebellum institution that the United States has surpassed but a particular historical form of an ongoing crisis involving the subjection of personhood to property."[28] Slavery does not, nor can it, just go away. It remains embedded as a function of law and other social institutions and, therefore, as a feature of U.S. culture. One telling manifestation of this crisis appears in the doctrine of corporate personhood.[29] Over a series of cases decided between 1873 and 1886, the Supreme Court established that the Fourteenth Amendment protected corporations as "persons"—persons who could be bought and sold *and* buy and sell. Master and slave merge in a technically raceless body that, while the slave body is no longer a site of commerce, can circulate legally.[30] In their 1927 work *The Rise of American Civilization*, historians Charles and Mary Beard argued that the privileges and immunities clause, the focus of successive lawyers' claims for corporate rights, came to protect bodies that were by then on their way to hegemonic status: "Just how this provision got into the draft of the Fourteenth Amendment was not generally known at the time of its adoption but in after years the method was fully revealed by participants in the process," they wrote. "According to evidence now available, there were two factions in the congressional committee which framed the Amendment—one bent on establishing the rights of Negroes; the other determined to take in the whole range of the national economy." The Beards condemned John A. Bingham, a member of the House from Ohio and a railroad lawyer "familiar with the possibilities of jurisprudence," who constructed the "mysterious sentence containing the 'due process' clause in the form in which it now stands" and the one "who finally forced it upon the committee by persistent efforts."[31] The Beards assumed that the amendment was actually designed to protect "corporate" persons as opposed to people who had been considered property. This idea, which became known as the Conspiracy Theory, was, according to constitutional historian Howard Jay Graham, "daily gossip, an article of national faith and popular enlightenment" by the mid-1930s.[32] Thus the notion that the government was commuting former slaves into engines of commerce took hold as a part of the ephemeral generative forces of popular culture. At the same time, it illustrated a widespread intuition that there was something problematically expansive about what slavery had done to society's foundations.

Marx's suggestive concept of objects in which people are concealed lends itself immediately to an analysis of the persistence of the figure of the slave within regional and national imaginaries. Marx supposedly borrowed the idea of the fetish in "commodity fetish" from French proto-anthropologist Charles de Brosses's 1760 work titled *Du culte des dieux fétiches ou Parallèle de l'ancienne religion de l'Egypte avec la religion actuelle de Nigritie*. If this is true, the European eye on Africa informs deep recesses of economic and cultural theory. Regardless, both the slave and the commodity fetish are things for sale in which people have been obscured by the processes of production. (In the Three-Fifths Compromise, "chattel" competes with "person," "person" winning out by two-fifths; but "person" would become increasingly obscured by processes of social production—government, law, and custom.) After Emancipation, the commodity fetish reappears in nostalgic objects like the "Alabama Coon Nigger," a mechanical toy popular between 1915 and 1917, which William Leach describes as the "first huge international mass market toy 'success'" in the United States. (Philadelphia merchant John Wanamaker remarked that his store made a "killing" on it.)[33] Slaves as animate property gave way to commodities as slaves.

Moving through the final part of the nineteenth century and into the present, the plantation, as both symbol and physical place, intersected a series of modern phenomena: industrialism, consumer culture, film technology, segregation, nostalgia, tourism, and convict leasing and the twentieth-century penitentiary. The dynamics of ownership associated with and summed up by the plantation financed, for example, the successes of Storyville's octoroon brothels. Around the turn of the century, when the practice of convict leasing had become so disreputable that states could no longer engage in it, southern prisons like Parchman Farm and Angola enfolded plantation landscapes and enforced plantation disciplinarity. The plantation became popular as a film set in the early to midtwentieth century and, later, as a tourist destination. At each of these sites, strange things happen to property—to physical property, to the memory of property, and to people. Counternarratives and unexpected hybrids overload attempts to re-create the plantation as a nostalgic setting, a signifier of national unity, or the scene of an uncomplicated hierarchy.

To investigate the theoretical possibilities within my superstitions about the nature of the evolving plantation, I look at texts especially given to intuition and "illogic," grounded in information arriving through irrational channels as well as prone to *being* illogical and (as such?) influential channels that shape how people think about and see the world—in a word, fiction, as well as film, tourist performance, and oral history.[34] I use these texts to consider property in the United States as a locus of possession—by which I mean an admixture of ownership and what we might call spirit possession.[35] For possession is so much more than ownership.[36] Plantation slaves were engraved on banknotes from across the Confederacy; thus scenes from plantation slavery related the true meaning of "states' rights,"[37] and it was no secret that the Confederate economy was and would be, God willing, all about slavery. These abstractions of value reveal the slave as quintessential commodity—the object of financial exchange and the very embodiment of commerce. Money, touched intimately by slaveholders and nonslaveholders alike, becomes a kind of commodity fetish in its own right. "Spirit possession" seems appropriate in describing the consequences of enslavement, fetishized otherness, and property on the postslavery plantation, as it is a term that emerged in white outsiders' accounts of Vodou.[38] It is the language of the (at least somewhat alienated) observer, and I mean it to invoke, in part, the often uneasy differential between what whites thought they knew about property and what was really going on. Possession expresses a complex of money, fetishism, and being owned, in a sense, by what you own. At the same time, the profound, ultimate impossibility of owning another person has unmoored the conceptual products of the slave system from their physical referents. (In the stress of expressing something impossible, the signifier detaches from the signified and becomes mobile.) The ownership of people has generated a culture in which people may become possessed by what we call history, and the plantation itself remains haunted by property.

Faulkner's novel *Absalom, Absalom!* helps to illustrate this concept of possession. When Faulkner was writing the novel, with its much-discussed links between antihero Thomas Sutpen and the Haitian Revolution, images of Haiti suffused U.S. culture.[39] The marines occupied this independent nation between 1914 and 1939, and through political, economic, and cultural contact, images of its history and culture—factual, mythical, and erroneous—began to circulate more widely in the United States. They captured the imaginations of Arna Bontemps, Langston Hughes, and Zora Neale Hurston, as well as readers of marine John Houston Craige's accounts of Haiti, *Black Baghdad* (1933) and *Cannibal Cousins* (1934), and those who watched Victor Halperin's *White Zombie* (1932); later films like *The Walking Dead* (1936), *Revolt of the Zombies* (1936), *I Walked with a Zombie* (1943); and Eugene O'Neill's *Emperor Jones* (with Paul Robeson playing the lead onstage in 1924 and on film in 1933). Faulkner helped make "literary" a cultural preoccupation with Haiti as a scene of shocking violence and mysterious practices shrouded in darkness—race as a figure for moral decay. Faulkner never visited Haiti, and in fact his version of Haiti and its southern consequences is instructive, I think, because of this absence of firsthand experience (which is not to say that firsthand experience would guarantee "authenticity") and thus for what it appears Faulkner has absorbed from misinformation circulating in popular culture.

In *Absalom, Absalom!* the presence of Haitian slaves on Sutpen's Hundred conveys in shorthand that Haiti is a frighteningly unpredictable place. (Sutpen himself even fathers a kind of cannibal tribe that consumes itself through sexuality, murder, and finally fire, and the self/personhood gets consumed by possession along with everything else.) As Faulkner makes clear in the rhetoric with which he enshrouds Sutpen's half-Haitian son Charles Bon, the white family possesses Bon as an object to be displayed and fondled, if only with the mind. At the same time, through Bon, Haiti becomes a force that overcomes and inhabits white characters. Bon's desire to be recognized by his father, to claim a bloodline, and to escape his indeterminate status between past and present, embodiment and ephemerality, are played out through Sutpen's less resistant surrogates—his white family Henry, Judith, and their mother, Ellen. Ellen refers to him "as if he were . . . one inanimate object for which she and her family would find three concordant uses: a garment which Judith might wear as she would a riding habit or a ball gown, a piece of furniture which would complement and complete the furnishing of her house and position, and a mentor and example to correct Henry's provincial manners and speech."[40] Bon's urges are reciprocated by the family's powerful, blinding desire to possess him— both to own him as a kind of commodity that confers status and to possess him sexually. They do not yet (consciously) know him to be already a member of the family or to be "black," only exotic, foreign. Their desire for otherness is sufficiently profound that it does not require the presence of a physical body. Henry and Judith are "seduced simultaneously by a man whom at the time Judith had never even seen."[41] Ownership becomes not only interactive but mystified. Ellen and Henry also experience the urge to use Bon as a substitute for themselves that would perform acts the "white" self cannot or will not. In fact Bon is already a critical part of the "white" self. Faulkner describes Henry's relationship with him using the metaphor of a diseased limb "which he knows must come off,"[42] an originary but ultimately, if painfully, detachable element of Henry. While Bon is Henry's diseased limb, however, he is also its prosthesis. As he closes the gap between referent and reproduction, he becomes a simulacrum of vanishing whiteness *and* blackness that illuminates the troubled hybridity of life within what Antonio Benítez-Rojo calls the repeating island.[43] (As Cécile Accilien, Felipe Smith, Ian Strachan, and Catherine A. Reinhardt have shown, throughout the circum-Caribbean, in Louisiana and Martinique, Guadeloupe, the Bahamas, and Jamaica, there has been a trend toward the deliberate effacement of the history of slavery at sites where slaves lived, labored, and died, from plantation houses to burial grounds.)[44]

Perhaps some of the fascination with Haiti in the United States emerged from the fact that, as popular images of Haiti—on the page, on screen, and onstage—make clear, there is something mysterious and unquantifiable that pervades the collective consciousness of societies that have known slavery. In a reading of labor issues in post-Emancipation Cuba and Louisiana, for example, Rebecca Scott reveals race as a floating signifier, "a construct whose political meaning could shift sharply over time and space, rendering inclusion or exclusion in the polity historically contingent."[45] The concept of race in the postslavery context is such a restless traveler that even the most concerted efforts to detain it meet with varying degrees of failure. Zora Neale Hurston's description of U.S.-occupied Haiti includes an account of Dr. Reser, a former Navy pharmacist's mate, originally from Arkansas, who had decided to stay on in Haiti as "officer in charge of the state insane asylum at Pont Beudet."[46] "He had been in Haiti seven years by the calendar," Hurston writes, "but in soul he came from Africa with the rest of the people."[47] Reser is both doctor and *houngan*, and Hurston describes him "in the psychological state known as possession."[48] Michael Taussig argues that "Europe and its colonies, white and colored, reflect back stunning fantasies of each other's underworlds from conquest and slavery onward";[49] here it is a circum-Atlantic reflection in a white American eye, this mirroring of an other's forbidden. Both the *lwa* Guedé and, it seems, blackness itself work as agents of possession. Hurston continues,

> A new personality burned up the one that had eaten supper with us. His blue-gray eyes glowed, but at the same time they drew far back into his head as if they went inside to gaze on things kept in a secret place. After awhile he began to speak. He told of marvelous revelations of the Brave Guedé cult. And as he spoke, he moved farther and farther from known land and into the territory of myths and mists. Before our very eyes, he walked out of his Nordic body and changed. Whatever the stuff of which the soul of Haiti is made, he was that. . . . He was dancing before his gods and the fire of Shango played about him.[50]

A white person may become black, since race is not only property but, as Hurston appears to say, possession.

The idea of race as an externalizable, transient force becomes explicit in a description of the possessed Langston Hughes. In February 1930, Hughes sailed for Havana in search of a black composer to create the score for a "singing play" he had planned about the fall of the controversial Haitian revolutionary leader Jean-Jacques Dessalines. (It would premiere in Cleveland in 1936 as *Troubled Island*).[51] Hughes met with Amedeo Roldan, but Roldan did not think of himself as "black." Hughes found a kindred spirit, however, in the poet Nicolas Guillén, who interviewed him for the literary supplement of a local newspaper. In the interview, Hughes describes his realization during a stay in Africa that his true calling was to write the black experience. "I live among my people," he avers; "I love them and the way they're treated hurts me deeply so I sing their blues and I translate their sorrows, I make their troubles go away. And I do this like my people do, with their same ease. . . . I write what comes from within. I sing it the same way old people do. I don't study the black man. I 'feel' him."[52] Guillén accompanied Hughes to a black dance hall and described the experience for the newspaper: "From the very moment he enters, he acts like he's possessed with the spirit of our people," Guillén writes. " 'My people!' he exclaims. For a long time he stands next to the band which is wildly playing a Cuban *son* and is gradually overcome by this new spirit within him. Afterwards, while he looks at a black man dancing rhythmically he exclaims with an air of insatisfaction: 'I'd like to be black. Really black. Truly black.' "[53] "True blackness" is kinesthetic memory, the rhythmic pulse of Africa completely and effortlessly embodied in diasporic performance; it is evidence of an intact genealogy. By contrast, Hughes seems to view himself as an actor playing a role. But his search for racial identity reveals a crucial factor in the experience of "plantation America"[54]: the syncretic cannot just replace but can also become that which is original and "pure." Possession points to the only partial ability of language to describe what is emerging from a creolized interculture, as well as to the way in which purity is seen to exist specifically at sites of creolization. The promiscuity of apparently "real" forms of difference appears through the lens of possession.

These chapters describe an eclectic, unconventional plantation tour. I begin in late-nineteenth-century New Orleans, where the perceived rights of plantation slaveholders, including sexual access to women of color, had traveled into historically black neighborhoods and officially sanctioned brothels. I visit a variety of transformed plantations in Louisiana and Mississippi and explore Elvis memorials. Leaving the South entirely, I investigate the encroachment of plantation ideology on the frontier and end at the Louisiana State Penitentiary at Angola. The landscapes of Louisiana and Mississippi are prominent here because in these states' renewed plantation economies, the plantation's range of adaptations becomes especially clear. It supports tourism and refineries, confines prisoners, and supplies the ground for at least one major university, even as cotton and cane still grow where they were first planted by slaves' hands. In focusing on these areas, I set up the exemplar that I hope will make plantation descendants in other parts of the South even more apparent. While both are considered the Deep South, these two states are marked by different historic influences and signify differently in the popular imagination. With its history of French and Spanish governance and the New World port of New Orleans, Louisiana not only has a varied southern history but has even been referred to as "not part of the South." The source of the quote is my mother, from South Carolina, who uttered these words as I was preparing to move to New Orleans for graduate school. Since then, however, I have heard the same idea voiced by a demographic including southerners and nonsoutherners alike (though what I mean by "southern" is now open to question) and people who expressed actual fear at the idea of visiting Mississippi or Alabama but none at coming to New Orleans, which was known, at least until hurricane Katrina, as a "murder capital." Meanwhile, Mississippi's white influences were mostly Anglo, with the exception of the Gulf coast. Mississippi is a more rural state, and its history of civil rights violence made it a national symbol of stereotypical southern backwardness. At the same time, Mississippi has experienced a twenty-first-century influx of industry, particularly companies like Nissan and BMW and their suppliers. I also touch on Virginia, viewed as perhaps less southern and more American within the nation as a whole in part because it was the home of founding fathers, and because of its proximity to the nation's capital. This expanded focus helps illustrate the relevance of these ideas about the plantation across an even broader spectrum of southern cultures, emphasizing the South as a heterogeneous region that blurs not only into other parts of the United States but into the larger plantation region of the Americas.

Chapter 1 examines the plantation as a figure of memory that informs representations of women's bodies at a time when hysteria over white slavery, meaning forced female prostitution, was growing intense. The ideal of white women as naturally inferior to and chattel of white men had stood as one of the key underpinnings of the paternalist justification for black slavery, but its equation of white with black complicated whites' post-Emancipation narratives of white identity, as contemporary writing by women reveals. At the same time, white men's historic sexual fascination with women of color continued to inform their sexual proclivities and served as stimulus for a nostalgia-fueled, legally sanctioned consumption of women's bodies.

Chapters 2 and 3 explore the physical spaces of plantation houses as they have become integrated into twentieth- and twenty-first-century popular culture. The plantation house today is often a site of the erasure of slave history, but, as I argue, careful readings of plantation images suggest that slavery's physical and psychic violence is always active within scenes of nostalgia. Tara McPherson notes that "in many ways, Americans can't seem to get enough of the horrors of slavery, and yet we remain unable to connect this past to the romanticized image of the plantation, unable or unwilling to process the emotional registers still echoing from the eras of slavery and Jim Crow. The brutalities of those periods remain dissociated from our representations of the material site of those atrocities, the plantation home."[55] In fact, I show how the plantation is reduced to a "home" precisely as part of the process that attempts to separate slavery from the meaning of the plantation. Touring plantation houses along the Mississippi River, visiting Graceland, and watching Bette Davis movies, among other encounters, clarify some of the rightfully disturbing effects of such rewritings of plantation history. The final two chapters consider "southern frontiers," cross-pollinations between ideas about the South and myths of the West. In the nineteenth century, American slavery was moving westward. Residents of the Indian, Utah, Nevada, and New Mexico Territories were slaveowners, and heated discussions took place in Kansas, Oregon, and California over whether slavery should be permitted there.[56] The plantation was recognized as a social model that could be adapted to ranching and even mining.[57] Slave cowboys worked on Texas cattle ranches,[58] and members of the Creek, Choctaw, Chickasaw, Cherokee, and Seminole nations had black slaves, some of whom participated in the forced marches to Indian Territory, where Native people established plantations after the removal treaties of the 1830s.[59] By the first decades of the twentieth century, with *Birth of a Nation*, popular culture reflected that the investment in plantation ideology was indeed a national phenomenon, familiar on the frontier as in the Deep South. Its commercial appeal was certainly clear to M. L. Graham and his wife Adelaide, who opened the Coon Chicken Inn in Utah in 1925; business was booming, and they soon expanded to Seattle, then to Portland. A huge, winking darky head (only a head) stretched its huge, open-mouthed grin nearly the full height of the buildings' facades, as if inviting diners to eat or be eaten.[60] Chapter 4 investigates adumbrations of the plantation in early-twentieth-century representations of the frontier, focusing on Willa Cather's novels of New Mexico. Cather's family, including a grandmother who treasured Confederate relics on the prairie, moved westward from Virginia when she was a child, and Cather herself scripts an antebellum southern presence into her narratives of the "free" West. Chapter 5 explores an inversion of the South's westerly migrations in the southward journey of an archetypal frontier form: rodeo. Through rodeo, myths of Wild West freedom merge with plantation space at the Louisiana State Penitentiary at Angola. Angola Prison was formerly known as Angola Plantation, and the convergence calls to mind the fact that slavery is not forbidden in the United States; under the Thirteenth Amendment, it remains legal as punishment for a crime.

A fter hurricane Katrina, the landscape of Homer Plessy's ride presented a challenge to the concept of time's forward motion. Winds had peeled back the layers of billboards all over town, and former New Orleans Mayor Marc Morial, who left office in 2002, congratulated St. Augustine High School's basketball team on its victory at the state championship. A long-invisible neon sign for Bill's Coffee Shop & Hamburgers hung perilously over an abandoned storefront that was home to several cafes, none of them Bill's, during the past decade. In some ways the city as a whole had returned to Plessy's time. The local newspaper reported that the storm resurrected the geography of the late nineteenth century, before the development of former swamp and low-lying land brought it to its early-twenty-first-century size.[61] More than one hundred years since the *Plessy* decision, and more than fifty years since *Brown*, the place where Homer Plessy boarded the East Louisiana Railway remains unmarked.[62] In the fall of 2005, however, armed National Guard troops stood sentry over the site and fire trucks awaited calls to duty, as if now, at last, ready to respond to the emergencies of history.[63] New Orleans has sometimes been referred to as a Caribbean place, and certainly in images emanating from the inundated city, connections with other parts of the circum-Caribbean suggested themselves. Broadcast to the nation, these images seemed to shock the way that images of the floods in Haiti following tropical storm Jeanne the previous year had shocked (and images of Haiti in general seem to shock people in the United States). Citizens of New Orleans, most of them black, waded through polluted waters while governmental agencies seemed paralyzed. Such images reveal wounds of returning as they insist on the common history of the plantation—the implications of which have been, despite everything, easy to ignore. Following painfully delayed evacuations, people living in the Houston Astrodome, most of whom were black, resisted boarding cruise ships named Ecstasy, Sensation, and Holiday, which, in the normal course of things, travel from Gulf ports through the "Western Caribbean."[64] Even the idea of putting people on ships as a solution to an economic problem seems informed by an undercurrent of plantation logic. Of course it was ships that traced the genesis of plantation cultures—slave ships—and in their wake, cruise ships have followed, banking, like plantation tourism in the South, on a public appreciation of the picturesqueness of former scenes of slavery.[65] Oil pipelines called Plantation and Colonial flowing from the Gulf were disrupted by the storm and therefore appeared in the news, exposing how unabashedly the rhetoric of economies linked to slavery has been reiterated, as well as the uncanny ability of the plantation to maintain its original shape even over the course of centuries.[66] Ecstasy, sensation, holiday, plantation, colonial—leisure blends with commerce and motifs of oppression in the rhythmic pulse of postslavery geographies, reminding us to attend to the revelations of the mundane.

# 1. Sex and Segregation

Ownership is the most intimate relation one can have to objects.
*Walter Benjamin*

"New Orleans is paved with Negro skulls," said one American author. He
would have done better to say that New Orleans is paved with beautiful
women, although this would not disqualify the first observation.
*Baron Ludwig von Reizenstein*

I t was the end of the nineteenth century. Consumer culture was
emerging as a force to be reckoned with in the United States, and
the mechanisms of production were poised to outstrip demand, with
advertising about to step into the breach to inspire fresh desires.[1]
Segregation was congealing as social practice even as everyday
life was inevitably more complicated than an overview of the laws
would suggest. And the southern plantation was being renewed as
myth. White culture invoked evidence of the Old South as a bulwark
against encroachments of blackness into post-Emancipation "mainstream" culture—encroachments that, in fact, white culture found
very seductive. Women of color were still serving as cooks, nan-
nies, and maids in white southern households, and white men still
wanted to sleep with them. In nineteenth-century Louisiana, the
taboo against sex and intimate relationships across the color line
grew stronger as segregation grew more entrenched.[2] The social
difficulties involved in white men's cross-racial desires could be
managed, and the fulfillment of these desires facilitated, however,
through their confinement to certain spaces and geographies: brothels and, later, the officially sanctioned environment of Storyville, the
red-light district for which New Orleans would become famous.

Because female sexuality was critical to the exercise of power on the plantation, the reinvention of the plantation system necessarily involved women's bodies. In the antebellum South, wives and slaves were quite openly and deliberately entangled. Historian Stephanie McCurry writes that

> in the lexicon of metaphors for slavery, marriage took pride of place, a discursive construction historians have rarely recognized. No other relation was more universally embraced as both natural and divine, and none so readily evoked the stake of enfranchised white men, yeomen and planters alike, in the defense of slave society. By equating the subordination of women with that of slaves, proslavery ministers and politicians attempted to endow slavery with the legitimacy of the family and especially marriage and, not incidentally, to invest the defense of slavery with the survival of customary gender relations. In this sense, the subordination of women bore a great deal of the ideological weight of slavery.[3]

As McCurry's research demonstrates, this justification of slavery via white marriage also operated among whites who did not own slaves. Freedom and authority as essential qualities of whiteness were reflected in the inverted mirror of those whom whites could legally own—both slaves and white wives—whether or not they actually owned them. Because the apparent naturalness of the subordination of white women had been a critical justification for the naturalness of black slavery, Emancipation compelled a recalculation of social value in the South along gender as well as racial lines. But the fact that white women could still be unfree servants became a challenge to concepts of whiteness. Both the historic value of a white wife as measure of her husband's social status and the ideological force of paternalism, which regained momentum during the Lost Cause era as whites across the nation espoused increasingly extreme notions of white supremacy, continued to link the subjectivities of white and black women. Thus white women were in the position of upholding white masculinity by defining an aspect of post-Emancipation whiteness as linked to slavery.

The city of New Orleans has long been associated with transgressive sexuality. In part because of the lack of white women on the Louisiana frontier, European men had sexual relationships with Native American and African women, and the practice of *plaçage* was eventually institutionalized as a unique white Creole rite during the eighteenth and nineteenth centuries.[4] Under this system certain light-skinned women of color, called *placées*, were groomed as suitable consorts for men who would support them and the couple's children. Some Creole men had two families, one with a placée, the other with a white woman. (This is the arrangement by which Faulkner is fascinated/repulsed in *Absalom, Absalom!*; the otherworldly visit of Charles Bon's "black" "wife" to the Sutpens' Mississippi plantation sums up Faulkner's vision of New Orleans's difference from the rest of the South.) With the Civil War, however, racial tensions made plaçage less feasible.[5] In the social climate of post-Reconstruction Louisiana an acknowledged intimate connection between a white man and a woman of color became problematic, and white men's legal acknowledgment of their mixed-race children became more difficult.[6] But interracial intimacy persisted. As Alecia Long writes, "There was a range of historical situations and contexts in which sex across the color line occurred in New Orleans between 1865 and 1920. For the city's women of color, those situations could include unwanted sexual advances or violent rape, exchanging sex for money or other favors on an intermittent or ongoing basis, being a mistress to one or a series of men, marrying across the color line, which was legal in Louisiana between 1870 and 1894, or living with a man in a committed relationship without the benefit of marriage."[7] As law created fictions of racial identity as it mandated the meaning of blood, fiction helped generate attitudes about race and race relations that shaped the practice of everyday life. Local color writers played a key role in the evolution of public perceptions of slavery and the Civil War, and national interest in southern domestic and social scenes created a forum for women's writing. In detailed descriptions of southern society, women interrogated the consequences of plantation life, including unstable post-slavery relationships among property, gender, and sexuality.

Kate Chopin's novel *The Awakening* reveals the enduring problematic of paternalism embedded in late-nineteenth-century attitudes toward white marriage; it addresses white fears about a slippery slope from "racial equality" to miscegenation, fears related to the contemporary increase in lynchings. Yet the argument that in killing black men whites were protecting white womanhood served as an attempt to simultaneously cement all blacks and white women as property. In Chopin's depiction, female sexuality actively destabilizes the relationship between race and property upon which postbellum order still rested. After slavery, female sexuality could no longer be controlled with the ideals of asexual white women on pedestals and black women as self-perpetuating property. Chopin shares Thorstein Veblen's interest in women's roles as both "unfree servants" and emblems of masculine leisure.[8] Veblen does not develop a connection between race slavery and gendered surrogacy, but Chopin suggests that it creates a trajectory linking antebellum with postbellum domestic economies. The historic relationship between white wives and property is fundamental to the plot of *The Awakening*, and Chopin explores how gender complicates possessive individualism. According to Margit Stange, Chopin's description of Edna's struggle to realize self-ownership "unpacks the paradoxical logic of self-ownership in all its contradiction and impossibility. It is through her role as the wife—and marital property—of Léonce Pontellier that Edna first looks for a self that she might possess; and it is as a mother that Edna first declares her resolve to withhold some part of that self from the claims of others." In other words, Stange argues, "in her aspiration to self-ownership, Edna claims title to a self that exists only in relation to her status as the property of others."[9] Edna's liberation is not possible outside the confines of the white self as sexual property that she seeks to escape, but her entrapment in the post-Reconstruction world of people as valuable property necessarily references black bodies as chattel, exposing the connections between whites and the blacks they were trying to return to a state of virtual bondage. As white men degraded black men and women, Chopin's work suggests, they simultaneously degraded their white wives. *The Awakening* indicates that anxieties around the fact that white male bodies could be categorized as valuable property within a consumer economy in which everything was for sale got deflected onto women, who already *were* property.

It is possible to read Chopin's suppression of black characters in the novel as a suppression of the correlation between white women as property and people of color as property.[10] Edna is from Kentucky, not Louisiana; unlike her husband, she is not "Creole," and her psychic transformation takes place in a realm effectively unpopulated by people of color. Given Chopin's almost painfully meticulous observations of white Creole life, sentences such as "Mr. Pontellier's two children were there—sturdy little fellows of four and five. A quadroon nurse followed them about with a far-away meditative air,"[11] or "A maid, in white fluted cap, offered the callers liqueur, coffee, or chocolate, as they might desire"[12] sound like missed opportunities at the least. But perhaps "race is rendered narratively invisible"[13] because depicting a woman fleeing the bonds of property would be that much more difficult if, as Jim Crow law and custom amplified, Chopin had focused on things that Edna had in common with her colored servants, specifically their status as sexualized property.

While Chopin investigates ideological tenets of plantation life translated into urban space and postslavery society, the plantation and its racial and gender dynamics shadow the action without ever appearing—except, perhaps, in the form of Léonce's mother's house in the country where Edna sends her two boys and the nameless quadroon during the time in which she transforms her life and then ends it. For Grace King, however, the plantation is both an enabling and an explicit presence. Her story "Bonne Maman," set in New Orleans shortly after the Civil War, centers on an ancient, aristocratic former plantation mistress who has been left penniless. Refusing to ask her remaining relatives for help, Nénaine ("bonne maman") moves with her orphaned granddaughter, Claire Blanche, to New Orleans, where they live in a former slave cabin in the area known as back of town—"an obscured corner in which to thrust domestic hearths not creditable to the respectability assumed in the front part of town; where oil lamps could be economically substituted for gas, and police indifference for police protection."[14] These two fallen women (as it were) do piecework for the poor whites and people of color who populate the neighborhood. In essence and on principle, the grandmother, or good mother, imposes upon herself and "Bright White" a form of natal alienation (the rest of the family believes they are in France).[15] In King's image of alienated whiteness, bondage is associated with a plantation where whites are the slaves of blacks and former slaves do all the buying and selling.

Relocating a Creole plantation in the city of New Orleans and identifying it as a site of white oppression, King engaged the contemporary crisis of Creole identity as well as the postslavery relationship between race, gender, and sexuality. The woman who eventually became known as the "grande dame of New Orleans literature" was a Lost Cause loyalist and passionate Francophile; though not a Creole by birth, she began writing in order to refute George Washington Cable's ironic portrayals of Creole life and culture.[16] She published her first story in the *New Princeton Review* in 1886, after encountering well-connected *Harper's* editor Charles Dudley Warner at a Mardi Gras party.[17] As she told *Century* editor Richard Watson Gilder (also in town for Mardi Gras) when he suggested that some New Orleanians' vilification of Cable went too far, Cable "had stabbed the city in the back . . . to please the Northern press" with his "preference for colored people over white."[18] If Cable was pandering to antisouthern prejudice, King's stories, she determined, would enlighten northerners as to the "truth" about Louisiana.

Gwendolyn Midlo Hall's research shows that the term "creole" "derives from the Portuguese word *crioulo*, meaning a slave of African descent born in the New World. Thereafter, it was extended to include Europeans born in the New World. In Spanish and French colonies, including eighteenth-century Louisiana . . . *creole* was used to distinguish American-born from African-born slaves." And before long it became enmeshed in racial politics. During Latin American independence movements of the late eighteenth and early nineteenth centuries, it was used as a slur against those who wanted home rule in the colonies: "The Latin American elite born in the Americas was called the creole elite and was accused of being incapable of self-rule in part because of its racially mixed heritage. Rejecting this heritage, the creole elite of Latin American redefined the word *creole* to mean people of exclusively European descent born in the Americas."[19] Something similar happened in New Orleans during and after Reconstruction. As Virginia Domínguez writes, "Northern newcomers to the city and other non-Creoles began to insinuate rather openly and insistently that all Creoles had at least 'a touch of the tarbrush.' After all, many of the well-known politicians . . . called themselves Creole but were also colored. Although white Creoles did not exactly *look* colored, rumors spread that they had skeletons in their closets. Why, otherwise, would they continue to identify themselves as members of the same social group or category as thousands of colored people?"[20] In a climate of intensifying racial binarism, white Creoles needed to establish that Creole meant pure white in order to retain their social standing. Kate Chopin's husband Oscar was a member not only of the white Creole elite but, eventually, of the white-supremacist Crescent City White League—New Orleanians who effectively ended Radical Reconstruction in Louisiana in 1874 at the "Battle of Liberty Place," an armed insurrection against Governor William Pitt Kellogg's integrated administration. Louisiana historian Charles Gayarré gave a speech at Tulane in 1885 in which "he made thirty explicit references to 'the pure white ancestry of the Louisiana Creoles'" within an hour.[21] Meanwhile Creoles of color whose very existence white Creoles were trying to deny sought to distance themselves from "blacks," for as the category of blackness became reified, Creoles of color—a historically free group of people, members of which had lived and studied in France "as early as the 1740s"—watched their own relative privilege disappear.[22] The Louisiana State Constitutional Convention met in 1898 to determine an effective means of disenfranchising people of color without violating the Fifteenth Amendment. In February, a group of men of color presented a formal statement to the suffrage committee: "We are perplexed and discouraged when opposite courses are proposed to be pursued. When one insists that ignorance is a bane and the other that the most dangerous negro is the educated, that education unfits him for the responsibilities of citizenship, we confess ourselves in a dilemma and plead for that education which will enable us to shun the Scylla as well as the Charybdis." Their logic was brushed aside. The committee completed its task in early March after weeks of debate, breathlessly reported in the *New Orleans Daily Picayune*, and the day this antisuffrage plan was announced, coverage began, "The child is born."[23]

King's story was motivated by such emotional politics and fully committed to the assertion of white Creole purity, yet it exposes an uneasy racial hybridity. Claire and her grandmother survive only because of the unpaid labor of Betsy, a poor black woman who helps with housework and provides moral support. At the same time "Bright White" becomes slavelike as well: as she takes on her grandmother's work, she grows "blacker." Claire begins to feel drawn to the "loud, coarse, passionate" music coming from the nearby brothel run by a mulatto woman. "When I hear music like that," Claire cries, "it is as if my blood would come out of my veins and dance right there before me. . . . I want so much to get up and follow it, out, out, wherever it is, until I come to the place where it begins fresh and sweet and clear from the piano, and then dance, dance, dance, until I cannot dance one step more!" Even as she imagines a pure wellspring of jazz, Claire understands "blackness" as an infectious, miscegenating illness: "Oh bonne maman," Claire begs, "can't you give me something to make me stop feeling this way—to make the music let me alone?"[24] Metaphors of slavery and disease shape the white body.

And metaphors of racial identity emerge from the plantation house itself: approaching death, Nénaine calls to her granddaughter, "Claire, I wish I could see my little worktable again"—recalling her " 'corbeille de noces,' " a wedding gift that sat at the window of her room in the big house upriver, looking out over what was, for King, the ideally ordered world of slavery.[25] "You see, so much would come back to me if I could see my little table. I think sometimes, mon enfant, that the loss of our souvenirs is the worst loss of all for us women. . . . Even when our souvenirs are crumbling to dust they are fresher than we women are at the end. Mon enfant, I advise you, give up everything in life except your souvenirs."[26] For King, there is something more vital about the evidence of memory than about the living body. At the same time, the souvenir may be a living body—that of Nénaine's personal slave, Aza. "And it was Aza who first found it out—Aza," she continues. Aza, it seems (extracting meaning from the exasperating vagueness of the prose), had revealed the hidden compartment in the worktable that held the feminine equipment so exciting to young Nénaine. In fact Aza herself was a gift, bestowed when she was only a day old by none other than the slave's own mother. King's astounding solipsism is compounded in Nénaine's reflection that the baby "was more like a doll to me than a human being. . . . It felt so grand to have a live doll, just when I was beginning to tire of the others."[27] Rescuing the white plantation child from her ennui requires the willing sacrifice of the black mother's daughter, and the notion of the souvenir compresses a history of power into physical objects that may be human.

As she grew up, Nénaine recalls, "I could never put my hand out, so, without touching Aza."[28] Like the stone statues of mammies and monuments to faithful slaves that emerged from Lost Cause campaigns, at first glance King's fiction participates in redefining relations of property in terms of love, a postslavery paternalism intended in part to help shift the meaning of slavery from cruel to heroic in the public discourse of the postwar nation. King's commitment to proslavery ideology was such that she shunned her longtime mentor, Charles Gayarré, because he briefly depicted white cruelty to slaves in his memoirs.[29] And yet she insisted, "I am a realist *à la mode de la Nouvelle-Orleans*."[30] "New Orleans realism" was apparently not comprehensive but carnivalesque. On the urban plantation, Nénaine might still "put her hand out" and touch Aza, although she never realizes this. It is Aza who runs the quadroon brothel around the corner, from which the sensual epidemic of jazz emanates along with the moral disease of prostitution.[31] Aza has become a mistress—or rather, madam—while Nénaine has become a slave. But Aza's status as mistress demeans her, and this reversal balances slavery and white Creoles' supposed moral vacancy against the "real" social problem of prostitution. Through the figure of the quadroon madam, King recasts slavery as respectable. Prostitution and the brothel are the dishonorable doppelgangers of slavery and the plantation, as King lets her audience forget one of the most troubling sexual practices enabled by the slave plantation, white men's rape of black women.

King revisits the concept of human property in her depictions of both the madam and the faithful servant. The white women own Betsy only "by virtue of her dependence," and they "could pay her only with their thanks."[32] When dependence, not bills of sale, is what creates ownership, slavery becomes much more benign. But as King has already made clear, Betsy is not nearly as dependent on the white women as they are on her. She encountered the hungry and friendless child Claire soon after she had arrived in "this here quadroon faubourg."[33] "And what could a nigger do? . . . more in-specially a Baptist," Betsy says to herself. "Circumstances never permitted the childish appeal for assistance to cease, and an unselfish, tender heart never permitted it to meet with disappointment. It was three years now since that morning, but the sun, measuring their horizon, had never shown [sic] on a moment of distrust in either to their simple confidence, or of disloyalty to the pious obligation of serving, by fair means or foul, the proud old lady glorying in her lofty ideas of self-support."[34] Betsy knows the white women would be unable to survive without her, but she permits the old lady her pride. According to King, in enabling this illusion of self-support Betsy performs a duty that upholds her own self-worth; each rung in the hierarchy is equally invested in the overall stability of the system.

But our sense of Betsy's self-abnegation is undercut by a heated argument between Betsy and Aza over who has the most claim to the white matriarch, which takes place literally over her dead body.

Who owns this body and all it signifies? Aza, passing the white slave quarters, sees that one of its inhabitants has died. When she enters to pay her respects, she finds Betsy watching over the corpse. Betsy soon discovers that Aza is the madam from the nearby brothel. The two women argue their property rights in the white woman by comparing which one of them—her post-Emancipation servant or her antebellum slave—was most owned by her. "Don't you dare look at the face of my madam! Don't you dare touch her again!" Betsy commands. "Your madam! Your madam!" echoes Aza. "Don't you dare call her your madam. She was my madam! I was her Aza! I belonged to her."[35] At this, Betsy becomes nearly speechless with righteous indignation. "Your madam! Your—my God in heaven! And she lay a-dying here, and the mamzelle a-starving, and you her servant, what belonged to her, in that house over there! . . . A-scandalizing, a-rioting, a-flaunting yourself in carriages, you and your gals, right past this house!"[36] By contrast, Betsy claims a status "the same as if I were her boughten slave."[37] In attempting to make the case for slavery as an institution in which the highest ethical principles were brought to bear, and in which slaves and former slaves felt this profoundly bonded with their white masters, King suggests that the fact that whites had owned blacks meant blacks could claim property rights in whites. And if so, whiteness can be illegally appropriated by blacks. Aza thinks resentfully of Betsy, "How dared she steal the language and sentiments of the dead one in the coffin, and talk to her [Aza] like a mistress?"[38] King highlights slavery's crucial role in producing whiteness and even white bodies as valuable property; at the same time, she is forced to acknowledge that white property may circulate on the other side of the color line.

The rest of the story attempts to banish the specter of whiteness as black property. Aza returns to her original role as Nénaine's supplemental body when, at Nénaine's funeral, she facilitates the family reunion that the white woman failed to accomplish before her death: "A pauper's funeral had been ordered . . . but the family and friends summoned by Aza formed a cortège that filled the little street, and the service in the mortuary chapel where Aza directed the hearse to stop was such as only the wealthiest could command. At the end of the procession walked—where had Aza found them all so quickly?—a retinue of old slaves, the last, highest local affirmation of family worth; among them, one of them, in costume, race, condition, was Aza herself, bearing the conventional black and white bead memorial 'Priez pour moi.'"[39] The old plantation elite renews itself in the city. At the end of the day, Aza slips through the darkened streets to her brothel, "in her slavish dress, worn for the last time. The piano," King writes, "had already commenced its dances."[40] The value of whiteness remains reliant on slave bodies; their presence in the mourning procession is critical to establishing the worth of the dead. King resurrects slavery, staged like a play complete with costumes, and then shows that, for real, colored (never white) women's bodies continue to be bought and sold. Aza returns to her corrupted condition of madam; she can never truly be mistress.

Another plantation funeral was presented in Charleston in March 1865, a month after Union troops occupied the city. Newly free blacks celebrated Emancipation with a procession stretching over miles. They presented a terrifying vignette: three former slaves, two women and a child, were seated on an auction block and drawn through the streets. According to a contemporary account, "a black man, representing a negro trader" and himself a former slave, "rang his bell and cried out 'How much am I offered for this good cook? . . . Who bids, who bids?'" Seeing this, "old women burst into tears . . . and forgetting that it was a mimic scene, shouted wildly, 'Give me back my children! Give me back my children!'" But it was not a mimic scene—these women mourned children who had been sold and who had disappeared forever among the transactions, migrations, and deaths that occurred as slaveholders settled the southern frontier. Sixty men tied together in a coffle, "representing the numerous coffles that had marched through [Charleston] on their way to Louisiana," followed the auction, and behind them was a hearse bearing the words "Slavery is Dead."[41] Former slaves marking slavery's end so soon after freedom with reenactments of scenes from slavery suggest this performance as an expression of the right to claim bondage as collective memory. King's work attempts to dismiss the radical capacity of black memory by presenting a version of white antebellum nostalgia in which blacks are merely players. But, by turns repulsively retrograde and weirdly subversive, "Bonne Maman" is evidence of the volatile postslavery relationship between race and gender and the ultimate untenability of plantation nostalgia.

While King began her career in fiction in response to George Washington Cable's popularity, Alice Moore Dunbar (later Dunbar-Nelson) began hers in response to the popularity of both Cable *and* King. Dunbar, too, wanted "to tell her version of New Orleans culture."[42] Growing up in New Orleans in the 1870s and 1880s, Dunbar regarded the lifestyle of Creoles of color with longing and eventually blended into their midst while a student at Straight College (which became part of Dillard University) in the historically Creole Seventh Ward.[43] She embraced a society and culture that King and many white Creoles sought to obliterate by insisting it did not exist. Dunbar's early stories about New Orleans, as circumspect and even slight as some of them may seem, therefore constituted an intervention into the dominant rhetoric of race around the turn of the century. In effect, Dunbar publicly contradicted Charles Gayarré (among others), one of New Orleans's most respected historians as well as King's mentor. Gayarré's fiercely held notion that Creole meant white bespoke a feat of conceptual transformation from hybrid to "pure" that would echo in the claims of twentieth-century Creoles of color that theirs was a separate race, one that should not be contaminated by intermixing. Gayarré's views, as voiced in the 1885 speech at Tulane entitled "Creoles of History and Creoles of Romance," "quickly became so universally accepted as truth [among whites] that they found eventual ratification even in the pages of otherwise competent professional historians."[44] Although Dunbar's references to the race of some of her characters were subtle—the title character in her story "Little Miss Sophie" is described as "dusky-eyed," for example, while a character in "The Goodness of St. Rocque" is "dat light gal"—they would have been unmistakable.

"Little Miss Sophie," originally published in Dunbar's first collection of stories, *Violets and Other Tales* (1895), and reprinted in *The Goodness of St. Rocque* (1899), is a distinctly New Orleanian tragic mulatta story. When she enters a church seeking rest, Sophie, a poor seamstress, inadvertently witnesses the unnerving spectacle of her former lover, a white man, getting married. Later she overhears an exchange among a group of his acquaintances on the uptown streetcar: Neale is facing the collapse of his finances, career, and therefore possibly his marriage as a result of his affair with her. The men casually describe Neale's interracial liaison as "some little Creole love-affair" and Sophie as his "dusky-eyed fiancée."[45] The reference to plaçage is explicit, and Dunbar seems to suggest that these kinds of relationships remained at least somewhat common. Neale has not been exposed as immoral for having a relationship with a "Creole" woman of color; the problem is that he had given Sophie a gift, an object of which he is now in desperate need. *She* is not his property, but she possesses his property. "Yes, it's too bad for Neale, and lately married too," says one man to another. "I can't see what he is to do." When the other inquires further, the man continues, "Well, the firm failed first; he didn't mind that much, he was so sure of his uncle's inheritance repairing his lost fortunes; but suddenly this difficulty of identification springs up, and he is literally on the verge of ruin." "Won't some of you fellows who've known him all your lives do to identify him?" "Gracious man, we've tried," comes the response; "but the absurd old will expressly stipulates that he shall be known only by a certain quaint Roman ring, and unless he has it, no identification, no fortune. He has given the ring away, and that settles it."[46]

Reviewing antimiscegenation case law in her study of Creole New Orleans during the nineteenth and twentieth centuries, Virginia Domínguez concludes that the courts pursued their function of supporting the public good by keeping individuals from improvising on the theme of racial difference. The courts "approach their role as seekers of *biological truth*, and decide cases not with regard to the best interests of those individuals concerned but rather in terms of a body of laws designed to prevent people from drawing their *own* conclusions about the implications of particular 'blood lines.' " Domínguez continues,

A kind of paranoia seeps through these statutes, directly or indirectly, limiting nonwhite access to property held by whites. . . . But not until we study the full set of family and estate laws do we get a glimpse of what amounts to an unstated conspiracy. The problem . . . stems from the existence of widespread assumptions about the properties of blood—that identity is determined by blood; that blood ties, lineally and collaterally, carry social and economic rights and obligations; and that both racial identity and class membership are determined by blood. Clearly both the restrictive statutes on marriage, paternity, inheritance and adoption *and* the individual attempts over the years to circumvent those restrictions hinge on such assumptions. The point is that property is not just a corollary of racial classification; it is also a criterion of it.[47]

When property is a criterion of racial classification, if people legally classified as nonwhite can gain access to property historically owned by people legally classified as white, they may in essence become white. Playing out the judges' nightmares, Dunbar imagines a reversal of social norms in which white men are impotent. They have no voice with which to declare Neale's identity. Only a Creole woman of color is capable of restoring his property, and thus his privileged selfhood, to him. As in King's story, whiteness is an entity that requires a supplement, but this fact haunts rather than enables the white man, who has moved on to a white wife but remains stuck to his colored mistress. Yet the confines from which Neale cannot escape were erected by white men themselves, who have located their identities primarily within their right to own property, including property that is human. The system that has not just benefited but generated them has become a trap.

Dunbar imagines possible consequences of self-ownership as a foundational value within a society shaped by slavery: whiteness as property, she suggests, can get lost, possibly for good. "Shame" prevents Neale from trying to find Sophie and requesting the ring from her, and as it turns out, he will never be able to reclaim it. At the cost of her health, Sophie finally saves enough to recover the ring from the pawnshop where she took it during her father's illness. "Dear ring," she says, caressing it, "ma chère petite de ma coeur, chérie de ma coeur. Je t'aime, je t'aime, oui, oui. . . . Tonight, just one night, I'll keep you."[48] Sophie transposes the body of Neale onto his ring and loves him one more time, but true to the conventions of the plot, this night is Sophie's last. Neale can never retrieve his property/self; Dunbar insists on the objectification of whiteness as a consequence of the objectification of women of color.

As these three narratives depict whiteness as an ambivalent quality of property, they point to how, after Emancipation, the ownership of other bodies persistently remained a way in which white identity was organized and recognized. They also illustrate that the sexual and domestic dynamics rooted in the plantation as a model of power remained critical as a point of reference, even in the city. (While plaçage was not specifically a plantation phenomenon, its existence was made possible by the plantation model of white male sexual prerogatives, and it was practiced by men who were often also planters.) Even more important, perhaps, these stories reference the double-edged pleasures associated with owning human property, as they illustrate the nuances of white uneasiness. As Chopin, King, and Dunbar surveyed the complexities of whites' enduring plantation-based desires, the New Orleans city government attempted to regulate such gratification in the experiment that became known as Storyville, or simply "the District." In 1897, the unique excitement of sex across the color line—white men's antebellum "privilege"—became concentrated in this segregated vice district; the practice of buying a woman of color for sex at the fancy girl auctions or keeping a Creole mistress was modified in the temporary purchase of women for sex. Alecia Long writes, "As the states of the former Confederacy struggled to come to terms with Emancipation and a new, post-slavery economic order, New Orleans . . . ceased to be the nation's largest slave market and most permissive port. Instead, it became a tourist destination that encouraged and facilitated indulgence, especially in prostitution and sex across the color line."[49] Storyville indicated that antebellum forms of ownership remained current as objects of white fantasy, and it revealed that they were not sustainable even within a pleasure zone designed and patronized by the white elite. The post-Emancipation white dilemma born of the antebellum social similarity between white wives and black slaves was exacerbated by the fact that white and black women were actively for sale in New Orleans's "high class" brothels.

Before the Civil War, abolitionists had sometimes compared the entire South to a brothel;[50] to own human property was to engage in a transgressive form of sexuality, and transgressive sexuality became a metonym for the entire slaveholding region. During the war, General Benjamin Butler became famous for his "Woman Order." When he encountered white women's defiance of Union occupation in New Orleans, Butler announced that if they continued to resist, they would be treated as prostitutes. Just what he meant by this was a subject of scandalized debate. (He insisted that he wanted his officers to simply ignore the women, as any well-bred man would ignore a prostitute he met in public.) But in the years after the war, images of the differently feminized South aided the process of inter-regional rapprochement.[51] "Romances of reunion" in which southern white women married northern white men provided a sensual, inviting way for whites of both regions to imagine national unity.[52] Soon New Orleans's post-Reconstruction sexual politics would also become an object of widespread interest. New Orleans renewed its approach to the problem of prostitution by envisioning a spatial segregation of vice based on prevailing ideas about race, gender, and property as well as morality. As the South was reintegrated into the nation, New Orleans's transgressive, subversive, commercialized images of female sexuality—in fact, gendered images of ownership descended from plantation society—became part of the nationalized tourist network enabled by the railroad.

Storyville was not a new idea or a specifically postbellum idea; Sidney Story's ordinance actually reduced the limits of two earlier vice districts established in 1857 and 1890. Nor was Storyville a phenomenon unique to New Orleans.[53] It did not even make prostitution legal, but "neither legal nor illegal" within the new boundaries it established.[54] These boundaries took shape in part of the area called back of town, where Grace King had set "Bonne Maman" a decade before; in real life, enterprising madams like Lulu White and other purveyors of octoroons reconstituted plantation dynamics within the radius of the city. White herself sometimes claimed to be "West Indian," locating her enterprise within the circum-Caribbean scope of plantation-born hierarchies even as she attempted to distance herself from the rigid racial dynamics of the segregation-era South. In revised versions of the Old South popular during the Lost Cause era, the plantation was the primary symbol of white power, a power that translated into a postslavery belief in whites as the only truly legitimate property owners. The city government placed Storyville in a neighborhood that was home to many working-class people of color as well as a church, a school, and the oldest cemetery in the city, St. Louis No. 1, where Marie Laveaux was buried (and Homer Plessy now lies). The Story ordinance was intended to simultaneously protect white private property and white female virtue from contamination by "vice."[55] The geography it specified spoke not only to the lack of political influence within the community of color it occupied but also to the prevailing attitude among whites that blackness was a signifier of sexual depravity.[56] To be a prostitute of color was to fulfill stereotypes of black sexuality; to be a white prostitute was to be, on some level, black.

White men from all over were happy to take advantage. The desire to isolate vice from the everyday workings of so-called respectable society failed miserably when the District was incorporated into the city's transportation infrastructure. In 1908 the brothels of Basin Street became integral to the experience of arriving in New Orleans by one of several railroad lines that terminated at the new Canal Street station (Canal Street was the city's main shopping district). "I remember when the train used to pull into the sheds at the old station," a retired rail employee recalled of his youth. "I'd look out from the cab—we'd come in *real* slow—and there'd be the girls standing at the windows, all dressed up in fancy clothes—just posing, you know."[57] Through the combination of its visibility, its centralized location, and its apparent confirmation of widespread preconceptions about the character of New Orleans (permissiveness, excess), Storyville eventually "became an economic powerhouse that generated graft, enhanced the city's erotic reputation, and helped it become one of the South's most popular tourist destinations."[58] Storyville nationalized and relegitimized antebellum sexual mores. Though buying female bodies of color to own forever was no longer legal, it *was* possible to buy, for all intents and purposes, the body of a woman of color for a few hours in the District.

On an early autumn evening in 1890, the deluxe scent of night-blooming jasmine is like a lingering caress from a minor deity, the air still flushed with summer heat. Carriages clatter from Uptown mansions toward Lulu White's Octoroon Club on Basin Street for a sixteenth birthday party. (Though men of color also take their pleasure in the District, they are not allowed to frequent Lulu's except as musicians. Jelly Roll Morton, inventing jazz, as he claimed, played hidden behind a screen. Of course, he figured out a way to see anyway.) The boy turning sixteen expects a unique initiation—he will become a man tonight when he has no ordinary sex, but sex with a goat. All Lulu's girls are dressed in white gowns like those worn by the fashionable women in Paris—all but one, nude except for heels. Eventually she excuses herself, disappearing up the stairs. The room grows louder. Full of Lulu's expensive liquor, guests balance the women—practically indistinguishable from white women—on their knees, dance with them, and buy more champagne. Precisely at midnight, a drum roll sounds. The young man, drunk and blindfolded, is led to the foot of the staircase. The naked woman descends.

In its emphatic, dramatic, quite consciously constructed liminality, this performance reinforced and exploited the limits of the city's social and racial divisions. In addition to the provocative suggestion of bestiality, the term "goat" had another meaning inside the brothel. According to at least one Mahogany Hall prostitute, in the brothel's vernacular it was an abbreviation of "scapegoat." The goat was a surrogate victim unique to a society managing the after-effects of Emancipation through conspicuous consumption—in particular, the conspicuous consumption of "other" bodies. She is quite literally a receptacle for past transgressions of the larger community: the historic transgressions against slave women's bodies that created something called octoroons in the first place, as well as the transgression against black bodies that was slavery itself. The fact that the octoroon prostitute is, in the post-Reconstruction South, a purchase that can be made by white men is a form of redemption for the slave system, a special "privilege" legally reiterated at the turn of the century a few blocks from the sites of nineteenth-century slave auctions—the St. Louis Hotel in the French Quarter or the slave pens just across Canal Street. Profits from the rents in Storyville accrued to property owners that included some of the city's leading white businessmen, as well as the Catholic Church and Tulane, flowing in the same direction that money from the sale of bodies always had even as it made some madams, both white and of color, very rich.[59]

But, inevitably, the ritual leaks some of its tension, some of the meaning that its audience meant and wanted it to have. Perhaps the young man has already had sex; word has likely gotten out that the "goat" is actually a beautiful woman.[60] Maybe she is not an octoroon, but a white woman passing. White-appearing prostitutes were so highly in demand, so well paid, and so difficult to tell apart from legally white women that some white prostitutes simply declared themselves to be octoroons, even as legally black women were doing the opposite in order to get better-paying "respectable" work.[61] A man having sex with an octoroon in Storyville may therefore have been engaged, even more than usual in such circumstances, with his own imagination. The sexual appeal of light-skinned women that Alice Dunbar and Grace King allude to and that Kate Chopin carefully omits was writ large in the octoroon brothels of Storyville. But the fact that bodies of all colors and "of all nations," as the madam Emma Johnson optimistically advertised,[62] were objects of financial transactions in the District signaled the failure of attempts such as King's to reconstitute a recognizably antebellum culture near the turn of the century. Storyville spoke not only to the desire to return to the old ways but also to the limits of white southern society's ability to restructure itself around one of its historic "rights."

Evidence of both longing and failure eventually became an embarrassment. The existence of the goat was only preserved in oral history; it may have been one of the more scandalous details that the first Storyville historian, Al Rose, collected and then chose not to include in his book *Storyville, New Orleans*.[63] In a draft of the manuscript that Rose donated to Tulane, he writes, "The fact is that as raw as the report is, the *most* extreme details have been consigned to the wastebasket, not because the author chose to 'draw the line' somewhere, but because they represented individual deviations and were not characteristic of large numbers of inhabitants of the District."[64] By the time Rose started his research in the 1960s, the existence of Storyville had been in some cases deliberately erased from the landscape and from documentary effects. Rose describes his discovery that references in the New Orleans public libraries' newspaper collections had been quietly excised, relevant pages in the plat books at City Hall had been removed, and the *Times-Picayune* had tossed its photographs from the Storyville era in 1938 (the paper makes a practice of throwing out photos every so often). In the early 1940s, markers of Storyville were literally wiped off the map when politicians changed the names of the streets that had bounded the District.[65] But Rose himself apparently made multiple tapes of interviews with former prostitutes and others who had firsthand knowledge of Storyville that have never come to light. Of the nineteen oral histories he claims to have recorded, he published seven; the remaining twelve disappeared. Rose's manuscript states that these tapes were donated to the Howard Tilton Memorial Library at Tulane; but they are not there, and there is no record of the accession. Diana Rose, the executor of her husband's estate, referred to these tapes somewhat mysteriously in conversation with me and other researchers, including the curator of Tulane's Hogan Jazz Archives, but never produced them. Perhaps, not unlike the anonymous vandals in the public library, Rose himself "had a stake in suppressing the information" they contained, and for some of the same reasons. His interpretations of life in the District, particularly concerning race relations and the degree of integration that was actually practiced even within some of the brothels themselves, were inaccurate, as historians writing within the past few years have discovered, as was his assertion that the birth of jazz had nothing to do with brothels.[66]

The development of Storyville took place within a national context of sometimes unsuccessful attempts to regulate the geographies of both race and prostitution and, relatedly, of a shift in attitudes toward leisure. Leisure became, as John F. Kasson writes, "more vigorous, exuberant, daring, sensual, uninhibited, and irreverent."[67] The primary sites and symbols of this transformation, Kasson argues, were amusement parks, which "emerged as laboratories of the new mass culture, providing settings and attractions that immediately affected behavior. Their creators and managers pioneered a new cultural institution that challenged prevailing notions of public conduct and social order, of wholesome amusement, of democratic art."[68] In contrast to mass leisure complexes like Central Park in the mid-nineteenth century and the Columbian Exposition of 1893, which sought to affirm the status quo and keep an unruly populace in line,[69] amusement parks offered temporary opportunities to break out of social confines, though racial segregation delimited the extent of the release. The shift from "productive" to "unproductive" leisure paralleled, as Mason Stokes writes, "a broad shift from a reproduction-based sexuality to a pleasure-driven heterosexuality." And the developing concept of heterosexuality did not necessarily assist in maintaining geographies of segregation. Even as government, law, and white public opinion at the turn of the century insisted on rigid meanings of race, "the system of desire unleashed by a newly emergent heterosexual pleasure principle threaten[ed] the purity upon which whiteness depends."[70] Growing anxiety about prostitution across the nation during this time seemed to reflect a sense that heterosexual pleasure had the capacity to alter social order by bringing ethnic and racial "pollution" into contact with whiteness. Yet the original attempts to segregate Storyville, while still on the books, were more or less ignored until the very end of its existence, and thus Storyville established what was essentially a racially mixed sexual amusement park drawing male tourists from across the country in search of precisely that which endangered white racial ideology: nonreproductive desire and sex across the color line. Louisiana historian Katy Coyle's research suggests that the District was the scene of widespread integration despite the laws intended to prevent it.[71] The already impure products of America went even crazier. Looking back, a white pimp recalled, "Well, I didn't have much education, but I wasn't stupid. And I see how these broads was with money and I begin to understand how all these big-shot pimps got all those broads workin' for 'em and them guys buying theirselves diamonds and sharp clothes and like that. So one day them broads have a real fight over me. . . . So I slug 'em both until they both cryin' and I tell 'em they better do I like I say or I'll go away and leave 'em both. By that time I understood that nothin' had to make sense no more."[72] A crib woman, the daughter of slaves, commented, "Well, shit, you know how it is with these here 'hos. Every one of them got a man she give all her money! I ain't no different, I give *my* man my money. One time I buy him a box back suit, and you know what he do? He punch me in the head and tell me he don't need no suit, he need money. After that I just give him my money. I don't know why. I just give him my money."[73]

The bodies for sale in the District—which were both male and female—were not commodities in exactly the same way that they had been within a system that presented human beings as reproducible, if not uniform, goods. Storyville translated the appeal of the slave hierarchy into the postbellum consumer economy, within which white girls could be auctioned off, as one survivor of life in the District memorably describes. At age twelve she and a friend were sold as a pair of virgins by the madam Emma Johnson. "So, Emma she had a big mouth," she recounts, and "a loud voice, [and she] made a speech about me and Liz and how everybody in the District knew we was virgins, even though we did all these other things and if the price was right, tonight was the night and she'd have an auction. Some snotty kid bid a dollar and Emma had one of the floor men slug him and throw him out in the street. One man bid the both of us in, honest to God, for seven hundred and seventy-five dollars *each*! A lot of johns bid, and he wasn't gonna be satisfied with just one."[74] Occurring around 1916 in a brothel in a prostitution district that actively traded on New Orleans's slave history, this event directs us to a relationship between the social consequences of African slavery and the larger context of emerging consumerism.

The issue of prostitution became a lightning rod for concerns about the rapid transition to consumer culture; as Ruth Rosen writes, a "common theme in discussions of prostitution was discontent with the shift from a producer orientation to a consumer orientation, emphasizing the accumulation and display of luxuries and the pursuit of expensive pleasures."[75] A primary objection of antiprostitution reformers was that the paradigm of the commodity had come to apply to people, as if it had not applied to people throughout the nation's history. "To middle-class reformers," Rosen observes, "prostitution became a cultural symbol of the birth of a modern industrial culture in which the cold, impersonal values of the marketplace could invade the most private areas of people's lives. Reformers discussed prostitution in terms that reflected their acute anxieties about other unresolved ills and problems of the day: unrestricted immigration, rates of venereal disease, the anonymity of the city, the evils of liquor, the growth of a working-class urban culture, and most important of all, the changing role of women in society."[76] The development of the consumer economy had made everything in it, including white people, something for sale. Mark Connelly suggests that the authors of the *Chicago Vice Commission Report*, a landmark document in antiprostitution literature published in 1911, had intuited the Marxist concept of reification, "the necessity in capitalist society of turning all relationships into relationships between things, or commodities. Ultimately even human beings, relationships between human beings, and human attributes become commodities to be exchanged or bought and sold."[77] In other words, people can become commodity fetishes. The association between consumer culture and female prostitution was explicit: the Chicago vice commission had argued that department stores were a particular "breeding ground" for prostitution, and for many Chicago residents, the fact that Macy's department store had "opened in the neighborhood of what was once a notorious red-light district" seemed to confirm this belief.[78] The Louisville, Kentucky, vice commission report released in 1915 bemoaned "the commercialization of almost every phase of human life."[79] In *Prostitution in the United States prior to the Entrance of the United States into the World War* (1921), Howard Woolston launched a staccato series of phrases that have become (or already were) clichés: "Everything has its price. This is the day of the dollar. Money talks." The real problem for Woolston was that rampant consumerism had also succeeded in commodifying those who were not engaged in vice. "Even virtue has its market," he complained. "Men barter their brains for good incomes; women trade their hospitality for social position; candidates for public office modify their principles in view of preferment."[80]

As a tourist attraction, Storyville had its own guidebooks. The most common were called Blue Books, a combination of tour guide, semierotic literature, and promotional booklet. Later editions featured photographs. As these entries emphasize the female body as a product, they sometimes use almost exactly the same terms as advertisements for other luxury goods included in the Blue Books. "She comes from the south and is very well made. . . . The warm place at her side in bed is never without a wealthy occupier," reads the copy for "Miss Cora Dewit." A few pages later, there is an advertisement for "Highest Grade Havana Cigars Cuban Made."[81] Charlotte Perkins Gilman and Jane Addams had argued that women's desire for consumer goods turned women themselves into consumer goods—that commodity culture turned women's bodies into commodities, as prostitutes.[82] (On a trip to Chicago in the early 1890s, Max Weber noted that the bodies of prostitutes were arrayed in windows, like the consumer goods in department store windows, "with the prices displayed.")[83] But as we have seen, women's bodies had long been linked to commodities through slavery, as a way to justify slavery. And though prostitution took different forms depending on region—the western frontier, particularly as a result of the Gold Rush, as well as the immigrant boom in northern and midwestern cities, challenged the national infrastructure and national values—"slavery" was at the heart of the problem with prostitution in the United States as a whole. Prostitution in Storyville helps clarify how the specter of everything, including people, as priced to sell in a consumer market put pressure on the post-Reconstruction dilemma of constructing differences between whites and blacks. These differences had to be based on criteria other than the fact that one group consisted of commodified or potentially commodifiable things, while the other grounded its identity in its right to be buyers of these things. Once a large percentage of the public regardless of race had a price, a crisis of whiteness necessarily ensued, and it was known as "white slavery."

Between the year Kate Chopin published *The Awakening* and the beginning of World War I, the nation experienced a surge of white-slave hysteria—hysteria because there was never any real data to support the widespread notion that "respectable" white girls were being trafficked in huge numbers. White slavery, according to Connelly, was a way that people explained to themselves what had happened to daughters who went to work in the city and never came home, and it conveniently placed the blame for this symptom of economic transformation—the surge of massive factories, department stores, and new patterns of consumption—on nonwhites (Jews, Chinese, and other "others" were believed to be the primary white-slave traders).[84] The term "white slavery" had been used before the Civil War by advocates for women's rights like Angelina Grimké and Lydia Maria Child, but by the time Reconstruction had ended, white slavery meant white prostitution.[85] White society was gripped by a "near-obsession with the view that in the booming market economy of the early twentieth century, woman constituted a form of private property acquired through the market"; "with its lurid depictions of economic exploitation and its urgent calls for reform, white slavery literature is a nightmarish reflection of a social order overrun by business."[86] The literature of white slavery both obscures the social dilemmas of free blacks and exploits the power of the figure of the black slave, even as it conceals black slavery. "While

46 *Sex and Segregation*

interest in and agitation for black rights had dramatically declined in the post-reconstruction era," writes Gabrielle Foreman, "progressive organizations and their constituencies rallied behind anti-white slavery efforts." This replacement of black slavery with white occurred to such an extent that the Department of Justice's chief investigator into the problem of forced prostitution asked Congress to invoke the Thirteenth Amendment in an effort to combat it. At the same time, echoing big business's use of the Fourteenth Amendment, "the Supreme Court, southern Democrats and the executive branch actively eroded this same legislation as it applied to the ex-slaves whose rights it was drafted to protect."[87] (Meanwhile the Fifteenth Amendment was being nullified in the South by literacy requirements, poll taxes, and intimidation.)

A 1914 cartoon by Thomas Bellows illustrates the extent to which slavery had become white in turn-of-the-century America. A languid white woman reclines on a sofa, one hand resting on a book in her lap. Standing above her is a plump black woman wearing a fine hat and a fur stole.

"But if you have never cooked or done housework—what have you done?"
"Well, Mam, Ah—Ah's been a sort of p'fessional."
"A professional what?"
"Well, Mam—Ah takes you for a broad-minded lady—Ah don't mind tellin' you Ah been one of them white slaves."[88]

Sexuality completely overwhelms race in Bellows's wry commentary, and the figure of the free black is eclipsed by that of the enslaved white. "The white 'slave' is the most extreme victim of the property system," argues Margit Stange. And yet she can only be the *most* extreme victim in a system that values whiteness more highly than blackness; in her otherwise insightful analysis of connections between property and racial identity, Stange misses the fact that white-slave hysteria referenced a breakdown of the system set in place to control black bodies. The concept of whiteness as valuable property had become embedded in law and custom over more than two centuries, but now white womanhood was potentially stolen property—and the virtue lost by white slaves was unrecoverable, as Alice Dunbar's work suggests. It becomes clear that white fears about the potential reach of commodity culture are inextricable from fears associated with the aftermath of Emancipation.

In New Orleans, various regulations attempted to spatialize the differences between prostitutes and potential white slaves. Katy Coyle and Nadiene Van Dyke write that "on Sunday afternoons . . . prostitutes shopped along fashionable Canal Street. In doing so, they ostentatiously breached the barrier between the sporting world of Storyville and respectable society. Presumably in response to this well-known practice, between 1911 and 1917 Newcomb [College's] 'Rules for Student Residence' specifically prohibited the students, even those escorted by chaperons, from 'walking on Canal Street on Sunday.' In 1918, the year after Storyville was dismantled, Newcomb lifted the restriction."[89] As Al Rose wrote in an unpublished early version of *Storyville, New Orleans*, "One middle-aged lady of New Orleans's true upper crust recalls how her mother used to take her dressmaker to opening day at the Fair Grounds [in the 1890s], the better to copy the latest styles from the costumes worn by the demimondaines. 'The only way you could tell one of *them*,' an elderly Creole grandmere recalls, 'was that they would be more quiet, more fashionably attired than the wives and daughters of our leading citizens—but *then* we only saw them from a distance. Today they sit *next* to us, my dear.' "[90] Or, in the words of a Storyville prostitute, "They all *putas* too!"[91] (By the late 1930s, *Mademoiselle* would feature two new lipsticks from Volupté called "Lady" and "Hussy," and the consumer was free to choose both simultaneously: "Each of these two categories being as much a matter of mood as a matter of fact.")[92]

That Storyville was anything but gone and forgotten more than a decade after the War Department put down its ironclad foot— and that New Orleans's apparent loucheness remained an object of widespread fascination—was clear in articles that appeared in popular magazines during the mid-1930s. In "Uncovering the Vice Cesspool of New Orleans," Edward Anderson, writing for *Real Detec-*

*tive,* invited his reader to "watch [the prostitutes] as they lean out from shuttered windows and doorways, beckoning, posturing, calling—enticing sex-hungry males to a feast of flesh for the price of a couple of decks of cigarettes. . . . Reader, you are witnessing the nightly saturnalia within the New Orleans red-light district in the fall of 1934. Wide-open vice is running riot almost under the shadows of the century-old walls of Old St. Louis Cemetery and Our Lady of Guadaloupe Church."[93] Anderson is fascinated by the fact that vice is such an integral part of New Orleans culture. He notes that despite Huey Long's battle with the city's corruption—not just openly practiced prostitution but the way money from such illegal activities flowed into the city government—most residents were not holding their breath waiting for things to change. If Anderson's narrative is to be believed, the "most notorious" of the brothels in this reconstituted district was called Uncle Tom's Cabin, where, presumably, sex across the color line was still readily available and gleefully disturbing references to plantation slavery were perfectly explicit.

In a 1934 article for *Vanity Fair,* "New Orleans Is a Wicked City," Marquis Childs writes, "Corruption is familiar in New Orleans; traditional, one might almost say. And New Orleans accepts it all with a resignation that is difficult for the Northerner to understand." According to Childs, the city's wickedness began with the "birth of its quadroon prostitution," which he describes as "a strange institution comparable to nothing else that has come into being in America."[94] The intersection of blackness, sexuality, and commerce has evolved but endured in New Orleans from the antebellum period to the twentieth century, making the city a singularly unsettling place, presumably not only for Childs. A glance through the issue of *Vanity Fair* in which his article was published, however, makes clear that white bodies have become accepted as vehicles of commerce. The focus on sex for sale in New Orleans brothels is undoubtedly not supposed to remind the absorbed reader of what prostitution might have in common with the use of female bodies in advertising. In fact, it seems that New Orleans, with its long history of profligacy, functioned as a site where the problematic connections between white bodies commodified within a consumer economy and colored bodies for sale in slavery could be quarantined. "New Orleans Is a Wicked City" emphasizes New Orleans's distance from the rest of the country—"in many ways, New Orleans occupies the same place" it always had as a symbol of sin emanating from race mixing and prostitution. "This last spring I went down the river," writes Childs, "and I, a Yankee from the North, was amazed to see how brazen New Orleans still is, though in a less glamorous and more strictly commercial way. It was incredible to me that public vice existed in America on so large a scale. Not unlike the naive visitors of a century ago," he writes, "I sensed the foreignness of the city, its carefree, casual way of life, its wickedness and corruption."[95] Images of New Orleans have participated in the nationalized construction of difference between racially ambiguous bodies of prostitutes and bodies for sale within the normal operations of a consumer economy. In New Orleans the two merge, and consequently the city does not quite belong to the United States. This is a place where the sale of bodies is part of the fabric of life, and it is a "foreign" place for just this reason, titillating to visitors who can return to their by comparison sane and orderly worlds. "Ever since New Orleans first entered the American imagination, during the time when the territory later to be acquired by the Louisiana Purchase was under the rule of France," wrote novelist Hamilton Basso in 1948 with a touch of native pride, "it has been regarded as a place apart; for over a hundred and fifty years now, it has stood as a symbol of exotic alienness in the national mind."[96] Because of its history, New Orleans became a repository for widespread white unease associated with the link between whiteness and property and the attendant reminder of a connection between whiteness and racial otherness. For different reasons, natives and nonnatives alike had a stake in emphasizing, and helping to maintain, New Orleans's reputation as a world unto itself. The singular octoroon at Lulu White's serves finally as a metaphor for the city itself as it helped the nation to incorporate the capacity, in fact the need, of a consumer economy to turn all bodies into things—beginning, as in Veblen's analysis, with women, but not stopping there, as we inhabitants of the millennium know only too well.

Hackneyed images of New Orleans as a prostitute, which even Faulkner helped perpetuate, attest to the way that the city came to trade actively on its history of legitimated vice. In an early prose experiment, Faulkner imagined it from the perspective of "The Tourist": "she" was "a courtesan whose hold is strong upon the mature, to whose charm the young must respond. And all who leave her, seeking the virgin's unbrown, ungold hair and her blanched and icy breast where no lover has died, return to her when she smiles across her languid fan."[97] Though his experiment was not entirely successful, Faulkner effectively summarized some of what it means to miss New Orleans as he reproduced an image that the city would come to actively promote.[98] Louis Armstrong International Airport honors a son of Storyville, and the sounds of traditional jazz—a term that some say first meant sex—accompany visitors through its thickly carpeted walkways, perhaps to Lulu White's lingerie shop, which sells last-minute gifts in Concourse B.[99] The octoroon madam lit up with diamonds like the St. Louis Exposition, her fortune made from white men's unslakable urge for white-appearing women, becomes, in the postmodern zone of the airport, a New Orleans stereotype.[100]

The evolution of this previously destabilizing signifier into an only slightly risqué, approachable icon of New Orleans's appeal to travelers speaks to the evolution of our collective comfort level with the idea of the body as a commodity. At a point when the consumer culture that had developed so rapidly around the turn of the century had become ordinary and seemingly permanent, images of Storyville returned to public consciousness in a show at New York's Museum of Modern Art. Part of the power of Ernest Bellocq's photographs when they were publicly exhibited for the first time in 1970 lay in the way they reimagined Storyville as domestic space and represented prostitutes, at least some of whom were octoroons, as frankly sexual yet ordinary women. Bellocq's work both acknowledged a connection between prostitutes and "normal" women and

revalenced it. While the growing resemblance between the appearance and behavior of prostitutes and that of respectable women was
alarming at the turn of the century, the sexual revolution was making
the open display of female sexuality exciting in a mainstream kind of
way. This similarity became something much less frightening, something even to be celebrated. In her introduction to the catalog of
Bellocq's photographs, Susan Sontag remarks, "It could not be
detected from at least a third of the pictures that the women are inmates of a brothel." The women often present themselves, she continues, as "the wholesome-looking country women most of them
undoubtedly were."[101] Bellocq had allowed these women to be human again. (In fact, Bellocq's compassion may have been overstated;
it could have been Bellocq himself who obliterated the faces of his
subjects in some negatives, since the damage was done before the
emulsion was dry.)[102]

Leafing through the pages that follow Sontag's essay, Janet Malcolm writes, "I paused at a picture of a prostitute with her clothes
on, and it occurred to me to wonder whether she actually was a
prostitute. What evidence was there that she, or, for that matter, any
woman in the book, clothed or unclothed, was an inhabitant of a
whorehouse rather than, say, a cousin or a sister of the photogra-
pher, or a paid model?"[103] Malcolm discovers that the women have
been identified as prostitutes because the wallpaper in some photographs hung in Lulu White's Mahogany Hall. In Bellocq's images,
then, both racial and moral otherness is almost invisible.[104] Even as
these images point once again to the eye's habitual failure to apprehend meaning and remind us of ultimately hopeless yet profoundly influential turn-of-the-century efforts to legislate visibility,
the scene of Storyville today makes historical continuity painfully
obvious. One of its last remnants is Lulu White's saloon at the
corner of Bienville and Basin, which by the early twenty-first century had become a convenience store. Though the architecture of
Storyville itself is nearly gone, the history of racial injustice that
helped make it popular remains obvious in the housing project that
replaced it.

As it drew together racist oppression and tourist pleasure, Storyville forecast both housing projects and what might be seen as their opposite—perhaps the single most popular Deep South tourist attraction, plantation houses. These sites also trade actively on nostalgia for the Old South as they feminize the plantation experience. "Return to gracious living at Madewood Plantation," one brochure invites in flowery italics. "Experience a bygone era in the South's most beautiful setting," tempts another. "Enjoy her beauty and dream of her rich past!" While Storyville foregrounded and capitalized on racial inequality as it reiterated the antebellum appeal of bodies for sale, tours have attempted to suppress even slavery itself as they reconfigure plantation life for public consumption.

## 2. plantations without slaves

no whiteness (lost) is so white as the memory of whiteness
*William Carlos Williams*

---

The gift shop at San Francisco Plantation, on the east bank of the Mississippi River between New Orleans and Baton Rouge, sells pralines, postcards, and cookbooks. It also sells "Black People," miniature plastic boys eating watermelon and women wearing head rags that sit next to the cash register. Once slaveholders bought black people and brought them "home" to this very place; now tourists can take black people home, too, as slavery shrinks into a memory of leisure anchored by recommodified things. During the Lost Cause, the "white home" became a symbol that connected antebellum racial hierarchies with postbellum society. As Grace Hale writes, it "served as a major site in the production of racial identity precisely because there . . . racial interdependence was both visible and denied."[1] It is a very powerful thing to deny something obvious and have that denial accepted as truth. The white home as symbol reached its apex in the plantation house, and plantation houses and their tourist apparatus still call imaginary worlds into being.

The plantation tours, led mainly by women, that have become practically de rigueur for white tourists in the South are grounded in the inspiration of southern women who were part of the planter class, as Patricia West's account of the restoration of Mount Vernon points out. By the mid-nineteenth century, Washington's crumbling plantation had created a predicament for the nation as well as for southerners. Congressional efforts to buy it had come to naught; when the poor relation who inherited it offered it to the national government in 1853, "key members of Congress balked, predicting with some acuity that if government were to enter the business of preserving sites of historical interest, the process would snowball." Rumors circulated that "speculators" were approaching with plans to turn Mount Vernon into a fancy hotel. At this point, with the possibility that " 'Northern capitalists' were about to intercept the 'sacred property,' " southern belle Louisa Bird Cunningham and her daughter Ann Pamela Cunningham stepped in with an "appeal for help to 'Southern ladies.' "[2] Mount Vernon was saved, and the precedent was set for the restoration of other plantation houses as sites of national interest. When most people hear the words "Mount Vernon," their first thought is probably "George Washington," not "slave plantation." Plantations have become popular tourist destinations among whites because "historic house" or "unique architecture" or "romantic" comes to mind before the image of slavery does. And when it does, it will have been filtered through architecture and romance and perhaps not seem so disturbing any more.

Mount Vernon was an isolated case in 1853; by the early decades of the twentieth century, images of endangered plantation houses were more common. In *Absalom, Absalom!* Faulkner vividly describes the destruction of Sutpen's monolith by fire; but Faulkner himself had restored a plantation house and was living in it even as he described the fateful end of the Sutpen dynasty. The years after World War II witnessed a growing national interest in "heritage," though sometimes heritage had to be made from scratch.[3] Michael Kammen writes, "The immense influence of Disneyland made it more and more difficult to distinguish between what really happened in times gone by and what is *supposed* to have happened. In 1974, for example, the town of Medina, Ohio, emulated Disneyland and created new 'historic' structures that had never even existed in Medina."[4] By the twenty-first century, plantation houses (including Faulkner's) had been firmly established as national heritage sites— and, like downtown Medina, as mnemonic devices. To help remember their speeches, classical orators inscribed upon their minds real buildings, the features of which could serve as receptacles of content, translating abstract thought into physical space, and vice versa.[5] Like the loci used to perfect the "art of memory," plantation houses are transformed: like ancient politicians, plantation tour guides embed ideology in the chambers and ornaments they describe, the plantation becoming as much idea as place.

Plantations, as what we might call theaters of memory,[6] present corrective counterparts to the image of a malformed, backward, or just eccentric South, visible from Flannery O'Connor's poor white southern gothic to John Berendt's pseudo-ethnography *Midnight in the Garden of Good and Evil*. The pulp fiction "plantation novel," popular between the 1950s and the 1970s, followed Storyville in its recognition of taboo sexuality as a primary element of what got people interested in the plantation. In these novels, writes Christopher Geist, the white master and mistress are able to enjoy sex only with their slaves. While he turns to slave women, she turns to the "breeding stud" (as Geist identifies the character). In one novel, the master secretly barbecues his wife's lover. Discovering that what she has eaten is not pork but man, she faints and, falling into the barbecue pit, also dies the death designed for the slave. These books struck a chord; according to Geist, they sold in the "hundreds of millions."[7] Plantation tours, taking place at the sites that inspired such garish fantasies, use the persuasive evidence of their carefully reconstructed environments to normalize the peculiar institution and the fact of the war in which white southerners attempted to define themselves as unique enough to be called a separate nation, as well as to cancel out other peculiar things about the South ("squeal like a pig!"). In the late twentieth century, claims of southern difference were both renewed and reincorporated into the nation by Bo and Luke Duke in their undefeatable General Lee, a Dodge Charger emblazoned with the Stars and Bars; Confederate flags on license plates in Maryland, approved by a federal judge; and Confederate flags flying above the capitol buildings in Jackson and Columbia, which presidential candidates refused to condemn. In 1980, Ronald Reagan officially began his successful campaign for president at the Neshoba County Fair in Philadelphia, Mississippi, where Chaney, Schwerner, and Goodman were murdered in 1964. With their killers still at large Reagan declared, "I believe in states' rights."[8] Using leisure as a backdrop for retrograde politics, tours capitalize on the appeal of the strange and even dangerous South while converting southern difference into national difference through nostalgic invocations of partly fabricated histories in which blackness is irrelevant. Whites become the real laborers in a slave society, and they suffer as they claimed slaves never did.

Complaints about the hardships of slavery—more precisely, of possession—for whites were voiced by northerners and southerners alike before the Civil War. In 1856, for instance, Frederick Law Olmstead described a scene at a small plantation in Virginia where "during three hours or more, in which I was in company with the proprietor, I do not think there were ten consecutive minutes uninterrupted by some of the slaves requiring his personal direction or assistance. He was even obliged, three times, to leave the dinner table." When he returns, the planter complains, "To make anything by farming here, a man has got to live a hard life. You see how constantly I am called upon—and often, it is as bad at night as by day. Last night I did not sleep a wink til near morning. I am quite worn out with it, and my wife's health is failing."[9] In the hidden transcript of this scene, the enslaved have figured out how to exact a price from the slaveholder in return for the price he paid for them.[10] Perhaps, feigning incompetence, they will have shortened the lifespan of the master and mistress as forced labor threatens to shorten theirs, and made of their master a mammy. New Orleanian Eliza Ripley wrote of the loved-to-death Mammy Charlotte, who "often . . . remarked that no one in the house did more and had less to show for it at night than she did": "Guests were made to understand that if they required anything, from a riding horse to a fresh stick on the fire, from a mint julep to a bedroom candle, they had only to call Charlotte. She was never beyond the reach of a summons, day or night."[11] Ripley's Lost Cause nostalgia for the transcendent convenience of slave labor seems to more accurately represent the incessant demands on slaves than do some antebellum planters' remarks. Like Olmstead's host, prewar slaveowners described themselves as the victims of the slave system: "There could be no greater curse inflicted on us than to be compelled to maintain a parcel of Negroes"; "I shall get through my business as quickly as I can, and return to the miserable occupation of seeing to negroes, and attending to their wants and sickness and making them do their duty—and after all I have no prospect of being paid for my trouble."[12] As Union armies triumphed, a Louisiana woman imagined that the planter class, which included her, would become "slaves, yes slaves, of the Yankee Government."[13] Characterizing slavery as a boon to blacks, cared for and civilized by paternal planters, southern apologists could still cast it as a metaphor for ultimate oppression among southern whites. Mildred Rutherford, historian of the United Daughters of the Confederacy from 1911 to 1916, stated baldly, "The negro was the free man and the slaveholder was the slave."[14] Whites became slaves without sacrificing whiteness; blacks became masters without gaining status. Robert E. Lee fought for the South's right to slave labor. His grandson Robert E. Lee proclaimed that the South had stood for abolition: "If the South had been heeded, slavery would have been eliminated years before it was. It was the votes of the southern states which finally freed the slaves."[15] Had the real Robert E. Lee been kidnapped and his identity assumed by an impostor? "Anglo-Saxon emancipation" was necessary.[16]

In the face of the physical evidence of black slavery, both white tourists and white plantation employees still call themselves slaves. Jennifer Eichstedt and Stephen Small describe a series of white slave moments from their research: at a plantation in Virginia, when Eichstedt "inquired about the number of people who had been enslaved on the property . . . she was told that while there had been a study done at some point, neither of the two people she was talking to could remember how many had been there. The white woman then looked at the elderly white man and said, 'Of course, the slaves are still here—we're still here!' " At another Virginia plantation, after the guide had made available an optional tour of the slave quarters "a white male guest asked a white woman, who was apparently his wife, 'Do you want to be in a picture with the slave quarters?' She answered with a laugh, 'I feel like I should be in there!' He then said with a laugh, 'I want a picture of the girls in the slave quarters—it's only appropriate,' and they rounded up their daughters to take pictures."[17] Eichstedt and Small make the point that these people are "demean[ing] the experience of slavery." But as they demean black slavery, they testify to its reach. Wired to other symbolic appropriations of black slavery—Lost Cause images of whites as its victims, wage slavery, and white slavery as prostitution (in the example above, it is the wife who feels like a slave and daughters who are pictured in the slave quarters)—such offhanded comments become part of an American time machine. When we reemerge in the twenty-first century, slavery is a not-that-funny joke ("He then said with a laugh, 'I want a picture of the girls in the slave quarters' "). And the tired humor points to a key part of the problem with nonrepresentations of black slavery on the plantation: when plantations offer tranquil vacations, the roots of contemporary social problems are all the more easily blamed on some perceived intrinsic flaw in black culture.

And yet in the new plantation economy, tourists can view themselves as slaves but also as masters. At Louisiana plantations converted into bed and breakfasts, "a full traditional planter's brunch" may well be served by descendants of slaves. "Climb into a huge mahogany bed that has been in the family for generations"—and whose family has managed to hold onto this cherished heirloom despite the trials of more than a century? If you're white, it's yours.[18] James Scott points out that the public transcript is a highly flattering "self portrait" of the powerful.[19] While the wealthy are often the primary consumers of their own spectacles, through tourism everyone else can become eager consumers of spectacles of power too.[20] Slave quarters are disguised with air conditioning and bubbling bathtubs. Sometimes they have disappeared entirely. Guides at the popular plantation Oak Alley, when asked, produce competing accounts of what happened to them. One said they were "destroyed by a hurricane in the late 1800s," while a woman responsible for designing the tours responded that the slave quarters had simply "disintegrated and fallen down. There was hardly any point in rebuilding them" because they were "just a part of American history that is no more." Though slavery has become irrelevant to the plantation, the slaveless plantation house is central to "American history."

During biannual pilgrimages, "A Cherished Southern Tradition since 1932," in Natchez, Mississippi, "ladies in hoopskirts . . . welcome you to twenty-four beautiful ante-bellum houses, which still treasure the relics and furnishings of a vanished era. The colorful legends of these gracious, time-mellowed dwellings are enshrined in the history of the Natchez country." Though refineries have often become part of plantation landscapes, tours in Louisiana successfully construct their appeal along agrarian lines—even when, as in one case, the oil company owns the plantation. As "dwellings," the contents of the house become crucial to the narrative, and tour guides regularly assert that furnishings are "original to the home" or at least "antique" or "of the period," although it is not made clear exactly what the period is. One brochure boasts, "The furniture was either plantation-made by artisans or—later—of the finest European import." In this once again unspecified time, "later," which can only refer to post-Emancipation, it apparently became clear that slaves were not in fact all that necessary to the running of the plantation. Eichstedt and Small's analysis of plantation tours in Virginia found that there were "*thirty-one times as many mentions of furniture at these sites than of slavery or those enslaved.*"[21] Tours in Louisiana and Georgia produced "similar numbers." Furniture has replaced people as objects. The furniture becomes a kind of anti-commodity fetish—not for sale itself, it disguises the presence of people at the plantation who were. After the slaves "left," as an Oak Alley tour guide put it, there was still plenty of money with which to purchase the "finest" European furniture. Perhaps furniture was a consolation prize for the loss of human things.

The tour of Longwood, a plantation house in Natchez that was never completed, exposes the process of the production of nostalgia. The building of Longwood, a gigantic octagonal "Oriental Villa" capped with "a magnificent Persian dome," was halted by Union blockades.[22] As a result, the owners lived in the only finished part of the house, the basement, originally intended as the playroom for their eight children. The tour of the basement offers visitors an intimate view of family life, as they gaze upon the wife's child-birthing couch and peer into the upholstered chair in the master bedroom, its seat set aside to reveal a pink porcelain chamber pot. Unlike the many tours that claim to reveal plantation houses as they were when planters lived in them, a tour of Longwood offers the infrastructure of the house as the primary attraction. Novelist Ellen Douglas describes playing as a child in Longwood's upper stories, which were "still littered with scaffolding, dried-up buckets of paint, canvas carpenters' aprons, ladders, and tools," and "climbing among the rafters and floor joists and looking out from the windowed dome over abandoned fields and shaggy lawns."[23] The scaffolding and tools, their purpose aborted, have been preserved in order to dramatize the Civil War's effects on the southern economy —that is, to mourn the planters' rudely interrupted lives. The tour does not acknowledge that the scaffolding was erected and the tools set down by enslaved carpenters. But slave craftsmanship appears in the details of many thousands of bricks made by hand, which would have been concealed by plaster and stucco had the house been finished according to plan, and in the beams that curve toward the cupola.

Despite the architecture's eloquence and the dramatic contrast between the relatively tiny size of the quarters intended to house thirty-two blacks, visible alongside the 30,000 square feet intended to house ten whites—and this was only the family's summer home— it is because Longwood's white inhabitants were millionaires that tourists are urged to bemoan their misfortune. Packing crates fill the areas that were to be the library and dining room. As visitors walk across the bare boards and look up into the partially built upper floors, the guide encourages the group to imagine black and white marble tiles, a grand stairway, and the elaborate furnishings that never arrived to grace these rooms. The grandeur of Longwood is even more apparent because it never was. If they are receptive to the building's cues, tourists develop a vested interest in seeing the plantation as an opulent palace and, by association, legitimate the slave labor without which it hangs suspended like the villas of Pompeii.

As tourists in the bowels of the plantation become like family, they take the place of slaves in bearing intimate witness to the life of the masters, and the spaces occupied and used by slaves transform accordingly or disappear. At Oak Alley, the building that originally housed the kitchen still exists but has become unrecognizable as a garage (and is not mentioned on the tour). Edward Chappell, director of architectural research at Colonial Williamsburg, describes a similar treatment of former slave sites at Monticello. Great pains have been taken to preserve Monticello precisely as it was when Thomas Jefferson lived there. However, Chappell writes, "surviving in Monticello's south range are workers' dwellings for which detailed records of occupancy exist, and there are at least two workers' rooms in the main cellar, all directly accessible from exhibition areas. For the museum to continue using these intact spaces for redundant toilets, break rooms, and storage is, frankly, outrageous."[24] Documenting abuses of slave space at other tourist plantations, Eichstedt and Small include a photo of a sign that reads "Servants Quarters" (invoking the common euphemism). Below it hangs a smaller sign: "Rest Rooms." The designers of Longwood's tourist facilities also took advantage of the proximity of the slave quarters by converting them into a place for waste. At the same time, white waste may be elevated to the status of "heritage." At Chatham Manor in Virginia, a sign next to a substantial wingback chair conveys this information: "The wingback chair in front of you dates to the late 1700s. A circular hole cut into the bottom of the seat identifies it as having been a chamber chair. According to family tradition, George Washington, the Marquis de Lafayette, James Madison, James Monroe, Washington Irving, and Robert E. Lee all used this chair."[25] As strange as it is to imagine the nether parts of these famous men passing over the same pot, this historic segregated men's room becomes "tradition," while sites where slaves slept are effaced by modern plumbing.

Laura Plantation in Vacherie, Louisiana, presents itself as unique not only because it was owned by (white) Creoles rather than "Americans" but because it still has slave quarters. "Surrounded by sugarcane are Laura's 12 buildings on the National Register, including her historic slave quarters," the brochure notes enthusiastically. The slave quarters are still "her" property. African folktales of *Compair Lapin* were first recorded here in French by white Creole historian

Alcée Fortier, who, like Joel Chandler Harris with the Br'er Rabbit stories, then got most of the credit when he "collected and edited" them in 1895 as *Louisiana Folk-tales, in French Dialect and English Translation*. Despite the brochure's excitement over the existence of intact slave quarters at Laura, in contrast to so many of its competitors along River Road, slave quarters are not necessarily featured on the tour. In fact, they are more or less falling apart and filled with architectural refuse. When a Haitian colleague asked if there were plans to restore the cabins, our white guide quickly replied, "Oh no—you are welcome to visit but that will be left alone." Perhaps made self-conscious by this question coming from a person of color, the guide was unable or unwilling to offer any meaningful information about slavery at Laura. The fact that the slave quarters of which Laura boasts are not being restored—unlike the rest of the plantation (which was badly damaged by fire in 2004)—may be due to an official ambivalence about the implications of maintaining, and thereby perhaps seeming to authorize, the meager conditions in which enslaved people lived. Regardless, the virtual neglect of the quarters contradicts Laura's claims of inclusiveness.[26]

Some plantation tour organizers have recognized the commercial possibilities, if not the social responsibility, associated with illuminating the history of slavery. An article published in the *New Orleans Times-Picayune* in 2003 calls attention to the fact that "at San Francisco plantation . . . a new interpretive history of slavery will focus on a slave cabin on the grounds." The article quotes an assistant manager of San Francisco as saying, "I do think visitors want to hear the other side of the story. . . . Obviously, there used to be more on these tours about the beauty and the elegance of the house, but you have to be inclusive. . . . We are marketing to a new audience. Heritage tourism is a segment of tourism that is growing and of course, we don't want to be left out."[27] It would be easy to read San Francisco's apparent embrace of slave history as simple opportunism. Tours of the plantation now feature a "restored" slave cabin, and the article includes a photo of an African American woman leading a group of white visitors into it. This guide, perhaps a descendant of slaves herself, now reveals it to a market segment that has been targeted by its white owners. This is not to suggest that greater attention to slavery on tours formerly dedicated exclusively to "the beauty and elegance of the house," even attention marked by such profound irony, is not a step in the right direction. But within the larger structure of plantations as tourist attractions, the "addition" of slavery takes place within a framework that continues to privilege white ownership.

Evergreen Plantation, available only by appointment until the past few years, is one of the most unique of River Road's tourist plantations because it still has all of its original slave cabins in their original configuration. It is now the country home of a wealthy New Orleanian as well as a working plantation. Between the long double row of cabins under the old oaks, tourists trace the steps of slaves toward the green fields of cane. And some say the slaves' spirits linger. New Orleans *manbo* Sallie Ann Glassman writes of a visit to Evergreen, "I saw people standing on the porches, could hear children's voices, and heard songs being called. I poured libations, lit candles, and fed the spirits of the slaves—Vodou's early ancestors—in the slave quarters. It was clear that their spirits had moved out of these sparse cabins where so many had suffered and into the trees that line the alley. I thought how appropriate it was that these trees had become containers of spirits. No one had bothered to record or document the lives of the slaves, but their spirits had grown into the convoluted root systems and twisting limbs of the live oaks."[28] Yet the tour tells the story of the plantation from the perspective of wealthy whites (in the old kitchen, where the current owner hosts dinner parties, there are mammies everywhere you look). The tour is divided into halves: slave space and planter space. Our tour visited the cabins first and then walked up to the house. The guide, a white woman in her early seventies, was much more knowledgeable about the history of whites in the area, from the Germans who had cleared the land to the family feuds of the whites who built the big house, than about slavery. Providing details of slavery on this plantation would have altered the tenor of these stories profoundly, and the nonnegotiable aspect of most plantation tours is a sympathetic portrait of white owners. It was practically impossible for the

A slave cabin at Evergreen (photo by Adam Stone)

tour as it was set up to truly depict the lives of both those who suffered in slavery and those who benefited from it. Evergreen offers a rare glimpse of slave life, but in the context of the tour its impact lies mainly in the realm of spectacle and affect, not "history." The tour as a whole would need less of an investment in presenting the perspectives of the planter class, including its modern-day descendants, sympathetically in order to go beyond architectural authenticity in its account of slavery.

If some plantation tourists are now expressing a desire for a more "authentic" representation of plantation life, I would tend to believe that they still want it sanitized. For the most part, tourists at places like San Francisco do not want to hear much about its terrible realities as they contemplate the period furnishings. The *Times-Picayune* writer noted that in her tour of Destrehan Plantation, the guide "referred directly to the contributions of enslaved Africans and pointed out a recreated office like the one used after Reconstruction by the government's Freeman's Bureau to assist liberated

Evergreen slave cabins in their original configuration
(photo by Adam Stone)

former slaves," but "she made no mention of Destrehan's role in one of the ugliest incidents in Louisiana history. Following the 1811 slave revolt, the largest in American history, 21 participants were tried and executed at Destrehan. Their heads were cut off and hung along River Road as an example for other captive Africans."[29] More thorough counternarratives of plantation life do exist nearby, however. Kathe Hambrick founded the River Road African American Museum, which was located on the grounds of Tezcuco Plantation until, as the museum's website notes with a sense of what we might read as poetic justice, Tezcuco burned: "On Mothers' Day 2002, the Tezcuco Plantation was engulfed by fire. The fire destroyed the 4,500 square-foot main plantation house. The River Road African American Museum collection was spared. The owners of Tezcuco decided not to rebuild."[30] (The museum is now located in downtown Donaldsonville.) Louisiana State University history and African American studies professor Leonard Moore began to lead bus

The big house at Evergreen (photo by Adam Stone)

tours from New Orleans that focused exclusively on the history of slavery because, like Hambrick, he was "troubled by the lack of information offered on plantation tours."[31] Meanwhile, Oak Alley owner Zeb Mayhew made clear that *his* plantation's nonrepresentation of slavery's violence was quite deliberate. While "he is mindful of the surge in interest in slavery," he believes that "Oak Alley visitors, for the most part, are looking for a 'Gone With the Wind' brand of fantasy. 'They come for the hoopskirts, the grandeur and the elegance. That's a part of the story, and maybe a better part of the story for us to tell.' "[32] But what is "better" about this part, and for whom? The ritualized mourning of an apparently vanished past seems to maintain and legitimate elements of this past in a form of nostalgia for the present.[33] The very fact that slavery can be so easily detached from the history of the plantation suggests the peculiar choreography of memory through forgetting that French historian Ernest Renan argued is crucial to national unity. In 1882 (as white northerners and southerners engaged in regional reunion at the expense of black citizens in the re-United States), he wrote, "The essence of a nation is that everyone in it has many things in common and yet also that everyone has forgotten many things. . . . Every French citizen must have already forgotten Saint Bartholomew's Massacre, the Massacres of the Midi." Thus he assumes that the French will remember the very things that they must have already forgotten.[34]

Remembering through forgetting is not only a product of dominant culture's ability to hide things in plain sight, however, and the challenges of representing slavery in a plantation context stem from other factors in addition to white denial and disinterest. Rex Ellis describes creating black characters for "living history" presentations at Colonial Williamsburg in the early 1980s, a project that required Ellis and his fellow actors to play the roles of slaves and free people of color in the eighteenth century and interact with modern-day tourists. As they discovered, however, this living history was far too alive. Upon seeing black people costumed as slaves, Ellis writes, African American visitors to Williamsburg "were so ashamed" that they "walked away before hearing the presentation. Seeing the costume and knowing we were portraying slaves was enough for them." For African Americans, he points out, everyday life can serve as a sufficient reminder of slavery, and forgetting becomes a conscious strategy to temper the oppressions of memory. Ellis notes that black employees of Colonial Williamsburg who worked elsewhere also resented the actors' performances because "they apparently felt we jeopardized their 'roles' by causing visitors to assume that they were characters, too."[35] All the world's a stage, and these actors' antebellum parts became mobile, traveling through time and the landscape of Colonial Williamsburg, indiscriminately attaching themselves to anyone with dark skin. Nora Martin, an actor performing in modern-day Philadelphia's historic district, commented, "People see me, a black woman, and assume that I must be a slave. The discomfort, you can see it in people's faces."[36] Slavery may be "a part of history that is no more" from the point of view of many plantation tours, but all black people can still be slaves. Race is a force that possesses.

When a black person built the plantation, it may be even more difficult to come to terms with slavery. Melrose Plantation near Natchitoches, Louisiana, was built beginning in 1796 by a former slave, Marie-Thérèse Coincoin, who had been the mistress of a white planter. When he manumitted her and their children and gave her a large tract of land, she bought slaves herself. Now open to tourists, Melrose has one of the most visible black presences of any plantation in Louisiana. The twentieth-century artist Clementine Hunter was a cook and field hand at the plantation when it was the home of a woman who created a retreat at Melrose and hosted artists and writers like Lyle Saxon and Sherwood Anderson. Hunter gathered discarded tubes of paint from the artists in residence and began to paint on cardboard and other scraps of found material, and eventually she was commissioned to paint murals that cover the walls of Melrose's African House, which had been used as a "slave-fort."[37] Today one of the tour guides at Melrose is a descendant of Marie-Thérèse Coincoin; her face is the face of her ancestor, something I only realize later because she does not mention their connection during the tour. And so she was talking about her great-great-great-great-grandmother when she said, pausing at the door of the slave quarters, "She was a slave, and yet she owned slaves." This was all she said on the subject, but perhaps it was enough.

Cultural geographers, archaeologists, and landscape architects have begun to recover and interpret the remains of slave spaces in an effort to illuminate how Africans and their descendants shaped the land they inhabited,[38] though sometimes they remain only as text; John Michael Vlach notes that his study of slave architecture was inspired by WPA documentation of sites that have now vanished.[39] Even when slave sites *can* be completely restored in a tourist context, they might not be. Edward Chappell describes how curators suppressed "the refuse, disorder, and smells suggested by the artifact-filled strata at the Kingsmill [a slave dwelling site on the James River in Virginia], Monticello, and other excavated quarters" not only out of racism but also out of a fear that "preindustrial squalor will divert attention from more essential issues of race relations and personal survival," or that "limited visibility of physical resistance to forced labor may lead visitors to conclude that slaves supinely acquiesced."[40] Evidence of slaves' resistance and agency might be difficult to represent to casual visitors through object lessons, especially given the pervasiveness of images of blacks as lazy and (no longer valuable as chattel) "worthless"—even, as Rex Ellis's experience at Williamsburg suggests, as slaves.

When a descendant of South Carolina slaves returned in the 1990s to the plantation where his ancestors had labored for generations, he was moved to say, "This is hallowed ground. I feel like I'm walking in the footsteps of Jesus."[41] The land has been sanctified by labor and blood. Black communities are interspersed with tourist plantations along River Road, attesting to the fact that descendants of slaves continue to claim a place in the landscape. They may also claim a place within the plantation house. One of the tour guides at Oak Alley in recent years was a young black woman costumed in crinolines as an antebellum belle. In one sense, she took to its logical extreme the tour's insistence on disregarding slavery; it was almost as if her dark skin had simply gone unnoticed. At the same time, a black woman as surrogate for Oak Alley's white mistresses animated a quietly explosive text. Playing a role that whites have desperately guarded, she embodied the repressed fact that white power on the plantation was due entirely to the presence of blacks. But it is impossible to know what tourists thought as they listened to her stories.

As Aunt Jemima and Uncle Ben continue to make the loyal slave available for purchase at the local supermarket, mammy, in her red polka-dot dress and matching headscarf, can be bought at plantation gift shops to provide some help in the kitchen as a refrigerator magnet, cookie jar, teapot, pair of salt and pepper shakers, or simply decorative encouragement.[42] The mammy stereotype survives in part because the role of caregiver in white families is still often filled by women of color. The black women pushing white children in strollers down St. Charles Avenue or through Audubon Park in Uptown New Orleans testify to the duration of an economy in which black women are socially subordinate to wealthy white families, yet in a significant position of influence over them. One woman who had worked for an Uptown family for many years made her power explicit when she remarked that she felt her employers' children loved her "more than their own mother."[43] "Mammy" keeps the authority of black caregivers from becoming absolute.

The endurance of race-specific roles from antebellum days was dramatized in a tour of Nottoway.[44] The guide was an imposing black woman wearing a red dress and a matching headscarf. She strode majestically through the house, recounting the story of how Nottoway was spared by Yankee troops thanks to the bravery of its white mistress, Emily Randolph. Later she mentioned that since coming to work at Nottoway, she had discovered her own grandmother was a slave in this house before the war. Perhaps she watched from these windows as the cavalry rode past. For a moment, the tourist plantation and the Old South it claims to revive almost seamlessly blended. When I asked the guide what had drawn her to Nottoway, she replied that she simply "loved the old houses." It is also quite possible that the white family she describes in the tour are her blood relations. Like the antebellum mammies of plantation lore, our guide at Nottoway maintained significant control over the workings of the plantation house.[45] Throughout the tour, the plantation's history depended on her for its existence. She produced the stories that tourists would take home as evidence of what plantation life was like. As one woman gushed after the tour, "You really brought it to life for us!"

Hoopskirted guides and period furnishings are intended for nothing if not to bring "the past" to life. What returns, however, is not just the simplistic history that tours tend to promote, but a tangle of southern myths and stereotypes. As traditional as the image of moonlight and magnolias that tours draw on, and the stereotype of the Confederate-flag-waving redneck they politely rephrase, are eerie images of crepuscular gloom. Used to backlight live oaks draped with Spanish moss as the credits roll in movies about the South, the moon that shone so romantically on the magnolias turns ominous. Attempts to re-create plantation history as a primarily white history are not separate from white fears and superstitions about the consequences of slavery within a society in which black and white people continue to live in close proximity, and in which the upheaval and confusion following the Civil War sometimes seem not long past. In *Old Louisiana* (1929), Lyle Saxon describes overhearing a conversation between two old men sitting on a plantation house porch sipping mint juleps. " 'Look at our friends and neighbors,' " one says. " 'Once they had everything; now they have nothing. Think of your own family, and of mine. I had everything once, but the War ended all that. Yes sir! The War ended my good times.' The boy [Saxon] knows that Mr. Horatio is patting an empty sleeve; he has seen him do it many times before." " 'That's it, the War,' " responds the other. " 'But it is something else too, a sort of blight on us. I had nine children. They are all grown up now, and some of them are getting old. Only one is married, and the boy there is the only grandchild I have. Something is the matter with us.' "[46] Upon the lifestyle of the aristocratic Old South complete with its quintessential cocktail is superimposed a mysterious "blight" that has rendered whites infertile. Zora Neale Hurston's description of the hoodoo worked by a black man against the wealthy planter who abused the man's family springs to mind. The conjure drives the whites off the land and makes the planter's wife and children go insane and attempt to kill him.[47] Is Saxon actually suggesting that the recompense for enslaving black people is white impotence? That the white people he describes deserve to arrive at this literal dead end? Given Saxon's intention to rhetorically restore the old plantations and revive their inhabitants, it seems unlikely. Even so, he reiterates the foreboding theme: "In Louisiana one often hears the remark that such and such a family has 'gone to pieces.' As a child I used to picture that dire calamity in my mind. Did the men and women explode, I wondered—heads going in one direction, arms and legs in another? Or did they drop to pieces languidly, leaving a finger here and a toe there? . . . Later I learned what people meant when they said such things, but for some unexplained reason the phrase still brings to my mind the idea of bodily disintegration."[48] The bodies of plantation owners crumble, or detonate, in the aftermath of the Civil War. Saxon attempts to shake off this hex through exhaustive and sometimes exhausting iterations of family lore and tours of plantation houses. After one particularly extended litany of architectural detail, he says to the reader, "Here's my hand. Are we still friends?"[49] As the question suggests, his effort meets with at least partial defeat. Other reconstructions of plantation life, however, provide more satisfying answers to the questions that mark Saxon's text: What is the matter with "us"? And why do white bodies keep falling apart?[50]

The success of D. W. Griffith's film *Birth of a Nation* (1915), arguably "the picture that created the film industry," which Griffith intended as a way to tell history from the perspective of the losers, indicated how effectively the losers were shaping (white) public perceptions of the Civil War and race relations.[51] It also showed Hollywood studios the powerful appeal of a nascent genre, the southern.[52] The southern was eventually eclipsed by the western, in part because of the prohibitive costs of costume dramas, but only after *Gone with the Wind* began to influence popular ideas about the slave South, including those of today's tourists (there are still a lot of costumes).[53] A dissection of responses to the mystique of *Gone with the Wind* sheds light on the late-twentieth-century circulation of white property. New Orleans chef Leah Chase, who has lived long enough to remember the premiere of *Gone with the Wind* in segregated theaters, who cooked for civil rights leaders, and who in her eighties was a regular presence in the kitchen at Dooky Chase's, dedicated a room in her restaurant to Scarlett. Her menu featured drinks called Planter's Punch and the Scarlett O'Hara, "a lady's favorite." In a restaurant across from the Lafitte projects patronized by members of the black and Creole communities, Chase created circumstances in which the Old South could circulate as a sign of black status and leisure.

Chase's localized appropriation effectively challenged Mitchell's perspective while appearing to support her agenda; Chase seemed to be just a fan, and only when you examine context do the complexities of her intervention become visible. When Alice Randall attempted to publish a more direct and widely available response to *Gone with the Wind* in 2001, the Mitchell estate's lawyers accused her of stealing white property. Randall had committed "wholesale theft of major characters," argued attorney Tom Selz.[54] One of the Mitchell Trust's concerns was that if people invested in the mythology of *Gone with the Wind* read *The Wind Done Gone*, their perceptions of the original would be altered. According to the trust's attorney Richard Kurnit, the book "appeals to the market when readers are hungry to read about these characters. The people who are infatuated with Rhett and Scarlett will gobble any story about them"[55]—and, so gobbling, they may consume information about love and sex across the color line, racial passing, and perhaps even the disguises and sleights of hand that keep "the white man [from] trying to know into somebody else's business,"[56] whether or not these consumers agree with, enjoy, or believe Randall's version of events. Randall's Tara, called Tata, is another kind of memory theater. Garlic (Mitchell's "Pork") reveals that he is Tata's true designer: "There was no architect here," he tells the assembled former slaves at Mammy's funeral—Mrs. Garlic, Miss Priss, and Scarlett's mulatto half-sister Cynara. "There was me and what I remembered of all the great houses on great plantations I had seen. Bremo. Rattle-and-Snap. The Hermitage. Belgrove. Tudor Place. Sabine Hall. I built this place with my hands and I saw it in my mind before my hands built it. Mammy and me, we saved it from the Yankees not for them but for us. She knew. She knew this house stood proud and tall when we couldn't. Every column fluted as a monument to the slaves and the whips our bodies had received. Every slave being beat looked at the column and knew his beating would be remembered."[57] In Randall's representation, the plantation house emerges out of black memory as a memorial to suffering, endurance, and ingenuity; its carved columns symbolize not aristocracy but marks of the lash.

In *The Wind Done Gone*, Randall not only arguably trespassed on white property; she redefined the meaning of white property by imaginatively becoming a slave. Judge Charles Pannell, who issued the injunction forbidding circulation of the book, wrote, "When the reader of *Gone with the Wind* turns over the last page, he may well wonder what becomes of Ms. Mitchell's beloved characters and their romantic, but tragic, world. Ms. Randall has offered her vision of how to answer those unanswered questions. . . . The right to answer those questions and to write a sequel or other derivative work, however, legally belongs to Ms. Mitchell's heirs, not Ms. Randall."[58] The genealogy of this white property is carefully controlled through copyright; in Judge Pannell's reading of the law, Mitchell's version of events is protected against contradiction.[59] Any response to *Gone with the Wind* not authorized by the Mitchell Trust is likely to lead to litigation, and "parody" offers the only means of direct intervention in its monumental narrative. *Atlanta Journal-Constitution* columnist Cynthia Tucker wrote, "Though clever in places, Randall's book is not that funny. Some reviewers say it does not meet the literary definition of parody, either. (That's probably OK since *Gone with the Wind* doesn't meet the definition of literature.)"[60] But the parody defense does not claim that Randall's novel is hilarious. As the Supreme Court noted, fair use "permits [and requires] courts to avoid rigid application of the copyright statute when, on occasion, it would stifle the very creativity which that law is designed to foster."[61] Legally, parody is a critical "commentary" on the work it appropriates (rather than the reflection of a desire for self-aggrandizement, or simply laziness).[62] As Randall mocks the investment in white racial purity and obliviousness to enslaved people's consciousness evinced by *Gone with the Wind*, her work reads more like satire, "in which prevalent follies or vices are assailed with ridicule," according to the *Oxford English Dictionary*, or are "attacked through irony, derision, or wit," according to *American Heritage*. The Supreme Court held that "parody needs to mimic an original to make its point, and so has some claim to use the creation of the victim's (or collective victims') imagination, whereas satire can stand on its own two feet and so requires justification for the very act of borrowing."[63] A satire of *Gone with the Wind* would therefore be harder to defend.

On appeal, the Eleventh Circuit Court in Atlanta found that Randall's novel was legally a parody and determined that any damages Mitchell's work might have suffered could be remedied with money.[64] In the agreed-upon settlement, Houghton Mifflin donated "an unspecified amount" to historically black Morehouse College. In 2002, Mitchell's nephew also endowed a chair at the college in her name. A Morehouse press release describes the situation leading up to the bequest:

> The legacy left by an unlikely alliance between Dr. Benjamin E. Mays, sixth president of Morehouse College and Margaret Mitchell, author of the legendary novel "Gone With the Wind," continues to live on. On Monday, March 18, 2002, Mitchell's nephew, Eugene Mitchell, will present the College with a $1.5 million dollar gift. The money will be used to endow the dean's chair for the Division of Humanities and Social Sciences. The chair will be named for Margaret Mitchell and will celebrate her commitment to literature, scholarship and humanity.
>
> For more than a decade, during the racially charged 1940's, Dr. Mays and Margaret Mitchell corresponded through letters. Those letters led to dozens of scholarships for Morehouse College students, personally paid for by Mitchell. Later, Mitchell would give Dr. Mays more money, this time to aid in the education of young men at Morehouse wanting to pursue careers in the fields of medicine and dentistry.[65]

According to an Associated Press story, Mitchell had funded the scholarships secretly.[66]

During the Depression, romantic images emerging from Hollywood of a prosperous Old South offered a vicarious escape from hardship for white audiences. "The urban poor were unheard of in the Old South romances," and "New Orleans was but a delightful seat of aristocracy," writes Edward D. C. Campbell. Films made during this era continued the work of reunion begun after the Civil War, presenting an idyllic South—"rural, contented, and free from social ills."[67] Racial tensions are nonexistent, or so it would seem. In *Jezebel* (1938) Warner Bros. mobilized the publicity around David O. Selznick's *Gone with the Wind*, which had not yet been filmed. In fact, *Jezebel* was so effective a portrayal of the Old South milieu that "several reviewers suggested the filming of *Gone with the Wind* be delayed as *Jezebel* was bound to diminish the impact of Mitchell's bestseller."[68] Some felt that Bette Davis, who had lost her chance at the role of Scarlett O'Hara because of a feud with Warner studio head Jack Warner (but won an Oscar for her portrayal of Julie Marsden) "took 'the wind out of the sails of any prospective Scarlett O'Hara'" and that the film "stole 'quite a bit of the thunder of *Gone with the Wind*, still uncast.'"[69] The trailer for the film made reference to the uncompleted Selznick film: *Jezebel* is a "scarlet portrait of a gorgeous spitfire who lived by the wild desire of her untamed heart." But this Scarlett is ultimately the voice of a deeply conflicted rather than triumphant cinematic subconscious. Antebellum slaveholders had both complained about and feared their slaves, but *Jezebel*, and essentially every other film made during this period, portrayed blacks as unthreatening; indeed, in *Jezebel* the plantation owner eclipses the slave as the problematic element of plantation life.[70] The trailer even declared that Julie "was loved when she should have been whipped." This perversion of paternalism, the misuse of love and discipline, again linked the white lady with the slave, and Julie will be disqualified as a white wife when she refuses to submit to a white man's whipping.

After the opening credits scroll across moonlit moss-draped oaks, the camera moves down a street lined with vendors selling Mardi Gras masks and enters the bar of the St. Louis Hotel. In 1852, when the film is set, the hotel was a social hub in New Orleans because it was the site of slave auctions, including the tantalizing spectacles of fancy girls.[71] From this beginning, the theme of race mixing and sexuality is central to the film but always obliquely presented. We first meet the Jezebel of the title as she leaps off her horse at the front door of her New Orleans mansion and strides into a roomful of guests. Not only is she late for her own engagement party (she plans to marry up-and-coming young banker Preston Dillard [Henry Fonda]), but she refuses to change out of her presumably sweaty riding habit. Costuming in the film not only signals that Julie is headstrong (like the horse she rode in on); it also serves to mark an intersection of race and sexuality. Frustrated by Pres's refusal to go with her to the final fitting of her gown for the Olympus Ball (he *always* has to work), Julie decides to retaliate by wearing a shocking red dress instead of the white that propriety demands. Pres is scandalized. He and Julie argue—he gripping a walking stick he means to use to teach her a lesson—and she becomes even more determined to wear red. No man, especially not one threatening her while rehearsing clichés, can wield much influence with her. "Are you afraid somebody'll take me for one of those girls on Gallatin Street?" (a cheap prostitute) she taunts.[72] After Pres leaves the room, she calls her maid Zette (Theresa Harris), who, seeing the red dress laid out on the bed, exclaims gleefully, "Ooo-wee Miss Julie, this sure is the most elegantestest dress!" Julie says she will give Zette the dress if she takes a message to Buck Cantrell, her former fiancé. Impropriety is heaped upon impropriety, from Pres's uninvited appearance in the boudoir to Julie's insistence on wearing red to her solicitation of Cantrell's services as a gigolo. The disguised racial problematic associated with the dress is underscored by the black maid's delight and anticipation. Julie's choice dooms her to be ostracized at the dance; no one will talk to her or even stand near her because she is the wrong color.

In focusing on this relationship between color and otherness, the film references racial tensions through the body of a white woman. As Julie is marked as different, her body becomes (literally) a screen onto which unspeakable racial stress—stress that the studios were going out of their way to avoid—is projected. Since the film was made in black and white, the red dress just looks dark—black, in fact. *Jezebel* revisits the figure of the tragic octoroon, which "proved itself a moviemaker's darling" after its first appearance around 1912. In the traditional plot, a white-appearing woman is eventually doomed not only to social oblivion but often to death because of the invisible drop of black blood in her veins. *Jezebel* distills the idea of a concealed physical taint even further as the fatal drop of blood mutates into a red garment.[73]

Pres quickly rejects Julie when her true nature is revealed; she plunges into a depression that eases only when she and her entourage leave New Orleans. The city is rapidly succumbing to yellow jack, but her plantation, Halcyon, is "always above the fever line." Despite its name, Halcyon proves to be anything but a refuge. Fever moves steadily in that direction and with it Pres, who has chosen a particularly bad time to return to Louisiana from his new home in "Yankeeland." Julie still pines for him, and to welcome him back she puts on the fatefully rejected ballgown, an attempt to redeem herself by finally turning white. Unbeknownst to all, however, Pres brings with him his northern bride, Amy (Margaret Lindsay), who finds the South "strange and beautiful, and a little frightening," although it has "charming customs." The postwar motif of the North-South romance is rejuvenated, presumably to give equal weight to northern and southern perspectives on the South, a crucial element of the transregional marketing of the southern.[74]

Julie's reaction to the discovery that the man she hoped would redeem her is no longer available is to darken herself still further; blackness signifies both a racial and a moral taint. Insinuating that Pres made inappropriate advances to her after "punishing the brandy," she helps fan the flames of sectional strife that have arisen between Buck Cantrell and Pres and his brother Ted. Throughout the film Pres has been the voice of "modernization," and now he argues that "unskilled slave labor" is no match for northern industry, a viewpoint that does not recommend him to the southern cavalier Cantrell. As Pres is called away (yet again) to bank business in New Orleans, tensions reach a head. Ted steps in to defend his family's honor and Cantrell challenges him to a duel. Julie, now unable to affect the course of violence, turns to a large group of slaves who have been summoned to entertain the whites ("just another old custom," she tells Amy sarcastically) and leads them in a round of "Let's Raise a Ruckus Tonight." It soon becomes clear that this is how Julie herself will handle things. The obviously submissive slaves will not be raising any hell, but the white/black surrogate will. As she sings "Come along children, little children come along," Julie gathers the slave children around her outspread white skirt. The black actors form a mass of darkness juxtaposed against Julie's radical pallor, emphasizing not her whiteness so much as her failure to achieve whiteness. (Cantrell is a legendary shot, but the duel leaves him dead.)

Julie elides the problematic of male sexual aggression in the plantation context; instead of a white man, it is a white/black woman who pursues the white man as victim. Race is expressed in terms of sexuality here, and the depiction of Davis's character as a Jezebel subsumes the presence of black women as a site of white male desire, for an important part of the guilt that this image must expiate concerns the mixed-race descendants of slaveholders. But as the octoroon gets reinscribed at the heart of the text, the film's attempts to mask or channel the image of black women as sexual objects are only partially successful. Reversing the typical dynamics of ownership on the plantation—Julie as Pres's potential property as his wife, or even his potential property as a "black" woman—Julie claims that it is she who possesses the white man. In a scene highlighted in the trailer, she seductively argues that she, like the slave South itself, is "in his blood": "This is the country you were born to, Pres. The country you know and trust. Amy wouldn't understand. . . . Oh, it isn't easy like the North. It's quick and dangerous! But you trust it. Remember how the fever mist smells in the bottoms—rank and rotten? But you trust that, too. Because it's a part of you, Pres, just as I'm part of you." And the fever is indeed part of him—moments before this conversation, he has been bitten by a fateful mosquito. The discourse of plantation ownership is a discourse of possession in which property enters—even infects—its owner. Pres cannot escape an identification with the slave South, which means that he cannot escape the connection between owning other people's bodies and plague, but here possession becomes a way to distance slavery from the South as the film simply replaces it with yellow jack, asking, Can you deal with sickness? Not with the moral and possibly financial problems of slavery, but with fever? Louisiana's subtropical climate stands in for its primary social institution as the site of anxiety and disease. As Pres sickens in New Orleans, Julie secretly rushes to his side, aided by a faithful slave. Amy finds her there just before the authorities arrive to cart Pres off to quarantine on Lazarette Island. Though they struggle over the right to accompany him and try to save his life, in the end Julie convinces Amy to let her go. The southerner is the one who needs redemption, not the northerner, who is already pure. "Help me make myself clean again as you are clean," Julie pleads. As she and Pres are borne away on a rickety wagon, light illuminates her face with the beatific glow of a martyr. Like the title character in Dion Boucicault's play *The Octoroon; or, Life in Louisiana* (1859), Julie can be absolved of her black blood only as she engages with death because dying white people stand in for the pathology of slavery.[75] In the process they represent the "truth" of the South—for contemporary reviewers took the film "seriously" as a historical document.[76]

After World War II, belles and cavaliers faded into the background, replaced by images of "decadence and depravity in the South, old and new." Depictions of this haunted South "became a tradition that developed into a still flourishing genre."[77] Nominated for seven Oscars, the Bette Davis film *Hush . . . Hush Sweet Charlotte* (1965) is an example that can be read not only as a jaded retelling of *Gone with the Wind* but also as a sequel to *Jezebel*, a connection made explicit in the portrait of a youthful Charlotte that hangs in her father's study. It shows Davis dressed in the white ballgown from *Jezebel*, her hair arranged exactly as it was in her fateful scene under the fever moon with Pres.[78] The plantation is again the catalyst for desperate acts, but the supposedly noble motives of the earlier films have soured. Director Robert Aldrich imagined *Hush . . . Hush Sweet Charlotte* as a follow-up to *Whatever Happened to Baby Jane?* (1962), but Joan Crawford became ill on the set (mysteriously?) after feuding with Davis. Vivien Leigh, among other actresses, refused to work with Davis, but her friend Olivia de Havilland agreed to take the part. Thus instead of battling old Scarletts, we find sweet, self-sacrificing Melanie returning to the plantation having grown, as viewers slowly discover, into a blackmailer and a cold-blooded killer before she herself is killed by Davis's character.

The film opens with several views of an imposing white-columned house—in reality Louisiana's Houmas House (now a tourist attraction), transported back to 1927 as Hollis House, the pride of patriarch Sam Hollis (Victor Buono). As the camera closes in, we hear Hollis castigating the married man he has just discovered to be his daughter's lover as a low-class son of immigrants: "I'd sooner it'd been one of my *field boys*. Then I coulda *killed* him." At least the black field hands are disposable, unlike John (Bruce Dern), whose wife is Sam's social equal. But John will soon be dead by other means.

After the credits that follow this flashback sequence we find ourselves in 1964, the year of Freedom Summer, but the civil rights movement feels very far from the rural southern life this film depicts. Its concerns are with old, bitter feuds between white women, and with the vulnerability of the plantation house. Tara was threatened by Yankees; Hollis House is threatened by the state of Louisiana, which is determined to build a bridge right through it. Charlotte is alone in her conviction that the plantation house is valuable. For other people it is something antithetical to progress, a highly ambivalent symbol of wealth worth possessing—an obstacle to bridges, but more importantly, a locus of psychic terror. This plantation has been the site of gruesome death—not slave deaths, of course, but a white man's bloody end. Nearly forty years ago, on the night of a spectacular party, John was decapitated and his hand cut off with a meat cleaver, his death inseparable from his marital transgression. Davis's character is once again a Jezebel. On the night of the murder Charlotte makes her entrance into the ballroom stained red, but the white party dress has now changed color due to an outpouring of actual blood. Like the octoroon of *Jezebel*, Charlotte is completely ostracized by her community. Although she is not convicted of the murder in court, she has never been acquitted in public opinion. After the glare of publicity fades, Charlotte returns to Hollis House, where she lives alone, pining for a hopeless lover who has been absent now for decades. As the construction workers close in, Charlotte resembles a version of Scarlett to whom time has not been kind. She threatens the men with a rifle, her bullet pinging off the bulldozer in a scene reminiscent of Scarlett's attack on the Yankee with plunder and possibly rape on his mind. The object of rape and plunder here is the land itself, which the (white) workers are "plowin' up." But while Scarlett's act registers with the audience as self-defense, Charlotte is clearly someone who has "gone to pieces." Long gray hair flying, protuberant eyes rolling crazily, skin creased with age, she stakes her life on the plantation.

In a final attempt to stave off the blows of the wrecking ball, Charlotte writes to "the only kin [she] got left," her cousin Miriam (de Havilland). Miriam ostensibly helps Charlotte during the day, but at night she and Drew (Joseph Cotton), Charlotte's doctor and Miriam's old boyfriend, stage the return of John's unhappy, mutilated ghost. His amputated parts were never found, but the conspirators pose lifelike replicas along with a cleaver in the music room and play haunting interludes on the harpsichord. The plantation has become a theater of very bad memories. Once Charlotte falls over the brink of sanity, Miriam, as next of kin, will inherit her substantial assets. Sensing what's happening, Charlotte's devoted (white) servant Velma (Agnes Moorehead), cries that Miriam is "bleeding her white." Whiteness signals death now, not purity. At the end of the film we discover it was Jewel Mayhew (Mary Astor), John's wife, who killed him. Just days away from death, Jewel takes tea and releases her secret on the porch of her plantation house, which is actually Oak Alley. By chance or design, this fading southern aristocrat has the same family name as current Oak Alley owner Zeb; fiction and fact merge to create a forum for the resurrected past. The plantation is a place of warped and stunted, pointedly nonprocreative sexuality—a place of decay, of loss, of obsolescence. Its possibilities have apparently been played out. This film erases the plantation house from the landscape—in the end, the wrecking ball will have its way—and only death awaits the remnants of the planter class.[79]

Three decades later, however, the plantation reemerges onscreen inhabited by those who have known death but return nonetheless. In the adaptation of Anne Rice's novel *Interview with the Vampire* (1994), the recurring image of pathologically greedy whites—craving money, love, or life itself—illuminates its importunate relevance. A website for Cracker Barrel convenience stores imagines a journey through rural Louisiana: "Eagerly, your eyes search the landscape. In the distance it slowly emerges, indistinct and large: a hovering whiteness through the moss-draped oaks. As you draw closer you see the massive columns and experience a rare sense of wonder. You are in Plantation Country, a setting for the recent movie *Interview with the Vampire*. Is this the present or have you eluded time and logic and somehow slipped back to days gone by?"[80] The plantation, a hovering white mass just visible through the trees, is not so much haunted as haunting. Is this an entirely safe place? The passage suggests otherwise. "You" have stumbled into Plantation Country, which is also Vampire Country; it is possible that you have arrived here illogically, and your transportation back to the present is not entirely reliable. Vampire Country *is* a strange land, at least as Rice describes it. Robert Aldrich referred to *Hush . . . Hush Sweet Charlotte* as "cannibal time in Dixieland," but the phrase more accurately describes *Interview*, where procreation takes place through the erotic embraces of white men who live off the flesh of black women.[81] In the video version of the film, Anne Rice makes a brief appearance before the feature begins. In addition to plugging her latest vampire novel and emphasizing just how much she loves this movie (in response, or so it sounds, to her much-publicized dispute with its producers over the casting of Tom Cruise and Brad Pitt), Rice enjoins viewers, "Remember: It's not just about vampires. It's really about us." The not quite human slave is replaced by the not quite human white man, but even as white men are othered as they become vampires, they remain normative subjects—part of the amorphous, apparently universal "us."

Unsurprisingly, images of white privilege are accompanied by a minimized black presence, just as they were in so many other plantation films made over the course of the twentieth century, and now also in plantation tours. Plantation life in Vampire Country has to do with the related pleasures and pains of eating (other people) and sex. Slaves appear briefly as increasingly alarmed objects of white lust or wearing some costume designer's idea of African robes in a torchlit voodoo exorcism that lumps together circum-Atlantic symbols in an attempt to signify the essence of blackness. But the plantation owner as bloodsucking vampire is an almost too-obvious metaphor for race relations both during the era of institutionalized slavery and beyond it. These white bodies refuse to fall apart—they are already dead, so nothing can kill them—and in their refusal, they are damned. At the other end of the century from Saxon's melancholic ruminations, to be able to fall apart signals a state of grace. It turns out that what is wrong with "us" is intimately connected to the fact that remembering through forgetting is never a comfortable process, and the results it achieves can be terrifying.

# 3. Roadside Attractions

And while I had my back turned to him I said the only thing that I
could think to say, and the only thing I knew I really wanted. I said,
Elvis, can you stay awhile with me? And he talked back and said,
"Howard, I'm on a tight schedule."
*Howard Finster*

Tourist attractions are "precisely analogous to the religious symbolism of primitive peoples," remarked sociologist Dean MacCannell in 1976. MacCannell argued that the tourist is a model of "modern man in general" who, armed with leisure and disposable income, seeks to patch the cracks in modernity's master narratives. "*Sightseeing is a ritual performed to the differentiations of society*," he writes. "It is a kind of collective striving for a transcendence of the modern totality, of incorporating its fragments into unified existence. Of course, it is doomed to eventual failure: even as it tries to construct totalities, it celebrates differentiation."[1] MacCannell's insistence that visiting tourist attractions has become a means of understanding the order of things is borne out in the popularity of places of death and memorial with sightseers.[2] Visiting symbolic cultural sites, contemporary tourists perform "primitive" quests for self-knowledge: Where did we come from? Where are we going? And the answers they receive are inevitably incomplete, even thoroughly fabricated—by themselves. In nostalgia for the Old South, a clearly defined and singular "truth" appears to overcome the irruptions of a more troubling paradigm. The image of the plantation as an uncomplicated site of white achievement offers solace in the face of civil rights or affirmative action, but its attempt to construct a less heterogeneous time and place across landscapes irrevocably shaped by industrialism and globalization is necessarily futile: Gainesville, Georgia, part of "Georgia's Heartland of the Confederacy," is also the "Poultry Capital of the World," and most of the workers in its poultry industry are immigrants from Mexico.[3] And yet there is a comprehensive social genealogy to be found at tourist sites, in those places where the dead are prominent. The body exists as a means of remembrance, a location of collective memory. But it also gets dismembered, both literally and figuratively, and its pieces circulate through postslavery tourist economies.

In the aftermath of slavery, black bodies remained extremely vulnerable; when living black bodies ceased to be valuable property, dead black bodies became valuable property, as W. J. Cash tersely noted.[4] After Reconstruction, lynching became increasingly common in the South, reaching epidemic proportions in the 1890s (as if every act of lynching, no matter how isolated, did not bespeak something like a "pestilence" or "virus").[5] "By 1892," writes Fitzhugh Brundage, "the lynching of blacks had become . . . an everyday event. . . . With each succeeding decade, the proportion of lynchings that occurred in the South rose, increasing from 82 percent of all lynchings in the nation during the 1880s to more than 95 percent during the 1920s."[6] In *A Festival of Violence*, Stewart E. Tolnay and E. M. Beck calculate that 2,462 blacks were lynched between 1882 and 1930. Lynchings were carried out by whites across the class spectrum. (The Ku Klux Klan is sometimes dismissed as poor white trash—the national press represented the men who lynched Emmett Till this way, too—but Klan members and others willing to torture and murder black people were southern aristocrats and dirt farmers alike.) Over this period of time, the nature of lynching moved from "frenzied renegade outbursts or swift, corporal punishments" to become "highly ritualized tortures" featuring "hangings . . . beatings, mutilations, shootings, and burnings."[7] And the "lynching-bee," as a merchant in Valdosta, Georgia, described the killing of a pregnant woman, became a tourist attraction.[8] The expanding railroad infrastructure in the South made it possible for people to travel to a lynching they had learned about in advance. Beginning in the 1890s, lynchings were publicized in local newspapers, and sometimes special trains brought whole families.⁹ The new hobby of photography evolved into a critical component of lynching, and in pictures taken at the scene, spectators' enjoyment is written plainly on their faces. White people in modern dress smile at the camera within a few feet of dangling black bodies. This is not happening at some point in ancient history. These murdered bodies are not sites of mourning or of fear. The killers are showing their faces to the camera; they are celebrating; they seem to have nothing to hide.¹⁰

Lynchings produced their own apparatus of memory, and the souvenirs were not just representations of black bodies. They *were* black bodies. Fingers, teeth, ears, and genitals—all coveted remembrances; postcards with pictures of the dead were popular, too, "their prices varying according to supply and demand."¹¹ Such violence against black bodies constituted a public denial of the depth of the ongoing contact between blacks and whites, and between blackness and whiteness. If a white baby has nursed at the breast of a black woman, is he half black?¹² If a white girl lives and plays with a black girl, is she in danger of becoming black, as Lillian Smith's mother feared?¹³ If a black maid eats from the same plate that her white employers will later eat from, does her blackness overrun their kitchen cabinets?¹⁴ Gathering together, white people pointed out to one another what they thought they knew about the capacity of the black body, now unbound from slavery, to contaminate whiteness.

Susan Stewart interprets souvenirs as symbols of the loss of a direct, material relationship to physical experience—perhaps, in MacCannell's terms, as vestiges of the evolution from premodern to modern, or as evidence of the modern that survives into the postmodern age. "As experience is increasingly mediated and abstracted," she writes, "the lived relation of the body to the phenomenological world is replaced by a nostalgic myth of contact and presence. 'Authentic' experience becomes both elusive and allusive as it is placed beyond the horizon of present lived experience. . . . In this process of distancing, the memory of the body is replaced by the memory of the object, a memory standing outside itself and thus presenting both a surplus and a lack of significance."[15] But the ubiquitous souvenirs of slavery make clear how incomplete this process of disembodiment has actually been.[16] The black body keeps returning as a literal object of consumption, and nostalgia, at least in part, is what puts it there. In lynching souvenirs, a system of labor and culture is compressed into the body as fetish, but unlike Marx's commodity fetish into which the human body/laborer disappears, here the black body itself becomes a fetishized item with a price. Written on the back of one postcard of a lynching in which the body was burned was "This is the barbeque we had last night." Another offers a truncated genealogy: "He is a 16 year old Black boy. He killed Earl's Grandma. She was Florence's mother."[17] Lynching as a white tourist attraction forcibly articulates the memory of the body to the memory of the object because only the body as object can serve the kind of remembering at work here. Spectacle lynchings broadcast the message that the right to consume, to participate in the sensuality of consumer culture, was for whites only.[18] In his study of racist collectibles and memorabilia, "almost universally derogatory" images of African Americans in the shape of household objects, Kenneth Goings argues that these objects "*were surrogate African-Americans in people's minds*."[19] And they "originated in a very specific era—the period from the 1880s to the end of World War I."[20] Thus the national circulation of ceramic mammies paralleled the circulation of black corpses among southern whites; the objectification of the body in chattel slavery informed the objectifications of consumer culture.[21] The finger bones and severed genitals are part of a historic arc that now includes Aunt Jemima refrigerator magnets and little plastic black boys eating watermelon in the plantation gift shop.

Plantation tours actualize the assumption that all white people belong in the plantation house; in so doing, they point to what must be repressed in order to generate a vision of classless whiteness. In his book on Faulkner, Martinican writer Edouard Glissant locates Mississippi within the plantation regions of the Americas, part of a cultural organism shaped by the inevitable forces of connection crossing racial, social, and spatial boundaries. Reflecting on the rural South, he finds that the progress of the syncretic

> ... begins on the first bus a person boards, leaving behind this part of the world and heading for the nearest city, Memphis, for example; ... it lingers menacingly on the county's horizon; ... it has a name, Creolization, the unstoppable conjunction despite misery, oppression, and lynching, the conjunction that opens up torrents of unpredictable results; (like a tumultuous and boundless Mississippi); ... it is the unpredictability that terrifies those who refuse the very idea, if not the temptation, to mix, flow together, and share.[22]

Between "this part of the world" and Memphis so much has happened. Between the site of Homer Plessy's performance of whiteness and the Tennessee-Mississippi border the landscape is marked by slavery and segregation but also by what Glissant calls "Creolization" and the "terror" it has inspired: Medgar Evers Drive in Decatur, Mississippi, honors the NAACP field secretary assassinated at his home in Jackson by white supremacist Byron de la Beckwith; at Mt. Zion United Methodist Church, twenty-some miles north in Philadelphia, a historic marker commemorates the deaths of Chaney, Schwerner, and Goodman; Bessie Smith died in Clarksdale in a black hospital that is now the Riverside Hotel, a resting place for travelers to the "birthplace of the blues." And just past the Tennessee state line, signs point toward the plantation home of the archetypal White Negro.

The lawyer who finally convicted Beckwith in 1994 after two hung juries succeeded in part because he was able to obtain a new autopsy. Evers's embalmed body was transported north in secrecy from Arlington National Cemetery to the laboratory of a famous pathologist. There one of the doctor's assistants, "knowing only that the proceedings had something to do with Mississippi, took [the lawyer] aside and in all seriousness asked, 'Is this Elvis Presley?' "[23] The anecdote resonates with something—not just the assumption that all Mississippi's secrets have to do with Elvis, but the accidental fusion of a casualty of white supremacy with an embodiment of racial ambiguity that seems to sum up the incoherence surrounding the process of creolization. It exists, but how to visualize it, how to articulate it? Language cannot keep up with cultural evolution, and it is bodies that become both the stimuli for and the expressions of new ideas. In the tourist economies that have seeped into the spaces of slavery, bodies are souvenirs not only of the plantation but also of the "unpredictable results" of creolization. The theme of the body as a souvenir, a necessary or much-prized mode of remembrance, links things in the postslavery context that on the surface may seem unrelated, but which are nodal points in the transmogrifying complex of the body as property and as site of possession. In fact, Elvis and the phenomenon of his impersonation are impossible to overlook in a discussion of American wounds of returning, enacting as they do the relationship between the antebellum economy and mass culture as well as an essentially American approach to death. Besides, Elvis died in a plantation.

"There was no such thing as celebrity prior to the beginning of the twentieth century," writes Richard Schickel.[24] With consumer culture rose our modern icons: "certain [film] actors achieved unprecedented heights of popularity and prosperity almost overnight in the period 1915-1920."[25] Film was a conduit of seeming intimacy with public strangers, a technology that helped make Elvis Mississippi's most famous son. Within the confines of segregated and postsegregated society, Elvis encompassed and reflected "blackness." In a photo taken in a Las Vegas hotel room in the 1970s, Elvis playfully raises his fists against Muhammad Ali, who is wearing Elvis's bejeweled costume over his bare chest, the two men mirroring each other's iconic status. Was Muhammad Ali the first Elvis impersonator? Perhaps the "most photographed person in history,"[26] Elvis's white body continues to circulate as fans' property. The celebrity image of Elvis shatters into millions of fragments: records, movies, photos—young women even collected blades of grass from his lawn—and now that he is dead, reembodiment by Elvis tribute artists. Incessantly impersonated, Elvis was, Allison

Graham suggests, "like Jennifer Jones, Jeanne Crain, and Ava Gardner before him . . . a black impersonator."[27] Graham writes that during the civil rights movement, Elvis's southernness worked against his visibility: "Unable to sustain its romantic vision of the South in the face of graphic news footage from Oxford, Birmingham, and Selma, the studios ceded the territory to television. Never accorded the status of 'actor' in the first place, Elvis was virtually stranded in the mediascape."[28] Being recognizably southern was (again) something of a liability, as it (again) connoted both racial ambiguity and racial violence.

But while young Elvis was once "King Creole,"[29] young Elvis is now at the crux of a Confederate cross.[30] On average, 650,000 people visit Graceland annually, "ahead of Monticello but well behind Mount Vernon among historic homes," according to a *New York Times* report. Jefferson's classical plantation house is less popular than Elvis's "neoplantation Playboy mansion,"[31] and while Graceland may log fewer visitors than Mount Vernon, it has attained a level of pop culture recognition that Washington's more somber estate will never achieve. In fact, Graceland, its original name, did not start out as a neoplantation Playboy mansion. The "Greek Revival" (according to Elvis Presley Enterprises) or "Georgian Colonial" (according to a contemporary feature reporter for the *Memphis Commercial Appeal*) house was built in 1939 for Ruth Brown Moore and Thomas D. Moore, a Memphis socialite and her husband.[32] It was named Graceland in honor of Mrs. Moore's Aunt Grace. The architecture deliberately conjured up local plantation houses built in the 1850s, and the home was painted in neutral tones and "tastefully" decorated with family antiques.[33] Yet its tenure as icon of white gentility would be relatively short. In 1954, Elvis and his white trash family moved in and transformed it into something more complicated. Elvis's residence put antebellum architecture in the hands of people who, if we are to believe Faulkner, would not have been able to get through the front door under other circumstances. When young Thomas Sutpen went to deliver a message to the planter on the estate where his family was living and was turned away by a haughty house slave because his kind do not enter through the front, he went to Haiti and returned with his own slaves to build Sutpen's Hundred. Elvis paid $100,000 the year segregation was outlawed to buy his dream home from a member of the Colonial Dames.[34] The fictional Sutpen was trying to work off the elite's association of poor whites with black slaves when he fled to Haiti "to become rich." Teenage Elvis, living in the segregated Memphis projects, hung out on Beale Street and embraced black styles; when he moved into the plantation house, it was with the flourish of enough cash to buy acquaintances new Cadillacs made from being white "with a Negro sound."[35] And now everybody can come in through the front door.

Tours of Graceland begin at Graceland Plaza, a former strip mall rededicated to the incorporation of Elvis in the strictly commercial sense.[36] Tourists equipped with headsets are bussed across the street now called Elvis Presley Boulevard and up the long driveway. Isolated in our audial worlds, we begin to wander through the house. The ceilings are lower than I had expected. Only the first floor is accessible; the upstairs is the object of rumor and speculation. Priscilla redecorated before opening the house to tourists in 1982, eliminating the "violent Christmastime-lipstick-cherry-Coke-fire-engine-hellfire red" environment in which Elvis had been living when he died.[37] Now the Graceland brochure advertises "the cool elegance of the all-white living room." Graceland still produces, almost universally, a kind of wonderment, even if it is not stunned, starstruck, sentimental, or spiritual. This is the nexus of a massive network designed to channel and perpetuate a legend. At the same time, it forecloses the problematic hybridity that Elvis embodied. While inhabiting a quintessentially southern marker of status, Elvis banished the trappings of Old South gentility with extravagantly antinostalgic decor. His comment that he had had enough of "antiques" to last a lifetime after his childhood in Tupelo suggests an equation of things that are old with oppression—anything that is old, not just old things that are probably expensive and symbolic of class status. All things that have age are suspect. And yet, perhaps more than any of the "traditional" plantation tours, Graceland locates the plantation signifier as a vital force in the regeneration of national culture. It appears to demonstrate the validity of the claim that the plantation is accessible to all. Unlike Sutpen's white trash plantation, Graceland survives.

When Lisa Marie Presley married Michael Jackson in the mid-1990s, she caused a great stir among Elvis fans. The color line had been openly and explicitly breached, and the breach gave rise to untoward imaginings within Elvis culture.[38] For many fans, the marriage signaled disaster for them and even for Graceland. "That's the end of Graceland," one lamented. "Pretty soon Michael and his fans will be sleeping in Elvis's house and bed."[39] Overlaid upon the idea that Graceland is essentially a place for fans and that Jackson fans would overwhelm Elvis fans within it; upon the idea that what was, in more than one way, white property would become black property; and even upon the idea that the bed is a place for fans and their star, the wife being an interloper, is the image of homoerotic union between a dead man and a man who is both "androgynous" and performing whiteness in full view of a publicly recognized black identity. Lisa Marie became the mediator in a millennial version of Leslie Fiedler's erotic bond of nationalism, in which "a white and a colored male flee from civilization into each other's arms."[40] Reverberations of the plantation's past persist as racially indeterminate men connect at the core of the nation, defying its historic norms as they call attention to the fact that such transgression has always defined "us."

Tours of Graceland exit the house to wind through a space filled with Elvis's empty clothing. The shimmering gold lamé and the caped jumpsuits hang in climate-controlled suspended animation, endlessly mourning the body that filled them, unreachable as Eurydice a few yards away by the outdoor pool. Elvis is buried next to Vernon and Gladys and a memorial to the stillborn twin, Jesse, who Vernon insisted was identical.[41] The dead Elvis that was born first. Elvis's body was originally in the Abbey Mausoleum at Forest Hill Cemetery in Memphis, but it was moved to Graceland when a plot emerged to steal it and hold it for ransom. The dead Elvis as property valuable enough to steal. It is almost unbearably appropriate that Elvis was a twin, considering his doubleness: the problematic, ambivalent racial doubleness as well as the postmortem limbo. In the poetics of American culture, perhaps his brother's stillbirth was a necessary death. Is it possible to imagine two Elvises? Yet now he constantly multiplies.

Eric Lott proposes that assuming the body of Elvis constitutes "a sort of second order blackface, in which, blackface having for the most part overtly disappeared, the figure of Elvis is . . . the apparently still necessary signifier of white ventures into black culture—a signifier to be adopted bodily if one is to have success in achieving the intimacy with 'blackness' that is crucial to the adequate reproduction of Presley's show." Lott reads Elvis impersonation as a way in which white working-class men restore the eroded value of their masculinity.[42] "Many Elvis impersonators circumvent 'blackness' altogether in their performances," he writes, "eclipsing an imagined set of attributes to which they are, in fact, powerfully indebted and attracted. Their solution to the felt embattlement of white masculinity is an assumption of the figure of Elvis, which to a great extent buries his 'blackness' at the same time as it appropriates its power." In the vexed relationship that Lott describes—white men's avoidance, erasure, or ignoring of their own construction of racial otherness, "an imagined set of attributes" that is, however, ultimately necessary to their self-empowerment—blackness is incongruous with yet fundamental to white working-class identity, as it was in the nineteenth-century white laborers' protests against wage slavery that helped establish the meaning of whiteness.[43] The term "otherness" seems inadequate to describe this relationship of simultaneous incorporation, self-reference, and distancing.

But what exactly is the "power of blackness"? According to Lott, in order to recognize their whiteness, whites must understand it as connected, on some inchoate level, with the cultural force of blackness (again, what is this "cultural force of blackness"?) and then forget the connection—remembering through forgetting. The white self enters into dialogue with its own imagined other by reanimating a dead body. If Elvis remains necessary as a way for white blue-collar workers to approach blackness, perhaps it is because he serves as a wedge between black and white, and the simultaneous performance of the self and the coded other becomes a means of escape from the dialectic of whiteness and objecthood, a way out of the connection between whiteness and the black body as object, and between whiteness and wage slavery.

The town of Holly Springs, Mississippi, was a stop on the early railroad line and served as Grant's headquarters during part of the Civil War. Today, it is like many other small southern towns that the highways left behind: a few businesses still open around a public square, but a sense of people moving on. Vernon Chadwick, one of the organizers of the Elvis conference at the University of Mississippi, suggests that "anyone's home, if approached in the right spirit, can be a Graceland also."[44] Karal Ann Marling argues that everyone *already* lives in a Graceland: "the house is full of things that we all have or used to have, or used to want, or hate." Elvis is dead, she writes, but "we still live here, in these same places. . . . Graceland is our house now, bought and paid for with the price of a ticket. Elvis has left the building. The story that the silent walls have to tell is our story. Softly and tenderly, the ghosts call our names."[45] Elvis's plantation, according to Marling, is haunted. The democratic engagement of owning Graceland necessarily involves listening to the murmuring spirits of national history. But not just anyone and everyone would want a resurrected New South plantation.

A few blocks from the main square in Holly Springs is the attraction that the town might be most known for today, insofar as it is known: a symbiotic monument not only to Elvis but to Graceland itself. It draws Elvis fans, curiosity seekers, college students, and even a few celebrities. Some visitors, according to its architect Paul MacLeod, have pronounced it "better than Graceland." Like Graceland itself since Elvis's death, MacLeod's home, which he calls Graceland Too, is a memorial in a uniquely American vernacular. In *Signs and Wonders*, the catalog of an exhibit of "outsider art inside North Carolina," Roger Manley describes the intensity associated with people giving free rein to their impulses to create. The huge concrete sculptures, stone carvings, scenes in whiskey bottles, and living environments that this text explores might seem eccentric, exuberantly eccentric, but if so, it is not possible to dismiss them as just weird. These works "elicit powerful reactions, and they cannot be ignored."[46] (Perhaps they are impossible to dismiss because they speak to forces coursing under the surface of the dry day-to-dayness of life in a culture of conveyor belts bearing identical things, more than we can ever consume.) A phenomenon like Graceland Too, with its openhearted intimacy with a dead star and aggressive proximity to the vestiges of wealth, as well as to a troubled racial history, is unsettling. Paul MacLeod's house is an "antebellum home" (as the plantation tour guides say) that he is in the process of transforming into a model of Elvis's neoplantation. "My house, Graceland Too, was built in 1853," he told the audience at the conference on Elvis at the University of Mississippi in 1995. "It's 145 years old. We're gonna have it blocked, the roof changed, we're gonna have new columns put on it, a porch, a little wall out in front. Everybody's been complimentin' us. As the work gets done it will be an identical twin to Graceland."[47] On the postslavery plantation, the authentic is not fake enough to be real. By 2002, MacLeod had added blue plastic Christmas trees growing out of spray-painted piles of broken concrete along one side of the house, and shiny silver lions sat atop makeshift columns. Above the front door is posted the phrase "Graceland Too 1853." While Elvis tribute artists enact a relationship to the body of the King that both envelops and distances black culture, Graceland Too, as simultaneous homage to and reinvention of Graceland, re-creates working-class whiteness within the architecture of the plantation South even as it underscores Graceland's dependence upon antebellum social structures. It appropriates the culture of mass consumption as a means of individual expression, and the plantation house becomes both democratic and idiosyncratic.

Paul MacLeod is originally from Detroit. He worked on the assembly line at General Motors and supplemented his earnings with trips to Las Vegas. In Vegas he "got lucky," as he says: he was winning at the tables, and Elvis was performing regular shows. MacLeod had been an Elvis fan since the mid-1950s, when as a teenager he witnessed Elvis's "explosion."[48] After he retired, he moved to Holly Springs and began to build Graceland Too. Officially, it is open for tours twenty-four hours a day, seven days a week. Entering the foyer, visitors encounter what is only the beginning of an overwhelming, even claustrophobic display of Elvis artifacts. The ceilings have been lowered, and the windows are heavily curtained. MacLeod says his collection contains 10 million Elvis-related objects, from crumbling fragments of "the first flowers placed on his grave" to a program of his first public performance, dated 9 April 1953, at the Humes High talent show.[49] It was called the "Annual Minstrel," and images of exaggerated blackface figures underscore the reference to blackface minstrelsy. Not surprising, since this was Tennessee in the early 1950s, but ironic, as a hallmark of Elvis's early performances, presumably including this one, was an inversion of blackface.[50] And though greasepaint had become obsolete, the "power of blackness" continued to underscore white "talent."

MacLeod talks in a steady stream that is sometimes nearly unintelligible due to ill-fitting dentures. He offers photos of many previous visitors mounted on posterboard. The stories he tells of Graceland Too's history as a tourist site sometimes verge on the surreal. One involves a midnight carnival with limousines full of blondes parked in the street and "midgets serving drinks." Another accounts for the absence of the mailbox (which read "Graceland Too 1853"): according to MacLeod, diminutive Asian women stole it with a few well-placed karate chops. MacLeod also talks about the sacrifices he has made to maintain this—more than a collection or a vocation, it is an entire lifestyle. He is fond of saying, "My wife told me, it's me or the Elvis collection, and I haven't seen her since." The apparent ease with which he gave up his marriage after twenty-two years, this embrace of the celibacy of the Elvis priesthood, may be the most extreme proof he offers of his dedication. As Charles Reagan Wilson points out, Elvis has become not only a celebrity but an icon of faith, ascending to the level of a legend complete with relics. In a foray into southern pop culture, Wilson discovered a suggestive souvenir of Elvis: a "vial of sweat" purportedly from the King's own brow, or perhaps somewhere else. "Now you can let his perspiration be your inspiration," reads the text surrounding the tiny container holding a drop of liquid. "Yes, dreams do come true.

Inside Graceland Too (photo by Jessica Adams)

In loving memory, send this greeting and show the world you really care!"[51] The manufacturers of this artifact knew they were not actually bottling Elvis sweat, but they also knew what people wanted from Elvis and how closely it was connected with his complicated body. Created with tongue in cheek or not, it replicates the language and responds to the desires that pervade Elvis culture. Its incoherence reflects the powerful but hard-to-communicate impulses that the figure of Elvis provokes and satisfies. Describing the sweat as a "greeting" invokes disorienting images of a social system in which bodily fluids stand in for or supplement language, or perhaps in which the immediacy of the body circumvents the commodity fetish. The photo of Elvis on the card is that of the later Elvis in concert, presumably at his sweatiest and also at his whitest. As a part of the white body enters circulation, it is celebrated, "purified," yet still haunted by the power of blackness. The most authentic living Elvis may well be a black man: African American Elvis impersonator Robert Washington "has placed first in numerous 'Elvis Competitions' all over the country," and Clearance Giddens "has met with similar success and now makes a living by playing the impersonator circuit up and down the east coast." An episode of *Geraldo* that featured Elvis impersonators culminated in a vote for the " 'best impersonator of Elvis'—or as Geraldo put it, 'the most authentic Elvis.' "·The winner was Giddens.[52]

MacLeod's project is characterized by renunciation thoroughly enmeshed in accumulation. It relies on the achievement of material success and then the relinquishment of luxuries in order to take the practice of purchasing (Elvis memorabilia) to the level of religious devotion. In his presentation at the University of Mississippi conference, "Why I'm the World's Number One Elvis Fan," MacLeod declared,

> I gave up everything I owned in the world to keep doin' the collection that I've got, preserve it for history, for future archives and everything else. And you ask me what I gave up? I was lucky enough to give up my time to go ahead and devote myself to Elvis. And I gave up another house that I owned that was paid for, a ranch-style home. I had $120,000 in customized furniture in it. . . . I had a Harley-Davidson motorcycle, a boat, a camper, a swimming pool, all paid for, $30,000 worth of diamond rings and watches I got rid of, a gold Cadillac, a Cadillac limousine with VIPs and wraparound bars and the whole works.[53]

MacLeod achieved the American Dream and then found that the greater value lay not in achieving it for himself but in commemorating Elvis's achievement of it. This narrative of sacrifice is a standard part of the tour of Graceland Too, and it conveys the message that merit lies more in memory than in action. Out of the remembrance of someone else's life—by surrounding oneself with relics and vestiges but also from time to time by visiting the body itself (in "tribute")—the self emerges. In the unceasing wake of modernity's upheavals, origin myths are created around souvenirs.[54]

MacLeod has erected and lives in a memorial to the King that is simultaneously a memorial to and a scene of the perpetual reinvention of himself. The first part of the tour is dedicated to describing accolades that MacLeod and his son, Elvis Aaron Presley MacLeod, have received: "I first met Elvis at Graceland Too," or "Even better than Graceland." Graceland security guards' uniforms hang along the wall in one room; by way of explanation, MacLeod says that when the guards who wore these uniforms visited, they were so awed by his dedication that they disrobed right then and there and donated their clothes. MacLeod is also fond of pointing out similarities between himself and Elvis, and between Elvis MacLeod and Elvis Presley. Elvis MacLeod, he says, has the same encyclopedic memory that the other Elvis had and, as a child, looked so much like his namesake that "up at Graceland, they can hardly tell the difference" between their two early photographs. (The photos are juxtaposed on a wall inside Graceland Too.)[55] Paul MacLeod claims that he himself shares not only Elvis's sleeping and eating habits but also his racial heritage—the same mixture of "Cherokee, Scotch, and Irish." Photos of him dressed as Elvis hang on the walls. At the back of the house is a record player that is a regular stop on the tour. "Just see if I can't get some of the sound of Elvis's voice," he says as he lifts the needle and places it on a track. The music begins, and his eyes focus somewhere behind me in concentration. His voice drops, reaching for the notes: "I'm all shook up."

The collection contains a tremendous number of videos recorded by MacLeod and his son that feature Elvis on television or in movies, as well as what must be thousands of copies of publications, marked with paper clips, that mention him. My initial sense of the irrelevance of MacLeod's project was succeeded by a feeling that the burdens of postmodern remembering are writ large in this vast assemblage. Beyond testifying to the ongoing presence of Elvis as a celebrity, the endless stream of citations suggests how difficult remembering is when there are so many channels through which it can and therefore must be done: photographs, videos, magazines, newspapers, television shows, films, and recordings, as well as the clothes and crumbling flowers. At some point the value of all these signifiers becomes impossible to assess. "Modern memory is, above all, archival," wrote Pierre Nora; "fear of a rapid and final disappearance combines with anxiety about the future to give even the most humble testimony, the most modest vestige, the potential dignity of the memorable."[56] Rescuing pieces of this multiplying icon as they fly through cathode ray tubes and cyberspace, MacLeod expresses a symptomatic extreme of the fear that the past may disappear before we can figure out what it means, as well as a desire to reshape the meanings that we *do* recognize. In the disappearance of an older, more "natural" way of being—what Nora calls *milieux de mémoire*, environments of memory, in which things happen for material and organic reasons, not because some prompt has been inserted in the calendar, its original impetus gradually atrophying, becoming obsolete, and evolving into a commercial opportunity—connections to the cultural past become unevenly traced, the reasons we do things unanchored, occasions to memorize by rote. It is the process of disintegration and loss of our cultural and biological ancestors, but also of our own bodies. As Graceland Too suggests, obsessive archival memory is an attempt to shore up the borders of our mortal selves as well as a means of imagining the self into existence, and anxieties surrounding the body as a commodity remain even within an economy that takes the commodification of everything for granted.

When I asked him why he had embarked on this all-encompassing undertaking, MacLeod responded, "I'd give up my greatest gift [his own life] if Elvis could live again." He has amassed a vast collection of souvenirs related to the body, both living and dead, of Elvis, but the most important of these is MacLeod's own body, both a reminder of and substitute for Elvis's. Memory and substitution seamlessly merge: the surrogate, as the self, is explicitly imagined as a replacement for an already hybrid original. Graceland Too, the "real" antebellum home, begins to overlap with the "real" Graceland in a dizzying precession of simulacra.[57] MacLeod gives up the hallmarks of material success (the gold Cadillac, the swimming pool) even as he moves into the realm of the commercial in another, profounder sense altogether: by turning the embodiment of Elvis into a business. The racially ambiguous body is recommodified as spectacle in the big house.

I want to deliberately draw icons of "high" and popular culture into proximity or, rather, to draw attention to their proximity, for it strikes me as no coincidence that Graceland and Graceland Too are located within an hour of Rowan Oak, Faulkner's antebellum home. Its purpose today is to serve as "a place for people from all over the world to learn about his work."[58] On a summer day, the lavish scent of gardenias floats through the cool shadows of its columned porch. The fluted columns and the scent of the gardenias seem to provide the most salient clues to Faulkner's work, for the spare, silent rooms yield little, with the exception of the study at the back of the house. Faulkner wrote *Absalom, Absalom!* in part in this room (the other part in Hollywood), overlooking the pasture, the old detached kitchen, and the building that the visitor's guide calls the "Servant's Quarters." Rowan Oak was built by a planter named Robert Sheegog in the early 1840s; Faulkner bought it in 1930 and restored it. Photographs that he commissioned of himself at Rowan Oak depict him as the ultimate southern gentleman, riding his horses and posing with his black groom and with his daughter Jill in her bridal gown.[59] The authors of one history of Rowan Oak write, "Looking at [it] now, in its restored condition, one might be seduced into embracing the easy theory that Faulkner . . . saw himself as reclaiming the power of his family in plantation days."[60] They are quick to reject this "theory" even though there is clearly something to it. Jay Parini asserts, "Faulkner . . . had always yearned to replicate the Big Place that his grandfather had lorded over."[61] Reclaiming the glory of plantation days would not have been a straightforward process, and Rowan Oak is said to be troubled by ghosts. "At least a score of reliable witnesses, from family members to curators, have reported spectral visitations: piano playing, footsteps, cries in the night," apparently coming from the unquiet spirits of the plantation's original owner and his family.[62] Perhaps—and how could it be otherwise?—Faulkner wrote some of his best work in a haunted plantation.

But it wasn't only his plantation that was haunted. In 1956, in the wake of the *Brown* decision, Faulkner published an article in *Ebony* titled "If I Were a Negro." Sitting in his study at Rowan Oak, Faulkner reinvents himself as a black leader.[63] He urges *Ebony* readers to fight segregation "Gandhi's way," which in this case he believes to mean "send[ing] every day to the white school to which he was entitled by his ability and capacity to go, a student of my race, fresh and cleanly dressed, courteous without threat or violence, to seek admission; when he was refused I would forget about him as an individual, but tomorrow I would send another one, still fresh and clean and courteous, to be refused in his turn, until at last the white man himself must recognize that there will be no peace for him until he himself has solved the dilemma."[64] Faulkner remains invested in the survival of white power even as he attempts to understand black resistance; "the white man" needs to know, he argues, that "nobody is going to force integration on him from the outside."[65] He probes the limits and limitations of his own racial identity and understands the value of integration, but he insists on southern whites as the arbiters of their own fate. White men should be nonaggressively hassled into a solution, but what that solution might be is left unimagined. Faulkner seems obsessed with the notion of "cleanliness," a word he uses five times in this short piece and by which he seems to mean not only hygiene but a clear-cut separation between blacks and whites. (This from a man who loved his mammy to death.)[66] "If I were a Negro," Faulkner insists, "I would say to my people, 'Let us be always unflaggingly and inflexibly flexible. But always decently, quietly, courteously, with dignity and without violence. And above all, with patience. The white man has devoted three hundred years to teaching us to be patient; that is one thing at least in which we are his superiors.'"[67] Glissant remarks, "The Blacks he is talking to in this way have never left Yoknapatawpha, have never known the ghettos of New York."[68] The most important point in Faulkner's essay is that black people need to "learn to deserve equality."[69] And the only way "we"/they can do this, according to his logic, is by becoming "superior" to whites: "We as a race must lift ourselves by our own bootstraps to where we are competent for the responsibilities of equality. . . . Our tragedy is that these virtues of responsibility are the white man's virtues of which he boasts, yet we, the Negro, must be his superior in them."[70] Inflexible flexibility, superior equality—the rhetorical blackface indicates a mind addled by racial "disorder." Elvis as King Creole, Faulkner as White Negro—this strange commentary suggests another result of the plantation system in addition to segregation: the fact that, as James Baldwin noted, "the Negro-in-America is a form of insanity which overtakes white men."[71]

Yet race is not necessarily a stable sense of identification for anyone in the American grain. Visiting Ghana in the early 1950s, Richard Wright watched women dancing and thought, "I'd seen these same snakelike, veering dances before . . . in storefront churches, in Holy Roller Tabernacles, in God's Temples, in unpainted wooden prayer-meeting houses on the plantations of the Deep South. . . . Never in my life had I been able to dance more than a few elementary steps. . . . So, what had bewildered me about Negro dance expression in the United States now bewildered me in the same way in Africa."[72] To the question of what the power of blackness really means, Faulkner seems to answer "chaos," and Wright seems to answer "soul."

Journalist Grace Halsell reprised John Howard Griffin's *Black Like Me* in the late 1960s, and her memoir *Soul Sister* was also a best seller. As with *Black Like Me*, critics acclaimed it as a searing account of what it was like to be "really" black—ignoring centuries of writing by blacks with no need for disguise.[73] For white readers, a white person from a middle-class background trying to survive the passage into blackness seemed to offer more immediate and even convincing testimony. Halsell was a southerner who had been "born and grew up in Texas, a descendant of slaveholders and Civil War veterans." "But," she writes, "color was not a conscious fact in my early years. I never regarded Negroes as a part of my society. I had no particular feelings about them, one way or another. They were simply a part of the landscape."[74] This negative space became positive when Halsell read *Black Like Me*, however, and the unacknowledged other half of her world took on an obsessional visibility. "Being black has become an all-consuming objective," she records.[75] Blackness is white achievement; race is an object of ownership but also an unpredictable result of creolization. Halsell wanted to pass so that she could report on how black women lived in Harlem and in Mississippi—the most "black" environments she could think of because the most abject. First, she used prescription drugs that accelerated the effects of sun exposure. When the sun glinting off the pool at her Washington apartment complex failed to produce a sufficiently convincing tan, she flew to Puerto Rico. The Caribbean has become a place where white people go to escape their white skin while accentuating the privilege that accompanies it, and Halsell can only pursue "blackness" because she has time and money. She seeks it in long sessions on white sand beaches. "Back from the seashore," she writes,

> I bathe and close the shutters and remove my loose shift and stand before the mirror—and gasp in horrified disbelief! The skin, the precious, beautiful black skin, my labor of love, literally hangs like falling wallpaper from around my eyes. Frantically, tearfully, I grab for the pieces, try to paste them back into place, to restore the black face that was. As I sit looking at that face with pale, accusing eyes—self-indicted as miserable, ugly, unloving and un-lovable, not myself, not another, a no-body, and no-thing—the eyes condemn me, no longer able to see the person I have de-stroyed, only this unraveled, molting monster I have created.[76]

Halsell seeks "thingness"; as Laura Browder argues, she seems to need the language of bondage to represent black people and black culture.[77] When she becomes a no-thing, she has nothing left. The constructed racial self simultaneously doubles and disintegrates. It is forever unclear whether "the person I have destroyed" is the "white" self or the "black" self. As she passes out of range of racial identification, Halsell understands herself as inhuman, a "monster." White people keep falling apart under the strain of owning race. Before Halsell can arrive at her destination, her racial impersonation in chemically assisted blackface leads to disembodiment; at least for now, "the eyes" belong to no one.

Faulkner works on *Absalom, Absalom!* during breaks from his gig at Twentieth Century Fox, gazing out across Los Angeles and seeing Jefferson. Hattie McDaniel, who would become Margaret Mitchell's iconic Mammy, sings jazz with the George Morrison Jazz

Orchestra at the Cheyenne Frontier Days rodeo.[78] Warner Bros. flies the Confederate flag over Hollywood to promote the premiere of *Gone with the Wind*. Such anecdotal images of the frontier landscape merging with southern myths speak to a long history of interconnection between the plantation and the settlement of the West. Creek, black, and mixed-race people sang psalms in the Creek language to the tune of slave spirituals; Cherokee slaveholders issued an emancipation proclamation on 21 February 1863.[79] The next chapter explores the meaning of such hybrid moments taking shape in the literary imaginary, as the adaptive nature of the post-slavery plantation appears in the expansiveness of metaphor.

# 4. Southern Frontiers

> To ignore the frontier and time in setting up a conception of the
> social state of the Old South is to abandon reality. For the history
> of this South throughout a very great part of the period from the
> opening of the nineteenth century to the Civil War (in the South
> beyond the Mississippi until long after that war) is mainly the history
> of the roll of frontier upon frontier—and on to the frontier beyond.
> *W. J. Cash*

In the preface to his 1896 collection of short stories *Red Men and
White*, Owen Wister introduces his tales of the West with a
commentary on the post-Reconstruction South as a lacuna where
atavistic barbarism can thrive. Pondering the imminent historicity of
his own subject matter, Wister considers how pockets of the past
exist within a context of progress: "These eight stories are made
from our Western Frontier as it was in a past as near as yesterday
and almost as by-gone as the Revolution," he writes, "so swiftly do
we proceed." And yet, "While portions of New York, Chicago, and
San Francisco are of this nineteenth century, we have many ancient
periods surviving among us." Wister's examples of this premodern
survival lie in Appalachia, among "the Kentucky and Tennessee
mountaineers," and in Texas, where,

> not long ago, an African was led upon a platform in a public
> place for people to see, and tortured slowly to death with knives
> and fire. To witness this scene young men and women came
> in crowds. It is said that the railroad ran a special train for
> spectators from a distance. How might that audience of Paris,

Texas, appropriately date its letters? Not Anno Domini, but many years B.C. The African deserves no pity. His hideous crime was enough to drive any father to madness, and too many such monsters have by their acts made Texas justly desperate. But for American citizens to crowd to the retribution, and look on as at a holiday show, reveals the Inquisition, the Pagans, the Stone Age, unreclaimed in our republic. On the other hand, the young men and women who will watch side by side the burning of a negro shrink from using such words as bull or stallion in polite society.[1]

Reflected in the evolution of the West, Wister sees a tourist lynching. The victim's mutilated body makes a brief, unassimilated appearance, fading into the background as Wister turns from this "too serious" material to stories "about Indians and soldiers and events west of the Mississippi." But he would continue to monitor the connection between slavery and the western frontier in his novel *The Virginian*, published in 1902 and destined to become "one of the most popular novels in American literary history."[2] Wister wrote the preface for *The Virginian* in Charleston. Members of his mother's family were prominent plantation owners; his great-great-grandfather Pierce Butler, a U.S senator from South Carolina, had two large Georgia plantations and more than six hundred slaves, and his grandfather Pierce Butler inherited this wealth. Notwithstanding the fact that his grandmother left her husband and publicly condemned slavery, Wister seemed to view such southern institutions, as well as the city of Charleston, with fondness.[3] The hero of *The Virginian* is identified simply as "the Virginian" or "the Southerner," as if he was *the* southerner, a real man and a real gentleman. The novel does not allude to black cowboys or any other black characters, though they were part of the West that Wister visited (Bill Pickett was becoming famous for his bulldogging and would join the touring 101 Ranch Wild West Show with Buffalo Bill and Will Rogers in 1905). Yet signs of blackness are scattered through it. Riding on the range, the Southerner sings a minstrel song:

Dar is a big Car'lina nigger
About de size of dis chile or p'raps a little bigger
  By de name of Jim Crow.
Dat what de white folks call him.
If ever I sees him I 'tends to maul him,
  Just to let de white folks see
  Such an animos as he
Can't walk around the street and scandalize me

Great big fool, he hasn't any knowledge.
Gosh! how could he when he's never been to scollege?
  Neither has I.
  But I'se come mighty nigh;
I peaked through de door as I went by.

He gets interrupted by the villain just as he is beginning the third verse.[4] Later, a character named Scipio is quick to assure the narrator that his name is not what it sounds like—a slave name. Scipio's introduction includes proof of racial purity: " 'Scipio le Moyne, from Gallipolice, Ohio. The eldest of us always gets called Scipio. It's French. But us folks have been white for a hundred years.' "[5] Wister followed up his interest in matters of race in his next novel; an appreciative resident of Charleston, his thoughts turned to that city as the setting for his best-selling *Lady Baltimore* (1906). Wister approvingly reproduced Confederate mythology while portraying the North as corrupted by commerce. Charleston is a "little city of oblivion . . . shut in with its lavender and pressed-rose memories, a handful of people who were like that great society of the world, the high society of distinguished men and women who exist no more, but who touched history with a light hand, and left their mark upon it in a host of memoirs and letters that we read to-day with a starved and homesick longing in the midst of our sullen welter of democracy."[6] Democracy as a sullen welter—it is little wonder Wister's old friend President Theodore Roosevelt lost his composure upon reading this.[7]

Wister's implication that democracy, as opposed to the white southern aristocracy, gave voice to society's lowest common denominator seems to be a direct response to developments such as the constitutional right, however abridged in practice, of former slaves to participate in the political process. Indeed, the negotiation of freedoms—what freedoms, whose freedoms—that followed westward expansion and civil war was fundamental to a broad range of stories about the frontier. Frontier settlement and its relationship to slavery, connections between the violence of the West and the violence of the postslavery South, nostalgia for the supposed orderliness of antebellum society—Wister's work points us toward an understanding of "the South" as an entanglement of transregional myths, signifiers, and events, an understanding borne out in even incidental observations of place. The Ninth Cavalry barracks, home to the first all-black army company, later known as Buffalo Soldiers, was established in New Orleans in 1866 on land that had been the Foucher Plantation. The World Cotton Centennial took place there in 1884, and now it is Audubon Park. During the renovation of the park in 2004, the Audubon Institute erected a memorial to the soldiers who had departed this site for their posts on the frontier. Dedicated during Black History Month, the monument honors "African American Cavalry troops who defended America's western frontier in the 1800s."[8] From whom they defended it is left unspoken, and American history rests uneasily in the gap. As we look at the history of "Indians, soldiers, and events west of the Mississippi," we find the plantation persisting as a way of thinking, as a sometimes almost invisible part of postslavery environments that extend far beyond the South.

Between Georgia and New Mexico in mid-October the cotton harvest unfolds across longitudes. Sometimes the crop is compressed into big rectangular bales whose escaped white strands catch in the weeds by the highways; elsewhere it is still in the boll. The cotton fields stretching from Sea Island past the Rio Grande hint at the range of slavery itself. Black slaves and slavery were part of the fabric of society on the frontier, existing "in virtually every state and territory prior to the Civil War." Oregon, California, Utah, and Kansas witnessed "intense local debates about [slavery's] suitability" to their particular landscapes and economies. The plantation was a concept that could be applied to ranching and mining as well as farming.[9] The Seminole, Cherokee, Choctaw, Creek, and Chickasaw owned black slaves. Quintard Taylor writes, "Only a minority in each tribe were slaveholders. Yet for this minority, which often was each tribe's political and economic elite, slavery was a profitable labor system and a proud source of identification with the planter culture of the Old South."[10] In 1896, students at the Cherokee Male and Female Seminaries in Talequah, Indian Territory, put on a skit titled "De Debatin' Club," which they performed in blackface. These students were among the "political and economic elite" (and some had little Cherokee ancestry); many came from families who had owned slaves. The writings of female seminarians published in the school's periodical, *A Wreath of Cherokee Rose Buds*, refer to "hostile Indians," "wild and untutored Savage[s]," and blushing, blue-eyed Cherokee maidens. Meanwhile, descendants of Cherokee slaves in Indian Territory "could only attend the 'Negro High School.'"[11] The existence of Native American slaveholders and segregationists illuminates the reach of plantation ideology, even as its virtual absence from the sphere of common knowledge points to the isolation of the plantation's post-Emancipation effects as "southern." The social problems that this institutionalized inequality had created could be partially masked within popular culture not only by figuratively isolating blacks as southern, but by using Indians as a foil for blacks.

As popular images of the West iron out its racial diversity, they reveal the relative value of stereotypes. In their 1965 study of black cowboys, Philip Durham and Everett L. Jones write, "Approximately two thirds of the 3,158 dime novels published by Beadle and Adams between 1860 and 1898 are laid in the trans-Mississippi West, where they deal with frontiersmen, desperadoes, miners and assorted Texas heroes and badmen. Negroes appear only insignificantly in their plots—action-packed stories far more concerned with bloodthirsty Indians, virtuous maidens, ferocious robbers and leering Boucicault villains than with cowhands and six-guns."[12] While blacks might be demonized or made into props or objects of comedy within certain parameters, the West was apparently not a place where perceived "black" characteristics usefully animated narrative. This popular investment in the West as not black was shaped by white disquiet occasioned by the possibility, and later the actuality, of Emancipation. Between 1861 and Reconstruction, *Harper's Monthly Magazine*, the most widely circulated periodical of its day, put forth the idea that the West was "free" of blacks and therefore a place where freedom seemed less conceptually dependent upon slavery. As Kathleen Diffley shows, former slaves as depicted in *Harper's* were "visually inarticulate without a space to enter or structurally constrained from entering the space that was there. The only roads that were open led to citizenship and education, or run-down homes and hard work, and those almost always led south. Otherwise black figures . . . turned toward the ambiguous space outside of the picture place, as though they would discover what they sought up front by facing their predominantly white audiences, rather than somewhere out there on the range."[13]

In a similar way Frederick Jackson Turner's "The Significance of the Frontier in American History" (1893), a profound influence on popular as well as academic conceptions of the West, placed the frontier specifically in opposition to the conflict between North and South. Drawing attention away from slavery, the Civil War, and Reconstruction as defining factors in U.S. society, Turner simplified western history to reflect "free" open spaces more representative of democratic ideals. Despite centuries of contact between Hispanics, blacks, Europeans, white Americans, and Native American nations, when Turner argued that "in the crucible of the frontier, the immigrants were Americanized, liberated, and fused into a mixed race,"[14] the mixed "race" he was talking about was an alternative to the race mixing that had resulted from slavery.[15] The liberation of those from elsewhere, and the mingling of their blood with "American" blood, redirected white fears associated with a free black population. The same dynamics become desirable when reapplied to the space of the frontier—indeed they become the very forces that generate and maintain the idea of the nation. Thus a feature of U.S. society that was a liability for whites is remade into an asset in the West. Union

General James Lane and John Brown's slave-liberation raids across the Missouri border in the late 1850s and black soldiers fighting against Apache chief Victorio and with Benito Juárez were forgotten in Turner's vision of a frontier melting pot for whites. When he described the frontier as "a gate of escape from the bondage of the past," the bondage he was talking about was a form of white slavery.[16] Turner's translation of the black slave into enslaved whites effectively eliminated black presence from the idea of America. "When American history comes to be rightly viewed," he wrote, "it will be seen that the slavery question is an incident."[17]

Turner delivered his remarks at the American Historical Association meeting that took place in conjunction with the segregated Columbian Exposition. There, Frederick Douglass declared, "Men talk of the Negro problem. There is no Negro problem. The problem is whether the American people have honesty enough, loyalty enough, honor enough, patriotism enough to live up to their own Constitution." Simon Pokagon, a Potawatowmi elder, proclaimed, "On behalf of my people, the American Indians, I hereby declare to you, the pale-faced race that has usurped our lands and homes, that we have no spirit to celebrate with you the great Columbian Fair now being held in this Chicago city, the wonder of the world. No; sooner would we hold the high joy day over the graves of our departed than to celebrate our own funeral, the discovery of America."[18] Refusing to endorse the zeitgeist that had materialized in the exposition and recognizing corpses rising from the converted wetlands on which it stood, Pokagon realized that all Native Americans, whether they had emulated white society or not, were doomed to the same destruction. "The Red Man's Greeting" was printed and circulated in quantity both during and after the exposition. Unsurprisingly, however, Turner's stylistically dull but ideologically indispensable version of events won out.

From the point of view of some white commentators, the defeated Indian served as a useful disguise for blacks in claims to southern distinction. The Agrarians, like Turner, described an opposition between East and West, though for them "East" represented the South, while the West signified the menacing power of northern industrialism. Yet the same kind of racial reembodiment found in Turner's work is effected through the Agrarians' insistence on the rural South as both the real South and the essence of the nation. This emphasis makes, or rather should make, it impossible not to think about those who worked the land. Allen Tate and John Crowe Ransom, however, produced versions of southern identity in which slaves virtually disappear.[19] At the same time, Ransom articulated an alliance between whites and Native Americans in which white southern men become more like Indians than frontier whites. "Indians lead a life which has an ancient pattern, and had been perfected a long time, and is conscious of the weight of tradition behind it," he writes; "compared with which the pattern of life of the white men of that region, parvenus as they are, seems improvised and lacking in dignity. . . . Life for the white men depends on what they can buy with their money."[20] Native Americans are the "primitive" alternative to slaves, whose previously ascribed primitivism has now become less safe.

As Richard Wright describes Ghanaians watching an American western, the myth of the American West, all cowboys and Indians, is a source of great merriment. Familiar characters are "greeted as old friends," and "throughout the film the audience commented like a Greek chorus."[21] The audience deconstructs, reenacts, participates in, and parodies American frontier violence, perhaps recognizing the intrinsic, unintended parody that such images of the West already embodied.[22] Indebted to attempts to reduce the impact of slavery on the idea of America, this version of the West playing in Accra, a few hours' drive from Elmina Castle, acts out a trans-Atlantic commentary on the meaning of diaspora, and excavations of the hidden racial complexity of the western context circle back to a point of departure for New World plantations. Expanding the frame of popular representations of the West, we discover the error in using them as alternatives to the racial heterogeneity radiating out from the South.

Willa Cather's best-selling novels *The Professor's House* (1925) and *Death Comes for the Archbishop* (1927) were written during a period that witnessed a "vast outpouring" of literature romancing the frontier.[23] This overwhelming public fascination with the Wild West during the 1920s materialized not only as the West became increasingly settled, but also during a time of domestic upheaval stemming from, among other things, the effects of immigration and the Great Migration, which shaped cities striated by segregation and ethnic prejudice.[24] In the context of these changes, popular images of Native Americans offered shelter to those seeking to influence the impact of both slavery and free blacks on U.S. society. The West served white popular culture as a place where contemporary social conflicts did not exist (the conflicts were all historical). Cather grew up in Virginia between 1873 and 1883 and, later, within a community of Virginians who had migrated to the Nebraska plains, including relatives who transported both tales and artifacts of the Confederacy.[25] Cather "did not come out of Virginia for nothing," Eudora Welty wrote, "any more than she grew up in Nebraska for nothing. History awed and stirred Willa Cather; and the absence of a history as far as she could see around her, in her growing up, only made her look farther, gave her the clues to discover a deeper past."[26] Here, "Virginia" signals history; "Nebraska" is the impetus for the realization of Virginia in other landscapes.[27] Recent thinking about Cather's relationship to southernness and to slavery has focused almost entirely on what ended up being her last novel, *Sapphira and the Slave Girl*, the only one of her works that was actually set in the South. But her novels of the frontier offer not just a more detailed picture of what the South meant to Cather, for what that is worth, but, in the subtleties of literary language, a sense of the symbolic expanse of the plantation.

*The Professor's House* (1925) begins far from the madding crowds of immigrants in the northern cities, the oppressiveness of southern segregation, and even, apparently, the wide-open spaces of the West, although not from the exigencies of colonialism. Godfrey St. Peter is a middle-aged historian living with his family in a small town and teaching at a small college on the shores of Lake Michigan. He has just won a prestigious award for his series titled *Spanish Adventurers in North America*, a work St. Peter himself describes as a " 'dazzling . . . beautiful . . . utterly impossible thing.' "[28] Cather integrates the West into the scale of both domestic and intellectual concerns through flashbacks and memories as St. Peter and members of his family reflect on the phantom presence of St. Peter's student Tom Outland—a name that "seemed to suit the boy exactly" (97)—who had assisted in the research for these prizewinning volumes. Through the recollections of the St. Peters, we see Tom arriving in the Midwest tanned by the southwestern sun, a former cowboy who does not even know his own age. When the professor, fatigued by an old departmental feud, worn down by students, and chronically underpaid, breathes a whiff of the desert air that clings to Tom, he revives. Eventually Lillian St. Peter becomes jealous of her husband's other relationship, and their marriage is never quite the same even after Tom dies fighting at Flanders. He leaves his fiancée, the St. Peters' daughter Rosamond, the rights to the patent for an engine he was working on before he went to war. The man whom Rosamond eventually marries, Louie Marsellus—an electrical engineer and, as Cather is careful to specify, a Jew—pursues Tom's idea, and the engine eventually produces phenomenal profits. In death, Tom escapes "the trap of worldly success"; he is exempt from the "thousands of useless letters . . . thousands of false excuses," and the demands of "his fellow scientists, his wife, the town and the State" that would inevitably, St. Peter imagines, grow ever more oppressive (236–37). But even if Tom has avoided such eventualities, he has nonetheless "all turned out . . . dollars and cents" (112).[29] After Rosamond and Louie announce that their new country house will be called Outland, St. Peter tells his wife, "They've got everything he ought to have had, and the least they can do is be quiet about it, and not convert his very bones into a personal asset" (36). As Tom's dead body becomes investment property, the men and women of the St. Peters' set duel among themselves with furs, dresses, and even doorknobs. During a dinner party at the St. Peters' with their younger daughter Kathleen and her husband, Louie Marsellus says of Outland, " 'we got our wonderful wrought-iron door fittings from Chicago. We found just the right sort of hinge and latch. . . . None of your Colonial glass knobs for us!' Mrs. St. Peter sighed. Scott and Kathleen had just glass-knobbed their new bungalow throughout"

(39). The text is preoccupied with commodities. As the novel opens, the St. Peters are in the process of moving into the new house that Lillian has finally convinced her husband to build using his award money, though Godfrey refuses to move his study from the old house. Cather contemplates the details of modern life at length: indoor plumbing and central heat as well as the luxuries that the Marsellus's money can buy. When St. Peter accompanies Rosamond to Chicago on an "orgy of acquisition" (135) for her new home, he returns "absolutely flattened out and listless" (133). St. Peter had continually "carpentered" and tinkered in his old house, but the new one simply rises, perfectly formed, from the earth. Human life and labor have disappeared into the St. Peters' new home, into the furs and mass-produced glass doorknobs, but they are readily apparent in the marks of ancient cooking fires on the bottoms of Tom's Anasazi pots.

While Cather idealizes Native Americans as embodiments of the best of "human culture," however, they are also the opposite of cultured.[30] The highly developed but extinct civilization of the Anasazis, the ruins of which Tom Outland explored, is contrasted with its Native destroyers—the "brutal invaders," probably "some roving . . . tribe without culture or domestic virtues" (198). Both tribes are not Indians so much as "extraordinary meditation[s]" on the meaning of white Americanness.[31] The "good Indian" is white culture's classical ancestor. As Father Duchene, Outland's tutor and an apparent expert on Native life—he "had been among the Indians nearly twenty years . . . , he had seventeen Indian pueblos in his parish and he spoke several Indian dialects"—states authoritatively, "I have seen a collection of early pottery from the island of Crete. Many of the geometrical decorations on these jars are not only similar, but, if my memory is trustworthy, identical" (197). These are not like, they are, Grecian urns, and in due time Tom will deliver an ode upon them. Meanwhile, the "bad Indian" distances whites from acts of violence committed on the frontier. It is he who has destroyed this civilization, not colonizers and settlers.

St. Peter's "history of the Spanish adventurers" is "dazzling" and "beautiful," but it is also "utterly impossible," as the events of the novel themselves make clear. The inconsistencies and lack of cohesion within the complex of bodies as property, commodities, fetishes, and racial otherness on the frontier become explicit as Tom and his partner Roddy Blake explore what they call the Eagle's Nest, a small group of rooms above the Cliff City. Here they discover the mummified remains of one of its original inhabitants. "We thought she had been murdered," Tom remarks; "there was a great wound in her side, the ribs stuck out through the dried flesh. Her mouth was open as if she were screaming, and her face, through all these years, had kept a look of terrible agony. Part of the nose was gone, but she had plenty of teeth, not one missing, and a great deal of coarse black hair. Her teeth were even and white, and so little worn that we thought she must have been a young woman" (192). They call her Mother Eve, a corpse preserved in a wail of agony as a mother of Western culture. However appropriate this might be, it still seems odd that the mummy becomes one of Tom's most highly prized and warmly beloved finds. Father Duchene is also "greatly interested" in Mother Eve. His reaction to the screaming mummy is incongruous: "He laughed and said she was well named." The priest seems to authorize the identification of the mummy as Eve. And yet his theory of her death suggests that he considers her more of a Jezebel: " 'I seem to smell,' he said slyly, 'a personal tragedy. Perhaps when the tribe went down to the summer camp, our lady was sick and would not go. Perhaps her husband thought it worth while to return unannounced from the farms some night, and found her in improper company. The young man may have escaped. In primitive society the husband is allowed to punish an unfaithful wife with death' " (201). It is never entirely clear why Father Duchene finds the mummy amusing or Eve-like—unless he enjoys it as a spectacle of retribution for the biblical Eve's betrayal of Adam. (The knowledge is all on his side.) Cather wants the Blue Mesa to work as an indigenous source of "American" culture where the works of Virgil, autochthonous natives, and cowboys fluently blend, though Mother Eve suggests a different story: the history of white barbarism that Wister inserts into his meditation on the national importance of the West.[32] But in the end, the mummy will be incorporated into the novel's moral structure as a symbol of the ideal of whiteness as property—property with a value that cannot be commercialized.

Work at the mesa completed, Tom boards a train for the nation's capital. He feels it is his "duty" to alert the federal government to this archaeological find and to locate scientists who will "dig out all its secrets" (202). Aggression and a sense of responsibility effortlessly coexist in Cather's imagination. While in Washington, however, Tom grows disenchanted. A functionary tries to buy one of his ancient pots for an ashtray, and Tom cannot get the higher-ups at the Smithsonian interested in his discovery because they are fixated on getting funding for an "International Exposition of some sort" in Paris. Eventually Congress appropriates money to the museum, but it "wouldn't cover an expedition to the South-west" (212)— only "pilgrimages to the commodity fetish," as Walter Benjamin described the world's fairs that marked self-congratulatory efforts of industrialized nations.[33] Yet the Anasazi ruins themselves would soon be featured on a pilgrimage to the commodity fetish. Cather fictionalized not only the story of the ruins but her own story of finding out about them.[34] She may have reconfigured the facts because the timing of the International Exposition that she used to illustrate the callousness of the federal bureaucrats got in the way of her characterizations of the Native West as an unadulterated antidote to consumerism. The Paris Exposition she refers to took place in 1889, but by the time of the Chicago Exposition in 1893, the Anasazi Cliff City had been thoroughly incorporated into an official narrative of national identity. As Frederick Douglass denounced the color line, Simon Pokagon spoke out against imperialism, and Frederick Jackson Turner claimed the frontier as a primal American scene, the Anthropological Building advertised dead Indians. It contained a reproduction of the Cliff City painstakingly curated by Frederick Ward Putnam of the Peabody Museum at Harvard and his assistant Franz Boas (who would later encourage Zora Neale Hurston's anthropological innovations). The display was crowned with an American flag, and a lemonade stand was set up at the entrance.[35] The dichotomy that Cather so meticulously constructs between consumer culture and authentic national culture deconstructs when what Outland most wanted—scholarly, nationalized recognition for the Cliff City—comes about.

That Cather's critique of consumer culture is a critique of it as a force that enslaves becomes evident in her depictions of Tom's life in Washington. The Bixbys, the couple with whom Tom boards during his stay, "spent their life trying to keep up appearances," he recalls, "and trying to make his salary do more than it could. When they weren't discussing where she should go in the summer, they talked about the promotions in his department; how much the other clerks got and how they spent it, how many new dresses their wives had" (209). Describing their preparations for an evening out at an exclusive reception, Tom comments,

> They decided that for such an occasion she must have a new dress. Bixby borrowed twenty-five dollars from me, and took his lunch hour to go shopping with his wife and choose the satin. This seemed to me very strange. In New Mexico the Indian boys sometimes went to a trader's with their wives and bought shawls or calico, and we thought it rather contemptible. On the night of the reception the Bixbys set off gaily in a cab. The dress they considered a great success. But they had bad luck. Somebody spilt claret-cup on Mrs. Bixby's skirt before the evening was half over, and when they got home that night I heard her weeping and reproaching him for being so upset about it, and looking at nothing but her ruined dress all evening. She said he cried out when it happened. I don't doubt it. (210)

Women perform both "culture" and its flaws—on the historic frontier, as Mother Eve attests, as well as in modern urban life. But men themselves become feminized as they assign this role to their wives; according to Cather, Mr. Bixby is more of a "woman" than Mrs. Bixby. Consumption thus appears dangerous not only because of its threat to human culture, but because of its related effects on "real" masculinity, and on racial identity. It is continuous with modern-day Native Americans, whom the novel finds "rather contemptible." And even the Cliff Dwellers, as they gained "looms and mills," "possibly declined in the arts of war, in brute strength and ferocity." The bad savage dies out, and it is a slippery slope to emasculating buying sprees on credit. Cather seems to want it both ways: brute strength is necessary for the defense of so-called civilization, but it can also destroy civilization.

In the end, Cather turns the bad white man into the good savage and critiques white society by accusing it of not being white enough, even as she asserts that dead Indians are, and must be acknowledged as, national ancestors. As Cather attempts to dismiss unsavory others from membership in the body politic, her substitutions get away from her, and whiteness goes with them when the white wage slave appears as a solution to the "problem" of the free black. The novel expresses the trouble with conspicuous consumption using the language of blackness and enslavement configured as white. Of the War Department Tom remarks, "How it did use to depress me to see all those clerks come pouring out of that big building at sunset! Their lives seemed to me so petty, so slavish" (209). When "the clerks streamed out of the Treasury building and the War and Navy," "they seemed to me like people in slavery, who ought to be free" (211). Later, frustrated by Washington, Tom proclaims, "I wanted nothing but to get back to the mesa and live a free life and breathe free air, and never, never to see hundreds of little black-coated men pouring out of white buildings" (213). The capital is a great plantation worked by thousands of (white) slaves who are to be pitied, although they are not especially important; to be a slave is to be "petty." As subsequent archaeological digs have revealed, the capital *was* worked by hundreds of (black) slaves who built the Capitol building itself. When Cather talks about commodification, it seems she cannot help but talk about enslaved bodies. But because blacks are no longer slaves and consequently a focal point of white anxiety, black slaves are excised and slaves again become white. The identification of white workers as "slavish" and as slaves in the late nineteenth century echoes developing concepts of whiteness in the United States. As David Roediger describes, in the early days of slavery, slaves became signifiers of a preindustrial past that members of the master class both "scorned and missed"[36]—a time before masters became cut off from unscripted leisure, spontaneity, and contact with the natural world.[37] (We begin to hear those complaints about the slavery of mastery growing louder in the distance.) Ironically, whites perceived that they both lost and gained freedom as they became slaveholders. Even more ironically, slaves actually embodied freedom. In Cather's novel, Native Americans are now signifiers of this premodern past, and they are described as a way back to the lost white freedom—and out of the social pressures to which Emancipation has led. The almost gratuitous blackness of government workers and the large white edifices that centralize their labor are intended to establish the West as the locus of true freedom and authentic Americanness.

But the distinction between the mesa and the plantation to which Tom clings cannot hold up to his actual experience, and he finds that freedom, like enslavement, is inseparable from possession. When he returns to New Mexico, Tom finds that commercial concerns have been part of this apparently unpolluted space all along. Roddy has sold the Cliff City artifacts to a German collector and reveals that he had "always . . . meant to realize on them." He believed Tom's talk of money as they excavated and cataloged meant that Tom, too, was looking to translate their work into cash. When he discovers what has happened to the artifacts, Tom upbraids Roddy: "There never was any question of money with me, where this mesa and its people were concerned. They were something that had been preserved through the ages by a miracle, and handed on to you and me, two poor cow-punchers, rough and ignorant, but I thought we were men enough to keep a trust. I'd as soon have sold my own grandmother as Mother Eve,' " he cries. " 'I'd have sold any living woman first'" (220–21). The mummy is rhetorically protected by a bulwark of slavery or prostitution (or both). As Roddy "grimly" notes, Mother Eve remains outside the reach of the commodity: she, along with the mule carrying her to the railroad car bound for Mexico, plunged over the cliff into the canyon below. American origins lie here in bodies that can be owned, but they are disconnected from bodies that can be sold. The novel disavows slavery only through the double-edged expedient of making female bodies of any color into sellable alternatives to black and Indian bodies. Filtering through Cather's multiplex images of U.S. history in the West is "the South," and as such imagery inadvertently signals, black slavery was hardly a stranger either to the frontier or to the genealogy of nationhood.

Roddy, beaten down by Tom's condemnation, leaves him alone on the mesa. As Tom recalls, he now experienced this place anew: "that was the first time I was ever really on the mesa at all." "Something had happened in me," he reflects, "that made it possible for me to co-ordinate and simplify, and that process, going on in my mind, brought with it great happiness. It was possession. The excitement of my first discovery was a very pale feeling compared to this one. For me the mesa was no longer an adventure, but a religious emotion" (250). Tom is the only person on the mesa. Its other inhabitants are long dead or at the very least recently departed. Embracing this solitary sense of ownership, he is imbued with "a religious emotion" that is also possession, derived from the notion of private property and inseparable from racial identity.[38]

At the end of the novel, we return to St. Peter's study. His family is spending the summer on a tour of France while he remains home, poring over and ostensibly annotating Outland's diary of his life at the Cliff City. In the process, St. Peter becomes a "primitive." He experiences a "reversion" to "the first nature" and is now "only interested in earth and woods and water," and yet he is "terribly wise" (241). As his transformation occurs, St. Peter stops being able to exist in society. Like the Anasazi, he is superannuated. The primitive national ancestors that Cather has called forth in the earlier section of the novel return with a vengeance at its conclusion, crippling their white descendants. St. Peter becomes inert, exhausted, and finally suicidal; he has gone primitive and barely survived the journey. Even his state of liberation from the responsibilities of adulthood—his new self "had never married, never been a father"— is caught up in the contradictory text of freedom in America. A white man cannot be represented as free without also being represented as deeply oppressed. When a storm extinguishes the stove in his study and blows shut the window, the room fills with gas, and

St. Peter thinks, "He hadn't lifted a hand against himself—was he required to lift it for himself?" (252). The white primitive is a passive victim of his own violence, and though St. Peter overcomes his attack of melancholia in the sense that his body endures, he is "not the same man" (258); he is now, and for the future, "without joy" (257).

Cather's work links body with commodity in consumer culture, and reconnects freedom to slavery. In Cather's West, Indians are both Indians and camouflaged black slaves; the mesa, mission, and hacienda are themselves, but also screens for the slave plantation. In *Death Comes for the Archbishop*, the novel's main character, Jean Marie Latour, is, like Godfrey St. Peter, a refined pioneer. Cather modeled Latour after Archbishop Jean Baptiste Lamy, the first bishop of New Mexico. "I never passed the life-size bronze of him which stands under a locust tree before the Cathedral in Santa Fé without wishing that I could learn more about a pioneer churchman who looked so well-bred and distinguished," she wrote in a letter to *Commonweal* describing how she came to center her novel on the life of the bishop. "In his pictures one felt the same thing, something fearless and fine and very, very well-bred—something that spoke of race. What I felt curious about was the daily life of such a man in a crude frontier society."[39]

The narrative—Cather referred to the text as a narrative rather than a novel—opens in Rome in 1848, the year the United States won its war with Mexico. The political effects of this victory were momentous and would hasten civil war; yet Cather does not seem interested in politics, or rather, the only politics that seem to interest her are church politics. She chooses this charged setting to describe the settlement of the western frontier in terms of spiritual trials, and accordingly, freedom is a spiritual matter—it is not about "rights." The text manages to trace the "civilizing" work of Catholic priests in the nineteenth-century West without engaging the worldly events in which this subject is so closely implicated. As Cather herself noted, the book is written in the "style of legend," "without accent."[40] Her depiction of Latour and Vaillant's relative isolation in the initial stages of their entry into the Southwest serves as a way to distance matters of government from the seemingly self-contained world of the missions and their moral agenda. The incorporation of what is now the Southwest into the nation is reduced to half a sentence; seen from the perspective of European church officials in Rome, it is "a part of North America recently annexed to the United States,"[41] its importance calculated in terms of the potential reach of New World Catholicism. The Church's power will increase—"the Vicarate of New Mexico will be in a few years raised to an Episcopal See, with jurisdiction over a country larger than Central and Western Europe" (6)—and thus, within the scope of the novel's sympathies, military annexation cannot be a bad thing. Likewise, the Gadsden Purchase is simply a moment when "the United States took over from Mexico a great territory" (199), as if it had relieved Mexico of a burdensome responsibility. The significance of this transaction registers only in terms of personal hardship for the missionaries: "as the national boundary lines often cut parishes in two, the boundaries of church jurisdiction must be settled by conference with the Mexican Bishops. Such conferences would necessitate a journey of nearly four thousand miles." "It was no easy matter for two missionaries on horseback to keep up with the march of history" (199), comments Father Vaillant disingenuously, since the missionary journeys themselves were part of history's literal march. This divorce of cause from effect is evident even in the text's structure, which, Cather explained, was based on a series of Puvis de Chavannes frescoes;[42] one episode follows the next like a series of images unified by theme, not plot.

Yet the narrative itself makes the military aspects of frontier settlement, the work of the traders, and the work of Archbishop Latour into "coincident missions," as Joseph Urgo shows.[43] Latour himself explicitly aligns spirituality with military force: to his sister in France he writes, "All day I am an American in speech and thought—yes, in heart, too. The kindness of the American traders and especially of the military officers at the Fort, commands more than a superficial loyalty. I mean to help the officers at their task here. I can assist them more than they realize. The Church can do more than the Fort to make these poor Mexicans 'good Americans.' And it is for the people's good; there is no other way in which they can better their condition" (35–36). It has, however, been the fort that has transformed Latour himself into a "good American." Although the passage intends to create an image of a compassionate military interested in the welfare of nascent Americans, Latour's identification of the power of the Church with the power of the repressive state apparatus seems sinister, all the more so because this moment typifies the way in which historic violence expelled from the text returns as its willfully unacknowledged subtext.[44]

Conflicting attempts to at once hide and reveal problematic effects of frontier contact surface in Cather's description of the nearly dead pueblo that is home to Latour's Native guide Jacinto. After describing a number of "dark legends" (122) to which non-Native locals have ascribed the tribe's decline, she states, "It seemed much more likely that the contagious diseases brought by white men were the real cause of the shrinkage of the tribe. Among the Indians, measles, scarlatina and whooping cough were as deadly as typhus or cholera. Certainly, the tribe was decreasing every year. Jacinto's house was at one end of the living pueblo; behind it were long rock ridges of dead pueblo,—empty houses ruined by weather and now scarcely more than piles of earth and stone. The population of the living streets was less than one hundred adults." But a footnote interrupts these elegiac meditations. "In actual fact," it reads, "the dying pueblo of Pecos was abandoned some years before the American occupation of New Mexico" (123). Why revive Pecos only in order to kill it off? This jarring interruption of the "legend" speaks to the difficulty of writing about European settlement of the Southwest without calling attention to that settlement's profoundly negative effects. The U.S. government's persecution of the Navajo does come up at the end of the narrative, almost parenthetically, and Cather's description of the forced migration to Bosque Redondo states that "hundreds" died (291), while the actual number was in the thousands.[45] The death of Pecos, however, is the fault of some Europeans, not "Americans."[46] Americanization can remain a source of value through the unmixing of the white race; whereas Turner saw fit to merge whites on the frontier, Cather ascribes its problems to "other" whites. After the allusion to the impending death of Pecos, the passage offers a description of "Coronado's expedition" and their exploitation of "their hapless hosts" (123). It was precisely such Spanish expeditions that were idealized in *The Professor's House* as the subject of Godfrey St. Peter's life work, the source of his greatest intellectual achievement and, perhaps more importantly, of his bond with Tom Outland. Now Cather recalculates the value she has placed on the Spanish adventurers in order to sustain an image of both benevolent Anglo colonialism and the contributions of French missionaries, and to distance these influences from the pressing problems of postslavery America.

When Cather's friend Elizabeth Sergeant gave her a story to read that concerned "the experience of two white boys in an Arizona reservation during some secret ceremonial, Willa returned it, saying: 'Don't you remember I am not interested in this sort of thing?' "[47] The anecdote is enigmatic. What exactly is "this sort of thing"? Perhaps Cather's problem lies with the proximity the story described between whites and others—*that* sort of thing. For in *Death Comes for the Archbishop*, Native people appear to be distant and impenetrable. In terms of systems of racial proximity, the mesa looks like an ideal antidote to the plantation. Latour says a futile Mass before members of the Acoma tribe; looking down on the assembled, he sees them as "antediluvian creatures . . . types of life so old, so hardened, so shut within their shells, that the sacrifice on Calvary could hardly reach back so far. Those shell-like backs behind him might be saved by baptism and divine grace, as undeveloped infants are, but hardly through any experience of their own, he thought. When he blessed them and sent them away, it was with a sense of inadequacy and spiritual defeat" (100). For the purposes of the text as a whole, Latour's "defeat" is ultimately for the best: he is a symbol of race, meaning both whiteness and class, and as he embodies it race is stable rather than dynamic. The Acoma are sealed off from the developing national culture not only on their remote mesa, but in their very souls.

Latour soon learns that the huge church where he has just

preached was built on the orders of the egomaniac Fray Baltazar, who exacted a debilitating tribute from "his Indians" (113); his passion was his garden, and his special oppressions had to do with making the Acoma work in it. One evening, however, he accidentally killed a Native boy and the community rebelled, tossing him over the side of the mesa into a trash heap more than three hundred feet below (112). This would seem to indicate that the people thought their priest was, in fact, trash, but Cather insists that because he did not struggle as he was thrown away, he "retained the respect of his Indian vassals to the end" (113). (Even if Cather made this story up, she still does not recognize its implications.) The mesa begins to look more like a plantation, with a paternalistic planter/priest using the rhetoric of a "father" and his "children" bound by love as a way to explain as well as to veil his own, and the church's, oppressive tactics and to de-emphasize the problems with its dependence on forced labor.

The fears that such dependence engenders burst forth in an episode suggestively titled "Stone Lips." On their way to Las Vegas, where Father Vaillant lies ill, Jacinto and Latour are overtaken suddenly by a snowstorm: "The wind was like a hurricane at sea, and the air became blind with snow. The Bishop could scarcely see his guide—saw only parts of him, now a head, now a shoulder, now only the black rump of his mule. Pine trees by the way stood out for a moment, then disappeared absolutely in the whirlpool of snow. Trail and landmarks, the mountain itself, were obliterated" (125). "In the landscapes imagined by Cather and her white southern female contemporaries," Patricia Yaeger writes, "whiteness is both senseless and too mobile; it erupts with an excess of meaning and becomes *terrifyingly dynamic, vulnerable, agitated, tortured, vertiginous*. Or, it is *partial, fragmented, an intensive source of labor, a site of confusion that gums up the works*."[48] The frontier is not, after all, a site where whiteness fragmented by consumer culture, immigration, black mobility, and Native resistance can be reassembled. In the whirling snow, Latour becomes "blind and breathless, panting through his open mouth. He clambered over half-visible rocks, fell over prostrate trees, sank into deep holes and struggled out, always following the red blankets on the shoulders of the Indian boy, which stuck out when the boy himself was lost to sight" (126).

Latour is saved from this deadly white mass only by that which is not white: both Jacinto's body and a sanctified cavern known only to the tribe. Its entrance is "two rounded ledges, one directly over the other, with a mouth-like opening between" (126). "Slid[ing] . . . into the throat of the cave" (126–27), Latour is almost literally consumed by it, and once inside, he immediately feels ill and ill at ease. "Great as was his need for shelter," Cather writes, "the Bishop, on his way down the ladder, was struck by a reluctance, an extreme distaste for the place. The air in the cave was glacial, penetrated to the very bones, and he detected at once a fetid odor, not very strong but highly disagreeable" (127). The cave has entered him, and the *escape* from whiteness is itself "vertiginous," "a site of confusion," because the cave fundamentally contradicts the premise of Cather's text as it reveals Latour's own racial self as an "agitated" hybrid. Latour's race, that which first drew Cather to her subject, can only be understood, it seems, as connected to the "rough frontier society" from which she wants to differentiate it. Latour looks back on this experience with disgust, despite the fact that the cave had "saved his life." He "remembered the storm itself, even his exhaustion, with a tingling sense of pleasure. But the cave . . . he remembered with horror" (133). The frontier landscape, even in life-threatening form, is a source of pleasure. But in order for it to be pleasurable, certain elements must be excluded, in a "blinding" rush of whiteness. At the heart of the narrative is a point it cannot openly acknowledge: Jacinto reemerges to offer safe shelter. If his erasure is not temporary, the white subject must cease to exist.

Clearly defined images of what race means and normalizing depictions of bodies are disrupted by figures of speech. The narrative is no longer "without accent" in the secrecy of the cave. The men climb through sexualized "lips," "slightly parted and thrust outward," into a cave filled with "faggots" (128) (a word which by the time of Cather's writing referred to homosexual men). The cave contains a "curious hole" (131), an "orifice" (128) to which much attention is paid by both of them, and the bishop's proximity to these dual orifices is frankly illicit (128).[49] Latour experiences the near-death of the white subject as a terrifying pleasure. Jonathan Goldberg has suggested that the relationship between Latour and Jacinto is "not one in which the Westerner seeks to impose himself on the alterity valued in the Native. It is only at the level of unspoken, unspeakable emotion that union is possible."[50] In fact, for the westerner, the alterity of the Native is already part and parcel of (in this case) him, and the "unspeakable emotion" that unites them is duly spoken by an actual mouth that appears in the text. This site of locution broadcasts the horizontal comradeship that crosses racial lines to generate nationalism even while illustrating that relationship's challenges. The imperialist nostalgia on view in this text comes with a subtle elaboration of its sources.[51]

The archbishop chooses to "die in exile" (273) because France, despite its comforts, has "too much past" (272). New Mexico, by contrast, has a quality that is "soft and wild and free, something that whispered to the ear on the pillow, lightened the heart, softly, softly picked the lock, slid the bolts, and released the prisoned spirit of man into the wind, into the blue and gold, into the morning" (273). But Latour's liberation is not the opposite but the product of what Eudora Welty identifies in Cather's work as history—that is, "Virginia." *Death Comes for the Archbishop* turns away from the conflict with Mexico, genocide, and the Civil War, but these things appear nonetheless. Black slave culture looks like minstrelsy: Stephen Foster's "negro melodies" had passed, singer to singer, into the frontier, where they are performed by an aging southern belle, Isabella Olivares, to the sounds of the banjo plucked by a "yellow" boy, presumably a slave (177–82). And the Olivares's house is the one point of true respite for the priests on the frontier; they cherish their visits to what they view as an oasis of culture.

Cather does not hide the fact that slavery exists in New Mexico: a Mexican woman, Sada, is the only slave held by a family of Georgians who were "forced to sell all their Negro slaves" (214). As a Mexican alone shoulders the burden of slavery in Cather's vision of the West, the slave herself becomes a body that can be owned but not sold. In this vision of freedom, bodies are decommodified—but they may remain trapped in slavery through this process of decommodification. On the frontier, the slave is immutably a slave. Slavery is present but unspeakable. Though everyone knows Sada is being held illegally and cruelly treated, Latour refuses to intervene because he fears her Protestant masters will compromise Catholic interests (215). But also, in contrast to the self-liberated Acoma who defeat Latour spiritually because they must be defeated culturally and politically, the slave remains a slave because she offers spiritual renewal. Sada provides an antidote to revelations of intimate dependence—slavery now offers a way *out* of white psychic and physical reliance on an other. Latour has been subject since youth to fits of doubt and melancholy. While in Santa Fe he falls prey to one of these dark periods: "His prayers were empty words and brought him no refreshment. His soul had become a barren field. He had nothing within himself to give his priests or his people. His work seemed superficial, a house built upon the sands. His great diocese was still a heathen country. The Indians traveled their old road of fear and darkness, battling with evil omens and ancient shadows. The Mexicans were children who played with their religion" (211). As spirituality, the military, and human objectification make common cause in this text, Latour's crisis of faith is necessarily multivalent. In the end, his sense of spiritual barrenness amounts to an acute attack of Eurocentrism. Sadly but predictably enough, it can only be cured with evidence of Western hegemony.

Again on the verge of extinction, Latour is again pictured in a landscape of "frozen whiteness."[52] Late one night he goes to the church; picking his way through the December snow, he sees Sada hunched in the doorway. She has risked punishment to try to pray while her masters sleep. As she and Latour pray together, she sheds "tears of ecstasy" (214) over the altar; her piety and her deprivation cure Latour of his faithlessness.

He was able to feel, kneeling beside her, the preciousness of the things of the altar to her who was without possessions. . . . Kneeling beside the much-enduring bond-woman, he experi-

enced those holy mysteries as he had done in his young manhood. He seemed able to feel all it meant to her to know that
there was a Kind Woman in Heaven, though there were such
cruel ones on earth. . . . When the Kingdom of Heaven had first
come into the world, into a cruel world of torture and slaves and
masters, He who brought it had said *'And whomsoever is least
among you, the same shall be first in the Kingdom of Heaven.'*
(217) (emphasis in original)

Slavery becomes a naturalized condition of spiritual possibility. Because Sada can own nothing, is herself a thing, Latour is able
to understand the power of "things"—and the effect of this understanding is to reify a contemporary American hierarchy. If the
slave were freed, she would no longer be "first in the Kingdom of
Heaven"; in other words, she would not be as valuable in the
archbishop's own terms. Like Mother Eve, Sada is the unsellable
possession whose true value lies in its effect on the master's psyche.

Latour feels an expansive peace in this American landscape
(wishful thinking on Cather's part?) as he contemplates "the line of
black footprints his departing visitor had left in the wet scurf of
snow" (218). In both *The Professor's House* and *Death Comes for the
Archbishop*, slavery is expressed in bursts of achromatic language
that fix the mark of slavery on bodies that are not black. Cather
seems to find no other way to come to terms with either "the great
[wrong] . . . of black slavery" (290), which she mentions in the
context of the Navajo exile, or the place of emancipated blackness
within American culture. Slavery is there, in the very specific form
of the slave, but the slave is never black. The problematic portrayals
in *Sapphira and the Slave Girl*, in which Cather finally returned to
her old Virginia home, are foreshadowed in this evasive imagery.

Today, the house outside the Tesuque mission where the bishop
died in 1888 is "The Bishop's Lodge Resort and Spa," a "hideaway
ranked by *Travel and Leisure* as one of America's best retreats." "As
one of the finest hotels in the Southwest, The Bishop's Lodge offers
exceptional recreational opportunities, fine dining and contemporary accommodations in a traditional ranch setting. Experience a

true Santa Fe retreat with breath-taking surroundings and award-winning accommodations. And consider The Bishop's Lodge for a truly stunning wedding or event."[53] Tourism and consumer culture have caught up with the bishop, and the architecture of white power once again offers a comfortable place to get away to, as well as a place to live every day.

# 5. Stars and Stripes

Damn, these outlaws make good cowboys.
*Urban Cowboy*

A few miles from the Myrtles Plantation, "One of America's Most Haunted Homes,"[1] past pecan orchards and groves of old oaks, is another kind of haunted plantation, one that only occasionally opens to visitors. The Louisiana State Penitentiary at Angola, the nation's largest maximum-security prison, was once Angola Plantation, named for the homeland of its first slaves, as if in a mockery of homecoming.[2] The slave cabins that were used to house prisoners; the cellblock where men were sometimes packed six to a tiny cell, their journey's end just down the hall in the electric chair; and the men who have never left the penitentiary, buried in the cemetery called Point Lookout, indicate ongoing links between bodies and things. Angola was the "favorite Louisiana plantation" of Isaac Franklin, one of the most successful speculators in the interstate slave trade, who had six to choose from.[3] In 1869 Major Samuel James, a former Confederate officer, purchased the lease for all of Louisiana's convicts. In 1880 he bought Angola's 8,000 acres and used some of the convicts he leased to work the land. Today the prison is sometimes referred to as just "The Farm." Warden Burl Cain commented in a documentary on Angola, "It's like a big plantation in days gone by. We hate to call it that in a way, but it kinda is, because we have the, you know, the, it's inmates in prison."[4] Looking out over men working in the fields, Cain stumbles when he gets to what sounds like a reference to slavery, which would inevitably summon comparisons between the plantation and the penitentiary, between the conjoined histories of slavery and black criminality.

Most of Angola's inmates are black. Houston Baker describes the South "as an emblem or metonym for American disciplinarity," by which I understand him to mean that the plantation as an institution has proved itself ideally suited to the maintenance of order in general, an order that is disproportionately applied to black people.[5] Before the men who worked this land for Major James were convicts, many of them were slaves. The connection is readily apparent, but it can also be, as Cain's circuitous approach to the subject indicates, hard to talk about. There's a pause between "a big plantation in days gone by" and mention of what that big plantation has meant to southern society since the Civil War. The language of "days gone by" is the nostalgic language of plantation tours, but it collides abruptly with the reality of prisoners working the same fields worked by plantation slaves. "I'm free, praise the Lord, I'm free, no longer bound, no more chains holding me," sings the gospel choir on the film's soundtrack. Slavery serves as metaphor for both earthly existence and incarceration. During the last decades of the twentieth century, Angola became a place that people could visit for fun, but the leisured enjoyment it offers is alloyed with the immediacy of prison life, with the violence and sadness and pain of things that have gone wrong.

Before the Civil War, southern penitentiaries were almost exclusively for whites, who were, the theory went, uniquely capable of penitence.[6] Plantations were their own jurisdictions, and because slave workers were at once crucial to the economy, imagined by whites as naturally criminal, and private property, slaveholders and lawmakers, often the same people, did not see an organized mode of punishment—outside slavery—as necessary. W. E. B. Du Bois writes that, in a slave society, whites were "tacitly assumed" to be actual or de facto members of the police system concurrent with their actual or potential status as slaveholders. "The police system of the South was originally designed to keep track of all Negroes," he argues, "not simply of criminals; and when the Negroes were freed and the whole South was convinced of the impossibility of free Negro labor, the first and almost universal device was to use the courts as a means of reënslaving the blacks."[7] After slavery, black criminality, real and imagined, became the state's responsibility. When convict leasing began after the Civil War, the logic of the plantation as a means of organizing labor reentered the postbellum southern economy. The opportunism of the marketplace and the entrenched idea of white supremacy among whites together produced forms of labor exploitation that ushered the South into the era of industrial capitalism while relying on social tenets established by slavery. The state leased convicts to the highest bidder, and the lessor in turn contracted out convict labor to those with jobs to be done. Convicts had a reputation for providing reliable results in work that whites would not usually deign to or be asked to do. Alex Lichtenstein argues that convict leasing was not simply a "continuity of or replacement for slavery."[8] It was part of the machinery of "progress" and was "accompanied more by flexibility and contradiction than a fully developed world-view compatible with a specific mode of production." And, Lichtenstein writes, "unlike antebellum slaveholders . . . postwar beneficiaries of the convict lease had no 'way of life' bound up with dependence on convicts, no *particular* commitment to forced labor, other than that of the capitalist's balance sheet of investment, production, and profit. For the lessee, the convicts were merely 'machines for whose rental a certain price is paid.' "[9] In other words, the physical protections associated with paternalism were not operative in this world reduced to a basic equation of people with property. Thus convict leasing reproduced the essence of chattel slavery: human ownership stripped of sentiment.

Leased convicts performed many different kinds of work. For example, the railroad infrastructure that transported northern tourists to the South after Reconstruction was built using the labor of former slaves. A relatively small percentage of convicts worked on farms in the mid-1880s, while "the rest were employed in brickyards, lumber camps, coal and iron mining, the turpentine industry, and railroad construction—the very industries which had relied on industrial slaves before emancipation."[10] The labor that Samuel James administered was spread throughout Louisiana and adaptable to the needs of his customers. James, not the state, was responsible for feeding, clothing, and housing the convicts, but judging from his phenomenal profits, he was not one to let such concerns distract him from the bottom line. Just months after he took over the lease, he had made half a million dollars.[11]

In the 1890s, accounts of barbaric treatment under the lease system led to public outcry. Although practices in other southern states were by no means humane, George Washington Cable described the situation in Louisiana as a benighted tangle of mis- and missing information—"the system at its worst." "So complete . . . is the abandonment, by the State, of all the duties it owes to its criminal system that . . . it does not so much as print a report," Cable wrote.[12] In 1894 James died of a massive hemorrhage on the front porch of Angola's big house. His son took over the lease. Convict leasing was declining in profitability, however, and was nearing an end in Louisiana.[13] Plantation labor and the penitentiary were set to converge. Bordered on three sides by the Mississippi River and on the other by the "rattle-snake infested" Tunica Hills, Angola was ideally situated as a prison.[14] In 1901 the Louisiana Corrections Board ended convict leasing and purchased the plantation from James's heirs; convicts became the property of the state. Matthew J. Mancini argues that in Louisiana and Mississippi, "leasing's end was an act that combined political retribution with economic calculation. In both states the abolition of convict leasing was part of a radically undemocratic package of political changes cloaked in the garb of reforms, and it was made possible by the creation of vast state-owned plantations."[15] In the early 1920s, Angola became truly vast when the penitentiary's general manager Henry Fuqua purchased 10,000 acres of adjoining plantations after a series of devastating floods made property owners less interested in farming their land.[16]

Over the course of the twentieth century, Angola became notorious. Former inmate Wilbert Rideau wrote that "by 1973, violence was a brutal, daily reality. Double-bladed hatchets, swords, long steel knives, and Roman-style shields were commonplace. Men slept with steel plates and JCPenney catalogs tied to their chests; even in maximum-security cellblocks, men slept with their doors tied and with blankets tied around their bunks as a means of protection and security."[17] It was only in 1999 that a judge released Angola from federal scrutiny.[18] Today more than 5,000 inmates live at Angola. Roughly half reside in the main prison complex, and the remainder are housed in five outcamps, self-contained prisons spread out among the fields, along with some prison workers in a town they call "the safest in America."[19]

Statistically, men at Angola are likely to die there. In a radio documentary, Rideau explained, "Traditionally most prisoners serving life sentences have had the opportunity to go free after about ten years. But in the early 1970s, Louisiana politicians came upon what was then a novel idea. They decided to make life sentences in Louisiana mean precisely that—they did away with the possibility of parole. Today there are more than 2,500 men serving this so-called 'natural-life' sentence."[20] The prison has become, as the inmates to whom Rideau spoke described it, a place where time has stopped. Joe White, incarcerated at Angola since 1961, said, "If you were buried alive, that's what it would be like. Except for the television, we wouldn't know that there's a world out there; except for the radios, we wouldn't know. . . . This, this is a graveyard. A graveyard of time." Inmate Henry Patterson reflected,

> I feel like my life have been frozen in time. Like the Cosby show. I look at those kind of shows and I wonder sometime, 'Is it fiction? Is it really real?' You know, because I can only relate to that which I came out of in '61, and when I came here in '61, the restaurants were segregated. When I caught a bus, I caught the back end of the bus, I had to go to the back, I couldn't sit in the front. You look at the changes from that time that you stopped, and they say, "Well, they doing this today, they doing that," and you wonder, "Is it real? That's for real there man?"[21]

From segregation outside prison to segregation in the prison/plantation, inmates for life are part of a system in which time cycles back perpetually to the same sites and signifiers. In a prison built on a plantation, time is doubly arrested. Inmates are not only removed from the changes taking place in the world outside but relocated within a place where little has changed for centuries.

In the 1990s, Elmina Castle, point of departure for the Middle Passage, opened to tourism, and Robben Island, where Nelson Mandela was imprisoned for eighteen years, became a "living museum." Meanwhile, Angola's visitors enter a living history of antebellum plantations that maintains a link between the Middle Passage and postslavery society. It is hard to resist the idea that this literalness, an embodied history of violence, must be on some level what draws the general public here. They come "from all over the world,"[22] as the warden's office claims, not only to see a plantation or a penitentiary—as rare as it is for a member of the law-abiding general public to gain access to a maximum-security facility—but to witness a rodeo played out against the crops and razor wire.

We might say that rodeo is to the West what plantation tourism is to the South, a nostalgic performance of its mythology.[23] But the Angola Rodeo, in which inmates, some of whom have never ridden a horse before they enter the arena for the first time, are the contestants, connects rodeo's myths of freedom directly with the opposite of freedom—incarceration and the plantation as a "metonym for American disciplinarity." Western myths inform southern landscapes, in the process exposing the violence of nostalgia. As slavery and the penitentiary are magnified by violent desires of the frontier, it becomes obvious that, as Richard Slotkin wrote, myths have the capacity to "reach out of the past to cripple, incapacitate, or strike down the living."[24]

The existence of rodeo depends on talents with decreasing opportunities for practical use, due largely to changes in cattle ranching dictated by the rise of corporations. But cowboys have remained icons. By the 1880s, they had developed into such compelling figures in American popular culture that "a stage and an audience for cowboy performance were available even when cowboy work was not."[25] Buffalo Bill was the first to bring rodeo contests to a mass audience, as part of the 4 July 1882 celebrations in North Platte, Nebraska. According to Michael Allen, partly as a result of the kinds of men who were drawn to and employed by the Wild West Shows, the public, knowledgeable in the ways of the (already mythic) range, viewed rodeo cowboys with some skepticism. But "most Americans knew so little of cattle ranching by World War II that they could enthusiastically romanticize it and, in their confusion, somehow turn the rodeo man into a *real cowboy*," he argues. "Earlier generations knew better, but by 1945 the path was open to idolization of the rodeo man as a hero in the growing Myth of the West."[26] The skills displayed in rodeo therefore evolved as performance in part because of their superfluity, and rodeo upheld the cowboy's cultural worth as his social utility atrophied.[27] The term "prison rodeo" signals the dual incorporation of dreams about what America means within the bodies of those whom society as a whole has segregated, cast off, ejected from its center. Prisoners, largely invisible and isolated through the court system as lacking value, indeed as a form of waste, are among the social dead.[28] But the social dead still have a place in culture. As Peter Stallybrass and Allon White observe, "Low domains, apparently expelled as 'Other,' return as objects of nostalgia, longing, and fascination."[29] The rodeo becomes a means by which nostalgia, longing, and fascination can be openly indulged for the price of gas and a ticket; the frontier West and the expanse of plantation history meet in the immediacy of confined bodies in motion.

In the beginning, the Angola rodeo was a modest local event. While behind bars "double-bladed hatchets, swords, long steel knives, and Roman-style shields were commonplace," in the rodeo ring inmates competed against nature. Members of the prison community sat on the hoods of their cars to watch. According to former warden C. Murray Henderson, "No attempt was made initially to make a profit from or attract the general public."[30] In 1967 Jack Favor came to Angola more or less directly from the pro rodeo circuit to serve two consecutive life sentences.[31] He had been a well-known rider—the original pattern of Wrangler jeans was cut from a pair custom-made for him—and he catalyzed the professional rodeo aspect visible at Angola today. Henderson noted that Governor John McKeithen provided the funding to purchase equipment, and "big-name entertainers, many originally from Louisiana, were invited to appear at the performances, which helped to draw crowds once the rodeo was opened to the general public. Profits from the rodeo went into the inmate welfare fund and steadily increased each year. In good years we netted something like $30,000 for the inmate welfare fund, money used to purchase necessary items for the prisoners for which no funds were officially appropriated."[32] Now billed as "the wildest show in the South," the rodeo has grown so popular that a new stadium was built in 2000 to accommodate 7,500 spectators, almost double the capacity of its predecessor.

D riving toward Angola on my first visit, I came to a halt in traffic about a mile from the prison gates. Hundreds of people were headed in the same direction, and it took another forty-five minutes to reach the entrance and get cleared by the guards. Inside, a herd of black-and-white cows grazed serenely behind white wooden fences, and the meticulously groomed borders of the road were blooming with pansies. In the expanse behind them lay death row. As I neared the rodeo grounds, the fields and clear blue sky became a backdrop for long, low buildings enclosed in a dense wire web. I parked in a muddy grass lot that was already almost full and made my way to the arena, where I was searched for food, water, and weapons. Past the ticket booth, livestock smells mingled with the scent of onion rings. A mock cell containing a rudimentary bed and toilet offered tourists the chance to have their pictures taken "behind bars." In a beautifully ironic reversal, the photographers were inmates.[33] A few yards away stood the painted plywood image of two headless prisoners wearing striped uniforms. Visitors would supply the heads.

I wandered past the photo ops and fragrant food stands toward the hobbycrafts, laid out below a guard tower and bounded by high chain-link fences. Leather belts, wallets, and purses from the hides of Angola cattle, paintings, clocks, keychains, and things that might be called novelties were all made by inmates. Hobbycrafts are one of the rodeo's main advertised attractions. Behind the lengths of fencing that stretched upward toward a lethal froth of accordion wire, men sat on benches or folding chairs or leaned against the chain-link, watching the flux of the crowd. Some of these men, medium-

Waiting for the rodeo to begin (photo by Jessica Adams)

"Souvenir photos" (photo by Jessica Adams)

security inmates, had created the things on display, and they carefully observed the interest of potential customers, calling out a price or encouraging a sale. Their aggressive watchfulness brought to mind Walter Johnson's discussion of the agency of apparently disempowered human objects: in 1852, Johnson writes, the city of New Orleans outlawed selling slaves "on the sidewalks in front of the slave pens." " 'Scarcely anyone desires to pass such places,' as the *Daily Orleanian* explained, 'while to the ladies it is like running the gauntlet to be exposed to the prying, peering gaze of lengthened lines of grinning Negroes of both sexes. . . . They hardly await the passing of persons before their extended lines, ere they commence making their comments and thus eke out lengthy and amusing conversation for each other.' " "At the moment of their performance," Johnson notes, "the slave traders' carefully choreographed pageants were being interrupted by the slaves' unruly subjectivity."[34] In the commercial relationship inside the prison/plantation, it is the prison's disciplinary structure that gets upset by the agency of the inmates. As one inmate demanded of a potential customer contemplating a purchase, the proceeds of which, the inmate informed him, would go to his legal fund, "Don't you want to see me out of here someday?" The answer was almost certainly no, but the question made the connection between consumption and release explicit. Through souvenirs of a day in prison, the lines separating consumers from the social dead blur; it appears that consumption actually has the potential power to release the human life and labor entrapped in the commodity fetish. At one of Angola's annual spring arts and crafts festivals, an inmate was selling a painting that depicted the sorrow of death at Angola and burial at the prison cemetery. Not even the remains of the body, that last vestige of the self, ever get free.[35] Affixed to the painting was a note that read, "If you see this please take it home"—the art a surrogate for its maker and a symbolic means to freedom.

In order to buy, customers can first negotiate with the man behind the fence. The intermediary standing at the table then gives the buyer a slip of paper stating the agreed-upon price. Finally, at a booth at the end of the row, money changes hands. In such trans-

Inmates watching tourists shop for hobbycrafts (photo by Jessica Adams)

actions, the multiple stages of Marx's commodity fetish come to life. The world from which prisoners have been ostensibly banished is one in which they continue to labor. Prisoners make items used constantly in daily life outside. Inmates at Angola manufacture license plates for both the state of Louisiana and the commonwealth of Puerto Rico (yet another node in the circum-Caribbean plantation network). In other states, prisoners perform work as diverse as "data entry, manufacturing plasma, building stretch limousines, slaughtering ostriches for export, and booking holiday reservations."[36] But this labor goes uncredited and virtually unremarked. License plates seem to simply appear, like natural outgrowths of government. In the exchanges around the hobbycrafts tables, however, the original relationship between producer and consumer, between people known and visible to each other rather than, say, between the consumer and an anonymous person toiling on an assembly line or in a sweatshop in Korea or Indonesia, or even a robot, appears. The human producer returns to the sphere of the object for sale, only to vanish again into the disciplinary machine.

In this series of interactions, the eye becomes vulnerable as a measure of social distinctions. The intermediary who provides the slip of paper authorizing the sale may be an inmate, one of the "trusties" who have earned privileges based on a record of good behavior; some of the men at the tables, also trusty inmates, are selling their own work. They wear ordinary street clothes, and there is nothing to signal difference to the browsing customers. Where do "we" end and "they" begin? A black trusty prisoner is like a white businessman in the sense that they both might be free. Louisiana's one-drop rule instituted the basis of blackness in something invisible; segregation visibly separated "black" and "white" and in so doing helped generate separate meanings of blackness and whiteness. At Angola, the effects of the plantation system on society reemerge as enforced divisions between prisoner and citizen, which reiterate the divisions between free and unfree, master and slave. But, as in the Plessy case, where Supreme Court justices used sophistry to establish precedent, the distinction is not necessarily apparent, and power and status threaten to shift out of the control of the dominant group—the nonincarcerated—even in a context in which difference is stamped so forcefully on the landscape.

The ability of the eye to affect power relations between inmates and free people is acknowledged and codified at Angola. It is called eyeballing when the object of the gaze is a female guard or visitor, and the punishment is up to ninety days of solitary confinement. But the positive possibilities of looking are recognized by inmates as well: an editor of the *Angolite* told Daniel Bergner that he felt the problematic aspects of a prison rodeo were at least partially offset by the fact that outsiders actually see prisoners—"They lay eyes on us."[37] The eye's inability to make reliable distinctions between what is dangerous and what is safe have often resulted in the legal, political reduction of this difference to racial difference. As Angela Davis writes, "Within the U.S.—and increasingly in postcolonial Europe—the disproportionate presence of people of color among incarcerated populations has acquired a 'self-evident' character."[38] Angola's demographics clearly demonstrate this racial disproportion, while the rodeo both obscures and draws attention to it. Participants are selected at random from a pool of trusty inmates who have expressed a desire to compete. However, despite the prison's black majority, inmate cowboys seem as likely to be white as black.[39] Therefore, despite the fact that it illustrates a racial disparity—based on the evidence of the spectacle itself, more whites than blacks seem to become trusties—the rodeo presents an illusory image of an odd form of equality: that everyone is equally capable of being unfree.

As I walked among the hobbycrafts, observed and observing, I came upon objects that seemed to summarize bonds between socially constructed opposites. Some prisoners had made items for sale out of the transformed refuse of their personal lives. One man had created a delicate jewelry box and a heart-shaped picture frame from meticulously folded Camel cigarette packs. This is a traditional prison skill, he told me, reminding me that prison life abounds with the reframing and reuse of waste. A little farther down, two wooden cabinets were covered entirely in elaborate designs made of used wooden matchsticks, their burnt ends barely visible. What would otherwise have been trash thus reentered circulation, once again became valuable.

The rodeo began at two o'clock sharp, befitting a place where time is the organizing principle. The warden said a few words and the preacher prayed. The sun beat down; soft drink and hot dog vendors were doing a brisk business in the grandstands. The inmate band struck up the familiar chords of "the greatest song the world has ever known," and the audience stood in unison. Drums rolled. The music rose. At last, riders burst through the gates. The Angola Rough Riders, the inmate drill team, sketched cloverleaf patterns and threaded the needle at a full gallop. Then prison officials, professional barrel racers, and local residents on horseback circled the arena to the rousing music of the band. Patriotism displayed inside prison—inmates playing the Star-Spangled Banner and the audience rising reverently—is a curious hybrid. "Stars and Stripes" is the flag billowing in the breeze, repeating in color the black-and-white stripes of the inmates' shirts. Giving thanks for freedom in this opening ritual is fundamentally at odds with the circumstances, unless free spectators are thankful for the fact that they are inside voluntarily and only for a few hours.[40]

Cabinet covered with a design made of used matchsticks
(photo by Jessica Adams)

The announcer reined in his eager horse with one hand and
gripped a large cordless microphone with the other. His voice
boomed through the arena, mellifluous and disembodied, calling
out the time the men were doing even as they attempted to do their
best time.[41] Time multiplies as a measure of human worth. One man
described his desire to participate: "I just want to feel it, feel free for
just a little while. Maybe it'll take my mind off this fifty years I got."
But while they provide a break from otherwise relentless temporal
punishment and allow inmates to recalculate the meaning of the
time that defines them, the rodeo's quests for mastery reassert time
as a necessary marker of identity.[42] According to Warden Cain, the
rodeo is part of a program to maintain order. "It takes four things to
run a good prison," he has said: "good playing, good praying, good
food and good medicine. This is good playing"—a way to keep up
prison morale and provide catharsis.[43] At the same time, neither
audience members nor inmates themselves are permitted to forget
that the men in the ring are incarcerated, and the rodeo is not really
open to prisoners themselves as spectators. Some trusties sit in a

small segregated section of the stadium, while others must listen to radio broadcasts from the prison station. Presenting the spectacle of prisoners publicly punished with the apparent complicity of the performers themselves, the rodeo appears to display for free citizens and the prison community alike the morality of this particular prison, as well as the apparent rightness of the existing social order. Involving visitors to the prison as participants in the enforcement of social order itself enables an efficient reproduction of the status quo. Even as they are subject to the same rules that have produced the prison, visitors view the event from a position of power, reinforcing their sense of having a stake in maintaining this order.[44] Michel Foucault concluded that prisons represent the processes by which social order in general is achieved: "We are in the society of the teacher-judge, the doctor-judge, the educator-judge, the 'social worker'-judge. It is on them that the universal reign of the normative is based; and each individual, wherever he may find himself, subjects to it his body, his gestures, his behaviour, his aptitudes, his achievements. The carceral network, in its compact or disseminated forms, with its systems of insertion, distribution, surveillance, observation, has been the greatest support, in modern society, of the normalizing power."[45] Through the normalizing process, Foucault argues, discourses with vested interests in the maintenance of particular hierarchies generate social divisions. And these divisions start to look natural. The identities of those forces that have made the "normal" normal—how they got there, whom or what they benefit—tend to disappear.[46] The penitentiary performs the plantation's disciplinary function, but the introduction of rodeo's symbols of freedom insists not only on a larger frame of reference for this southern institution, but on the gaps in its disciplinary logic. While the basis for distinguishing difference becomes obscured, what *does* become visible is the ordering mechanisms of the carceral. The assumptions and hierarchies shaping the trajectory from chattel slavery through convict leasing through chain gangs (which briefly returned to Louisiana in 1995) to penal institution are no longer quite so naturalized.[47] The prison cells for tourists and the wooden cutout that enables them to pose as if they were prisoners openly display an intimacy between these otherwise almost always separate groups. As tourists stand in the cells or playfully complete the partial wooden effigy, they expose fractures within the normalization process by enacting a continuity of subject positions that provokes phobias about unstable social boundaries. They take pleasure, perhaps, in the fact that they are just pretending, in the fact that they can walk out. As with white visitors photographing each other inside plantation slave quarters, they explore, in their leisured way, the subjectivity of the "object." *They lay eyes on us.* These things seem superficial. How much thought do casual tourists put into their souvenir photos? Yet even if the thought is minimal, the convergence of leisure and discipline says something important about culture. Tourists do not have to put much thought into what they are doing, and this is the point. It is easy, desirable, and not even very remarkable to pose as a prisoner or a slave. These popular (sought after) images of interdependence suggest the underlying difficulties involved in the maintenance of social order—an endeavor much more challenging than structures like the prison would suggest.

The Angola Rodeo comprises ten events. Some are common to rodeo: bareback riding, steer wrestling, bull riding, and barrel racing, which is the only event in which women or professional riders compete. Others have been created especially for this rodeo. Inevitably, it is a different kind of contest when spectators are watching men without experience rather than professional rodeo cowboys. Bulldogging, which Bill Pickett is said to have invented—and he could wrestle the steer with his teeth—has been modified at Angola. Instead of a cowboy pursuing the bull on horseback with the help of a dazer riding alongside the steer to keep it running straight, then jumping from the horse to grab the steer's horns, inmate cowboys try to wrestle the steer from a standing position in teams. Two men wait, one on either side of a chute, for the steers to be released. With the steers each weighing at least five hundred pounds, this is a test of both strength and fearlessness. Wild Cow Milking is another event featured at professional rodeos like the Calgary Stampede and the Pendleton Round-Up.[48] "Why Milk a Wild Cow?" one Angola

Convict Poker (photo by Jessica Adams)

Rodeo program asks. "Because the fans love it!" Though pro rodeo cowboys perform this same silly move, when attempted by men who may have little or no history of working with cattle, "milking a wild cow" often becomes a reflection on their lack of expertise.

At the same time, there are intense displays of bravery and skill even within events that highlight inexperience, and the winner of the trophy buckle at the conclusion of the month claims not only talent but the toughness essential to surviving prison life, much less rodeo Sundays. The event called Convict Poker, introduced in the mid-1990s, tests a strength that is not so much physical as psychological.[49] Four men sit down to face each other at a card table in the center of the arena, into which a bull is released. A rodeo clown then tempts the bull toward the table. The sitting men cannot necessarily see the bull; they may only be able to intuit when it is running toward their backs. One by one, they are either injured or manage to escape injury by leaping up or dodging the bull's horns. The man who remains seated longest is the winner.

Like Convict Poker, the rodeo's finale, Guts and Glory, devised by Jack Favor, seems to owe something to both gladiatorial contests and tests of masculine courage. All the inmate cowboys gather in the arena, again with a maddened bull. On his forehead is a red chip worth one hundred dollars. The men attempt to detach it while avoiding the horns, and if no one wins one week, the prize money accumulates. Injuries are not uncommon, and tension is high in the audience as it is in the ring. Bonds between the inmates, not just competition, emerge; at one rodeo, a man was caught on the bull's horns, but as he crumpled to the ground, another contestant lifted him in his arms and carried him to safety, giving up his own chance at the prize.

On the subject of the rodeo, Daniel Bergner quotes editors of the *Angolite* saying, "Most of Angola's inmates suffer from attention deficit disorder, and whenever somebody's paid attention to them, it's been to beat them up in one way or another" and "One thing God gave all of us: a man's allowed to choose his own path to hell."[50] At the same time, according to a spokeswoman for the prison, inmates reject the notion that they are being exploited by the rodeo, and the participants whom Bergner profiles see the rodeo as a way to, for example, reconnect with family by redeeming themselves in the arena (Carey Lasseigne believed that if he could send the All-Around buckle to his son, the young man would want to visit him again). It even becomes a way to find romance (champion Johnny Brooks married a woman he met there).[51] For inmate cowboys, the skills they attempt to demonstrate in competition, however undeveloped, can perhaps substitute for the imperfectly executed skills that resulted in their incarceration. Outlaw behavior can translate into heroism. One event in particular seems to speak to the dream at the heart of this rodeo. In Buddy Pick-Up, which was designed at Angola, one man rides the length of the arena from the starting gate to an upturned oil barrel painted red, white, and blue, where his waiting partner crouches. The man on the horse attempts to maneuver close enough to the barrel for the other man to leap astride. If they are successful, they will stay on the horse as they gallop back to the starting gate as fast they can—judging is based on timing as well as agility. Watching this event, nonincarcerated spectators emerge as willing participants in a fantasy of dismantling the prison's rigid displays of difference. In one sense, they represent agents of confinement, the forces of prosecution and conviction, but in another, they function as a means of liberation, albeit partial and contingent. A scene played in prison of one man picking up his

Buddy Pick-Up (photo by Jessica Adams)

partner and racing toward escape cannot help but be subversive. As the man on the horse approaches the barrel, tension in the audience rises. At the critical juncture, the audience shouts, "Jump!" The waiting man leaps, and the two prisoners ride away to cheering if they make it without either falling off and to audible disappointment if they fail. The moment is a setup—it offers an illusion of freedom that is quickly snatched away—but it is a setup that likewise ensnares the audience. As they eagerly anticipate the inmates' leap and virtual escape, they participate in—and, by virtue of the fact that none of this would be played out without witnesses, they enable—the release of the segregated other. Caught within the structure of the performance, audience members root for the downfall of a system around which their daily lives revolve.[52] As it replicates the plantation as a site of twenty-first-century pleasure and disciplinarity, Angola exposes the impulse to connect across even the most apparently impenetrable barriers.

Joan Dayan maintains that the "practice of rendering certain groups of people as 'dead in law' " in the United States originated in "the 'black codes' of the Caribbean and the American South"; thus the segregation of prisoners on a plantation would identify all inmates, whatever their racial history, with slaves restrained within a circum-Caribbean system.[53] Inmates at Angola, as they live and work on a plantation, are heirs of slaves. They have been segregated from the mass of society, and the basis for their segregation is transgression (whether they are innocent or guilty); in being designated criminal, they take the place of slaves physically and socially. In this fraught environment, charged with individual ownership of the black body translated into the state's ownership of the criminalized black body translated into the potentially lifelong depersonalization ("Every man has a Property in his own Person, and this nobody has any right to but himself. The labour of his body, and the work of his hands, we may say, are properly his") of convicted violent offenders laboring on the plantation who are also mostly black, the free visitor plays out the social drama of possession. The desire for the forbidden that is visible at the prison/plantation when it opens to visitors reveals the impulse to manifest or bring to the surface those fundamental relationships that shape the self—the intimacy between apparent opposites like freedom and incarceration, master and slave, living and dead.

Researchers and members of school and community groups, if approved by the warden's office, can get more immediate access to the workings of the prison than is available in the mass experience of the rodeo, and they have a chance to talk more privately with prisoners themselves. (I once toured Angola with a group of college students whose professor told the trusty inmates speaking with us that they had come as part of their research into white-collar crime, provoking incredulous reactions: "Well, you're not going to find much white-collar crime here." I could only think that they had really come out of a morbid curiosity to which they were unwilling to admit.) Visitors are sanctioned as voyeurs in the otherwise concealed workings of the state yet are continuously monitored by the prison's administrative apparatus. At the same time, their gaze calls attention to the stark disparity between life inside and outside. In the trusty inmate dorm, they stand among the men's beds and personal belongings and stare into their bathroom, a wide hallway lined on one side with gleaming stainless steel toilets and on the other with shining sinks.

In the old, unused cellblock that housed the original electric chair, a replica of the chair had been positioned where the real one used to sit. Swallows flew in and out of the rafters, and the kind, chain-smoking guide whose primary job was to interface between inmates and prison administrators described how inmates were packed into tiny cells. During executions, they could hear everything. At the Arts and Crafts Festival, local parents brought their children on bus tours to see the electric chair and look through the glass picture window into the lethal injection room. The table resembles a padded black vinyl cross to which the condemned is strapped with restraints that look like seatbelts in an American economy car. But any pleasures associated with prison voyeurism derive from an awareness that a slippage exists between who you believe you are and who you believe you are not.[54] There is now a golf course on the prison grounds called Prison View, designed by a dentist at the prison and built by hand by inmates. Although inmates are not allowed to play on it, it is available to members of the public after they pass a background check. The tees are marked with handcuffs. According to a *New York Times* article, Warden Cain assumed that inmates would not be offended by this reminder of inevitable punishment. By way of explanation, he commented, "They wear striped shirts in the rodeo. They like it."[55] But inmate Lester Wright, one of the men who maintains the course, said to the reporter, "What are they doing with handcuffs out there? Everybody knows it's a prison. It really offended me when I first seen it. After that, I just passed by and mowed the grass, it don't matter. They're going to do what they want, we have to accept it, so—that's all it is. It's all in trying to stay at peace with them and yourself."[56] The gratuitous handcuffs dotting the landscape underscore the reason people would play the very safe game of golf here: to relish the proximity to danger and the possibility of the self as connected to that danger.

In her reading of ethnographic museums, Barbara Kirshenblatt-

Gimblett argues that displays of an other's daily reality reinfuse viewers with interest in what has become ordinary in their own lives. Decontextualized and placed within the frame of an exhibit, another culture's artifacts lose their aura of usefulness and become exotic. Museum visitors can imagine their own pots and pans and clothing and accessories in the context of a museum display and see their own culture differently.[57] This fascination with the everyday things of other people's lives as they are recontextualized and displayed appears not only in handcuffs strewn about the golf course but in an actual museum located just outside the prison gates. In April 1998, Governor Mike Foster cut the ceremonial ribbon opening the Louisiana State Penitentiary Museum—"The Gateway to Angola," as its website describes it.[58] "I tell you, I cannot get over the response we have had, just overwhelming!" its curator exclaimed to a reporter from the *New Orleans Times-Picayune*.[59] There is now a gift shop selling hats, t-shirts, boxer shorts, and stuffed bloodhounds inscribed "Angola State Pen." The museum itself contains exhibits describing past escape attempts and other events in Angola's history, portraits of former wardens, and artifacts confiscated from prisoners, including improvised weapons made from objects that would be harmless in other contexts, such as a typewriter carriage and the glass tube of a coffee maker. Even a bag labeled "Yeast" had been impounded, transformed into contraband as a home brew ingredient. A hollowed-out Bible in which a small ice pick had been stashed, a toothbrush filed into a knife, and a smooth plastic department-store model clothed in a striped prison uniform—refracted through the lens of prison life, common, apparently innocuous things reveal a fuller range of possibilities. The museum displays evidence of inmate violence in concert with implements of state-sanctioned violence. For the first several years of the museum's existence, the original electric chair, "Old Sparky," sat behind glass in a small room with its accessories: a leather hood, sponges to conduct current to the temples, and thick leather cuffs that restrained the arms. The display went for realism: on the wall behind the chair hung a clock, a phone, and a painted replica of the original fan—"for the smell," the curator told me in a confidential voice. The scene was labeled

"ELECTROCUTION." When the museum first opened, a poster with photographs of the many men and one woman who had been executed in this chair hung above it. State violence becomes uncannily normalized, as it were, and not only as it becomes museumized. The conservative local judiciary and juries facilitate death penalty convictions, which are then very challenging to appeal. According to a local mitigation investigator, during closing arguments in the penalty phase of a murder trial in 2000, the East Baton Rouge district attorney ended his remarks by telling the jury that his own father had abused him more than the defendant's father had abused the defendant, but the DA had not turned into a killer. He intended to negate any influence that knowledge about the convicted man's family might have on the jury's verdict, convincing jurors to impose death rather than life in prison. Indeed, this DA has successfully argued for more death sentences than any other state prosecutor.[60]

Society must explicitly identify distinctions between law-abiding citizens and transgressors of its norms precisely because these distinctions are not necessarily visible. The anxiety over racial passing has faded, replaced by or channeled into a fear of undetectable violence. A doctor who is quietly killing his patients, a charismatic serial killer, a devoted middle-class mother who drowns her children—these characters haunt the collective subconscious. The threat of violence from those charged with preserving health, peace, or domestic order emerged effortlessly in an anecdote recounted by the curator of the prison museum. As she chatted with a young couple staying at a nearby bed-and-breakfast, she ventured that she could tell them a story about their hostess, the ex-wife of one of Angola's wardens. The warden had once shot his wife almost fatally, and only her desperate performance had saved her life. "If she hadn't've *played* dead, she would have *been* dead," our guide informed the speechless couple. In fact, white culture's fear of itself (the doctors, serial killers, deadly middle-class mothers, and Angola wardens are inevitably white) seems to translate into paranoia about others' deviance, and into the appeal of a place like Angola. In souvenir photos, visitors can literally picture themselves as deviant, criminalized subjects, reinforcing the fact that they can choose the context of criminality and then leave it, but also exposing the disturbing/thrilling reality that those who appear "normal" may not be. Sam Jones (a pseudonym), the operator of Louisiana's electric chair between 1983 and 1991, when the state initiated execution by lethal injection, was, in his own words, "just a normal person that mixes in with a crowd, a normal John Doe that walks the streets everyday."[61] Sitting at the counter of a bar as he appeared on the television screen above it, he remained unrecognized by the woman serving his drinks. Jones described his job, so potentially controversial that he used an alias, in the most routine terms: "It's no different to me executing somebody and going to the refrigerator and getting a beer out of it." After each death, he went home and painted before sleeping "like a baby." "Some people jog," he stated. "I draw pictures and execute people."[62] His comments seem to hint at hidden conflicts, but at the same time his avowal of the absolute normality of the role of executioner exposes carceral order as something very strange.

Freedom is always unrecognizable without the specter—and the spectacle—of its absence. Perhaps sensing this abstract truth, tourists at the rodeo appeared overcome by the end of the day with a desire to leave the prison grounds. Even before the final event had officially concluded and with only scattered applause, audience members began to throng the exits. In the parking lot, a sense of panic rose as the large volume of cars and trucks created bottlenecks. Some drivers left the defined roadway altogether and plowed through a ravine, but they were soon blocked by the slow, steady stream of vehicles coming from the far end of the parking area. As dusk began to fall, the crowd seemed united in an accelerating urge to reclaim its place in the outside world. Like "a great plantation in days gone by," at Angola the "history of the present" is inscribed on the walls that divide people—in fact, this history *is* the walls. But leaving the plantation is more difficult than it might seem when its limits are so well marked.

Passengers disembarking at the V. C. Byrd International Airport on the island of Antigua arrive at a place that bears the name of a descendant of slaves. It is also the name of slaveholders, such as William Byrd II, an eighteenth-century Virginia planter and author of *History of the Dividing Line*, as well as the many Byrds, black and white, who have lived and died throughout the South, among them Henry Roeland Byrd, better known as Professor Longhair, and James Byrd, the victim of a twenty-first-century lynching in Texas. A large photo of V. C. Byrd smiles down on travelers making their way through customs, perhaps visiting Antigua on a honeymoon package or returning home after a visit to relatives elsewhere in the Caribbean, North America, or Europe. This is truly an international destination. Like many other sites in the Caribbean, from the ruins of sugar mills to high-rise hotels, it cites global connections that have emerged out of the plantation economy and continue to be retraced and reinvented by individual travelers, nations, and corporations.

As it references a shared history of slavery between the South and the Caribbean, this point of contact indicates other maps of "southern culture" and "American history." After the United States gained independence from Britain, slaveholding Loyalists left North and South Carolina and Georgia for Florida and finally the Bahamas, where they established cotton plantations.[1] When Union victory became clear in the Civil War, several thousand white Confederates left the South and went farther south, to Cuba and Brazil, where slavery was still legal. They became known as *Confederados*. The Confederados remain a recognizable presence in Brazil today; their descendants annually recall their southern heritage in hoopskirts and Confederate uniforms at a southern-style picnic, although many of them are now, as a result of generations of intermarriage, darker-skinned than any white plantation-owning family in the Old South could have been.[2] Southern cultures open up into the cultures of the Americas, connecting the particularities of nationalism in the United States with international understandings of race, origins, freedom, and even "Confederacy." Wounds of returning continue to mark the bodies of those who pass across these lines that tell the story of modernity. To return is to confront global as well as individual pasts—to move in time as well as in space through the effects of slavery, colonialism, imperialism, and the evolution of the technologies that enabled them. Such journeys are never made alone.

# Notes

## INTRODUCTION

1. Starr, "Bywater Neighborhood Boasts City's Last Plantation," 16.

2. The Ninth Ward also included T. J. Semmes, McDonogh No. 19, and William Frantz elementary schools, which were integrated over the aggressive protests of whites. See Thevenot, "McDonogh Three" and "Unintended Consequences"; also Caddell, "White Flight and the Desegregation of the New Orleans Public Schools."

3. See Rothman, *Slave Country*, 147.

4. For more about the relationships/tensions between New Orleans creoles of color and black "Americans," see Logsdon and Bell, "Americanization of Black New Orleans," 201–61. Joy J. Jackson mentions the railroad's participation in *New Orleans in the Gilded Age*, 201.

5. Accounts differ as to whether this person was a plant in the car, Plessy himself, or in one case, the conductor. See Jackson, *New Orleans in the Gilded Age*; Roach, *Cities of the Dead*, 185, 235; Robinson, "Forms of Appearance of Value"; and Medley, *We as Freemen*.

6. Eric Sundquist comments in a discussion of the case, "In the legal rise of Jim Crow, the South received the blessings of a Northern Court," while "in the cultural rise of Jim Crow, the North adopted Southern plantation ideology" ("Mark Twain and Homer Plessy," 124).

7. Locke, *Two Treatises of Government and A Letter Concerning Toleration*, 111. Emphasis in original.

8. The full quote reads, "The individual was seen neither as a moral whole, nor as part of a larger social whole, but as an owner of himself. The relation of ownership, having become for more and more men the critically important relation determining their actual freedom and actual prospect of realizing their full potentialities, was read back into the nature of the individual. The individual, it was thought, is free inasmuch as he (specifically he) is proprietor of his person and capacities. The human essence is freedom from dependence on the wills of others, and freedom is a function of possession." MacPherson calls this concept "possessive individualism"

(*Political Theory of Possessive Individualism*, 3). Gillian Brown notes that "though the term 'individualism' does not come into use until the late 1820s, when market society and forms of the modern liberal state are well established, the principles it encompasses were already instated" (*Domestic Individualism*, 2).

9. Saidiya Hartman remarks, "The question persists as to whether it is possible to unleash freedom from the history of property that secured it, for the security of property that undergirded the abstract equality of rights bearers was achieved, in large measure, through black bondage" (*Scenes of Subjection*, 119).

10. Quoted in Bailey, "Slave(ry) Trade and the Development of Capitalism in the United States," 212. Bailey writes, "Between 1768 and 1772, Massachusetts alone imported some 8.3 gallons of molasses—8.2 million gallons from non-British colonies in the West Indies" (212).

11. Gordon, *Ghostly Matters*, 7, 139.

12. Dobbin, "Future of Historic Home Unclear"; Elliot, "Jury Selection Begins in Killen Trial."

13. Frow, *Time and Commodity Culture*, 79–80.

14. In *Delta Sugar*, xiii, John B. Rehder writes that the South's last working sugar plantations are in Louisiana, but these are gradually being replaced by an agribusiness model.

15. Silber, *Romance of Reunion*, 68.

16. Blight, *Race and Reunion*, 221.

17. Silber, *Romance of Reunion*, 69–70.

18. Ewell and Menke, *Southern Local Color*, xxix.

19. Silber writes, "Northerners eventually cast southern blacks outside their reunion framework altogether, portraying them as strangers and foreigners, as a people who were best placed under the supervision of those southern whites who knew them best" (*Romance of Reunion*, 6).

20. According to Quaker Oats, current owner of the Aunt Jemima brand, Aunt Jemima was developed in 1889 by Chris Rutt and Charles Underwood of the Pearl Milling Company in St. Louis, Missouri. In 1890, Pearl sold the rights to Aunt Jemima to the R. T. Davis Milling Company. In 1914, R. T. Davis renamed itself the Aunt Jemima Mills Company. In 1926, Quaker Oats bought Aunt Jemima Mills and "began production at its new plant in St. Joseph, Mo" (see <http://quakeroats.com/qfb_PressRoom/brandinfo/BrandDetail.cfm?BrandID=22&section=brandhistory>). In approximately 1891, Rastus came to represent Cream of

Wheat, a product of North Dakota's Diamond Milling Co. (see Kern-Foxworth, *Aunt Jemima, Uncle Ben, and Rastus*, 45–46). Uncle Ben became the mascot of Uncle Ben's Converted Brand Rice in the 1940s (see Kern-Foxworth, *Aunt Jemima, Uncle Ben, and Rastus*, 49). See also Manring, *Slave in a Box*.

21. Blight, *Race and Reunion*, 289–90.

22. Johnson, *Soul by Soul*, 78–9.

23. Ibid., 155.

24. Lipsitz, *Possessive Investment in Whiteness*, vii.

25. Ball, *Slaves in the Family*, 431.

26. Harris, "Whiteness as Property," 277. Harris's essay delineates the ways in which whiteness qualifies as property under the law. The "bundle of rights" included in property ownership consists principally of the rights to quiet enjoyment, exclusion, and disposition (freedom is part and parcel of the legal concept of property), and Harris describes how whiteness qualifies on all counts. "In ways so embedded that it is rarely apparent," she writes, "the set of assumptions, privileges, and benefits that accompany the status of being white have become a valuable asset—one that whites sought to protect and those who passed sought to attain, by fraud if necessary" (279). She shows that in the United States, whites in general, not just slaveowning whites, came to understand their whiteness via slavery, and she points to the current "valorization of whiteness as treasured property in a society structured on racial caste" (287).

27. Marx writes that for the worker

> emerg[ing] from the process of production, the contract by which he sold his labour-power to the capitalist proved in black and white, so to speak, that he was free to dispose of himself. But when the transaction was concluded, it was discovered that he was no "free agent," that the period of time for which he is free to sell his labour-power is the period of time for which he is forced to sell it, that in fact the vampire will not let go "while there remains a single muscle, sinew, or drop of blood to be exploited." For "protection" against the serpent of their agonies, the workers have to put their heads together and, as a class, compel the passing of a law, an all-powerful social barrier by which they can be prevented from selling themselves and their families into slavery and death by voluntary contract with capital. (*Capital*, 415–16)

28. Best, *Fugitive's Properties*, 16.

29. Also see Best's discussion of this issue in his introduction to ibid.

30. Relevant cases are *In re Slaughterhouse Cases*, 83 U.S. 36 (1872) & 83 U.S. 36 (Wall.); *In re Sinking Fund Cases*, 99 U.S. 700 (1878) & 99 U.S. 700 (L.Ed.); *San Mateo County v. Southern Pac. R. Co.*, 116 U.S. 138 (1885); *Missouri Pacific Ry Co. v. Humes*, 115 U.S. 512 (1885). Finally, in *Santa Clara County v. Southern Pacific R. Co.* 118 U.S. 394 (1886), the court reporter's notes state that Chief Justice Waite informed counsel, "The Court does not wish to hear argument on the question whether the provision in the Fourteenth Amendment to the Constitution, which forbids a State to deny any person within its jurisdiction the equal protection of the laws, applies to these Corporations. We are all of the opinion that it does" (see Fairman, *Reconstruction and Reunion*, 725–27).

31. Beard and Beard, *Rise of American Civilization*, 2:112.

32. Howard Jay Graham, *Everyman's Constitution*, 26.

33. Leach, *Land of Desire*, 86.

34. Avery Gordon writes that literature is valuable to studies of society because "literary fictions . . . enable other kinds of sociological information to emerge. . . . In the twentieth century, literature has not been restrained by the norms of a professionalized social science, and thus it often teaches us, through imaginative design, what we need to know but cannot quite get access to with our given rules of method and modes of apprehension" (*Ghostly Matters*, 25). (Indeed, literature has never been restrained by the norms of social science.)

35. In *Modernism and the Harlem Renaissance*, Houston Baker articulates a link between spirit possession as ritual practice and as metaphor. "Possession operates both in the spirit work of voodoo [*sic*] and in the dread slave and voodoo economics perpetuated by the West," he writes.

> What is involved in possession, in either case, is supplementarity— the immediately mediating appearance, as spectre or shadow, of a second and secondary "self." In specifically diasporic terms, "being possessed" (as a slave, but also as a BEING POSSESSED) is more than a necessary doubling or inscribed "otherness" of the conscripted (those who come, as necessity, with writing). For in the diaspora, the possessed are governed not simply by script but also by productive conditions that render their entire play a tripling. Caliban speaks his possession as a metacurse:

> You taught me language; and my profit on't
> Is, I know how to curse. The red plague rid you
> For learning me your language. (53)

For Baker, the ownership of black bodies that is at the core of chattel slavery has, like spirit possession, produced a multiplicity of self. Through Caliban's outraged lines, Baker shows how the identity of the subjugated simultaneously contains a preexisting culture, an alienating language, and a resistance to that language *through* it. Caliban, however, has been given voice by Shakespeare and thus is even more multiple than Baker's analysis admits.

36. In a discussion of sentimentalism in *Uncle Tom's Cabin*, Gillian Brown writes that Stowe develops a "concept of possession" that is opposed to slavery: "In addition to denoting ownership and the owned object (or property), possession encompasses the states of being possessed and of being propertied—what might be considered the inspiration with which ownership invests its objects, and with which objects invest their owners." She notes that "the service and notarization familiar things perform make the difference between a house and a home, a commodity and a possession" (*Domestic Individualism*, 40, 47). In my reading, interaction between objects is always inflected by a relationship to human property, expressed in terms of the cultural context of the twentieth century in which the term "possession" took on a specific meaning related to the perception of an African diasporic phenomenon.

37. Louisiana State University's online exhibit of this currency can be viewed at <www.lib.lsu.edu/cwc/BeyondFaceValue/>.

38. As Joan Dayan writes, linking the discourse of property with the discourse of spirituality, "You cannot surrender your will, you cannot be possessed unless your body becomes the vessel for the master's desire. The body must be owned, made into property, for possession to take place. In vodou practice, however, such an instrumental seizure does not describe the relationship between a god and a mortal. And to talk about possession is somewhat misleading, since those who serve the gods do not use the term. Most often, the experience of being entered, inhabited, and seized by a spirit is described as being mounted (as the horse is by the rider)" (*Haiti, History, and the Gods*, 55–56).

39. See Renda, *Taking Haiti*, esp. chaps. 5 and 6, "Haiti's Appeal" and "Mapping Memory and Desire."

40. Faulkner, *Absalom, Absalom!*, 59.

41. Ibid., 73.

42. Ibid., 72.

43. Benítez-Rojo argues that the character of the heterogeneous Caribbean has been profoundly shaped by the common experience of the "plantation machine," an infrastructure established by the region's colonizers to maximize their profits. This system has produced, however, and continues to produce not only profits but a way of life. It generates both physical spaces and "the type of society that results from their use and abuse" (*Repeating Island*, 8–9).

44. Accilien discusses similarities in the repression of slavery among French Caribbean plantations, including Martinique's Habitation Clément, and plantations along Louisiana's River Road in "Survivance et importance de l'oralité dans les plantations"; Felipe Smith analyzes a tour of Jamaica's Rose Hall in "Economics of Enchantment"; Strachan discusses the tourist industry and popular representations of plantations in the Bahamas in *Paradise and Plantation*; and Reinhardt examines the remains of plantations in Guadeloupe and Martinique in *Claims to Memory* (see chap. 5, "Realms of Memory").

45. Cooper, Holt, and Scott, *Beyond Slavery*, 10.

46. Hurston, *Tell My Horse*, 246.

47. Ibid.

48. Ibid., 257.

49. Taussig, *Magic of the State*, 6.

50. Hurston, *Tell My Horse*, 257.

51. This work premiered as a play with both actors and dancers in a production by the Gilpin Players, a black amateur theater company, in Cleveland on 18 November 1936. According to Rampersad, *Life of Langston Hughes*, 2:330, though Hughes labored to bring it to the operatic form he imagined, his final attempt, a collaboration with composer W. G. Still, was ultimately unsuccessful. Meltzer, *Langston Hughes*, 261, states that *Troubled Island* was presented by the New York City Opera with a score composed by Jan Meyerowitz, though Meltzer does not provide dates.

52. Mullen, *Langston Hughes in the Hispanic World and Haiti*, 29.

53. Ibid.

54. See Smith and Cohn, *Look Away!*, 22.

55. McPherson, *Reconstructing Dixie*, 3.

56. In New Mexico, Mexicans and Native Americans were also held in slavery. See Taylor, *In Search of the Racial Frontier*, 53, 55, 75.

57. See ibid., 80.

58. See Taylor, *In Search of the Racial Frontier*, and Massey, *Black Cowboys of Texas*.

59. Slavery was already an aspect of Native cultures; Taylor writes,

> Slavery among Native Americans predated European arrival on the North American continent. Numerous Indian people regularly enslaved other native people from opposing tribes. By the 1600s the Cherokee, Creek, and other southeastern Indians welcomed runaway black slaves because initially neither group harbored suspicions about the racial inferiority of the other. Moreover, the black newcomers brought important skills. Fugitive slaves served as interpreters and negotiators with whites; they also knew how to repair guns and traps, to shoe horses, to improve agricultural methods, to spin and weave, to make butter, and to build houses, barns, and wagons. (*In Search of the Racial Frontier*, 62)

60. See postcard included in Goings, *Mammy and Uncle Mose*, color plate 15.

61. Russell, "1878 Map Reveals That Maybe Our Ancestors Were Right."

62. A New Orleans group, the Crescent City Peace Alliance, and students from Frederick Douglass High School with the New Orleans Civil Rights Memorial–Plessy Park Committee had since 2001 leased a thin strip of grassy land bordering Press Street to erect a memorial, but as of March 2005, the owner of the land, Norfolk Southern Railroad, terminated the groups' lease, according to Skip Henderson, executive director of the New Orleans Civil Rights Memorial; see Henderson, "Plessy Park Now Endangered." In June 2005, Governor Kathleen Blanco wrote a letter to the Douglass High School community endorsing the plans for a memorial. However, the railroad had already begun negotiating with a "prominent local attorney," John Cummings, who, it was rumored, wanted to put up condos on the site. According to *Gambit*, New Orleans's local weekly paper, "Cummings does say that he plans to reserve the half-block bordering the Press and Royal intersection as a memorial to Plessy and possibly turn it over to the state for maintenance. 'The state arrested him, so the

state can maintain it,' Cummings says, speaking by phone from Italy, where he was vacationing" (Etheridge, "Derailing Plessy Park"). As of December 2005, however, the area was overgrown and storm-battered, its future, like much else in New Orleans, uncertain.

63. The headquarters for the National Guard in the Bywater neighborhood were located at precisely the place where Plessy had boarded the train.

64. See the Carnival Cruise website, <http://www.carnival.com/De fault.aspx>.

65. This is not to say that the trajectory has been a simple and straightforward one, however; again, it has been marked by the evolution of hybrid identities and identifications across race and class apparent, for example, in moments such as a Puerto Rican boy referring to black Americans arriving on a cruise ship as "gringos," an anecdote related by Lowell Fiet of the University of Puerto Rico–Río Piedras.

66. Thanks to Cécile Accilien for pointing out the irony of the ships' names, and to Michael Bibler for alerting me to news about the oil pipelines.

### CHAPTER 1

1. See Cross, *All-Consuming Century*, 5.

2. Long, *Great Southern Babylon*, particularly chap. 1, " 'It's Because You Are a Colored Woman': Sex, Race, and Concubinage after the Civil War."

3. McCurry, *Masters of Small Worlds*, 214–15.

4. See, for example, Martin, "*Plaçage* and the Louisiana *Gens de Couleur Libre*."

5. Guillory, "Some Enchanted Evening on the Auction Block."

6. See Domínguez, *White by Definition*, 62–79.

7. Long, *Great Southern Babylon*, 10.

8. Veblen, *Theory of the Leisure Class*, 83.

9. Stange, *Personal Property*, 21. Mark Connelly writes that "by 1915 . . . true feminine modesty was not what it used to be. Many aspects of the prostitute's life-style, such as the practice of birth control, the independence from traditional familial control, the smart and forward language, the aggressive manners, and the suggestive clothing, were also evident, albeit in less extreme form, in the behavior of women who were not, even under

the broadest definition, prostitutes" (*Response to Prostitution in the Progressive Era*, 47).

10. For an opposite reading of Chopin's portrayals of African American characters in *The Awakening*, see Birnbaum, "Kate Chopin and the Colonization of Race."

11. Chopin, *The Awakening*, 4.

12. Ibid., 50.

13. Birnbaum, "Kate Chopin and the Colonization of Race," 323.

14. King, *Tales of a Time and Place*, 63.

15. See Patterson's discussion of natal alienation in *Slavery and Social Death*, 5–8.

16. Joan Wylie Hall notes that King "identified with Louisiana's French aristocracy and clearly regretted the Creoles' fall from prominence in her story collections *Tales of a Time and Place* (1892) and *Balcony Stories* (1893)" ("Louisiana Writers of the Postbellum South," 207). Robert Bush writes, "When [King] and one of her sisters visited the Gayarrés at their plantation on the Mississippi-Louisiana border, she learned what conversation was, and the French paintings and furniture of the country home reinforced her preference for French civilization" ("Patrician Voice," 9).

17. Ewell and Menke, *Southern Local Color*, 155, 154.

18. Quoted in ibid., 154.

19. Gwendolyn Midlo Hall, "Formation of Afro-Creole Culture," 60.

20. Domínguez, *White by Definition*, 141.

21. Ibid., 143.

22. Fabre, "New Orleans Creole Expatriates in France," 182. Fabre writes that "New Orleans *gens de couleur* studied and even expatriated themselves in France as early as the 1740s, but they resorted to emigration in sizable numbers only after 1840s, when measures aiming at containing their progress locally were enforced" (182).

23. *New Orleans Daily Picayune*, 4 March 1898, 1.

24. King, *Tales of a Time and Place*, 92.

25. See Coleman, "At Odds."

26. King, *Tales of a Time and Place*, 83–84.

27. Ibid., 82.

28. Ibid., 73.

29. Tregle writes, "Publication of [his] reminiscences of life on an antebellum sugar plantation led to a temporary alienation from the old man

because of her [King's] outrage at a passage in his account which described cruel treatment of blacks by a white master" ("Creoles and Americans," 182). For an analysis of how King's slavery apologist stance manifested in her fiction, see Coleman, "At Odds."

30. Quoted in Pattee, *History of American Literature since 1870*, 362.

31. For an overview of antiprostitution efforts during this time, see Connelly, *Response to Prostitution in the Progressive Era*; also D'Emilio and Freedman, *Intimate Matters*, "Part III: Toward a New Sexual Order, 1880–1930."

32. King, *Tales of a Time and Place*, 114.

33. Ibid., 96.

34. Ibid., 97.

35. Ibid., 107.

36. Ibid., 108.

37. Ibid., 109.

38. Ibid.

39. Ibid., 115.

40. Ibid.

41. Quoted in Deyle, *Carry Me Back*, 276.

42. Ewell and Menke, *Southern Local Color*, 297. Alice Ruth Moore married the poet Paul Lawrence Dunbar in 1898; Paul Dunbar died in 1906, and Alice married journalist Robert J. Nelson in 1916.

43. Alexander writes that Dunbar held "a racial prejudice against dark-skinned people" and that her "displeasure with her racial self contributed to the construction of a new ethnic identity. She decided to become Creole. Her . . . physical appearance . . . and the fact that she was a native of New Orleans gave many the impression that her ancestors were Creoles of color, and more likely free Creoles of color. She encouraged this speculation" (*Lyrics of Sunshine and Shadow*, 64, 66).

44. Tregle, "Creoles and Americans," 182.

45. Dunbar, *Goodness of St. Rocque and Other Stories*, 145.

46. Ibid., 143–45.

47. Domínguez, *White by Definition*, 89. Emphasis in original.

48. Dunbar, *Goodness of St. Rocque and Other Stories*, 151.

49. Long, *Great Southern Babylon*, 1.

50. See Silber, *Romance of Reunion*, 7.

51. Ibid., chap. 2, "A Reconstruction of the Heart: Sentimentality during Southern Reconstruction."

52. In *Southern Local Color*, Ewell and Menke argue that "turning South, the industrialized and disempowered northern male began to view the southern belle nostalgically, as an epitome of womanhood, recognizing in her a pleasing figure over whom he could exert control" (xxxii).

53. Long, *Great Southern Babylon*, 108, 106–7.

54. Al Rose, *Storyville*, 2.

55. See Long, *Great Southern Babylon*, 114.

56. Ibid., 138.

57. Quoted in Al Rose, *Storyville*, 161.

58. Long, *Great Southern Babylon*, 156.

59. Coyle interview.

60. Al Rose's informant "René," "the scion of an old and prosperous New Orleans family" (in the early manuscript version, Rose reveals that René himself was very successful "in the food business"), describes being taken by his father to Lulu White's when he was sixteen to be "initiated": "Of course, my father assumed that I was about to have my very first sexual experience with a female, but he was just as wrong as he could be— although I had never been with a prostitute, or even seen the District before" (*Storyville*, 154). Diana Rose acknowledged that the identity of the "goat" probably ceased to be a surprise at some point.

61. Coyle interview. This instance of legally white women taking advantage of the whiteness of the quadroon to gain greater mobility had a precedent in the antebellum era of quadroon balls, where white men courted colored women. Monique Guillory writes, "For the wives of these Creole philanderers, the quadroon mistresses became such a source of anxiety and mistrust that in a bizarre twist of passing, white women, guised as quadroons, would attend the balls to determine the whereabouts of their husbands" ("Some Enchanted Evening on the Auction Block," 10–11).

62. Blue Book, 9th ed., Special Collections, Tilton Memorial Library.

63. The story was related to me by Diana Rose, Al Rose's widow and collaborator, during the course of my research into Storyville in the spring of 1996.

64. Al Rose, "Storyville," n.p., Special Collections, Tilton Memorial Library.

65. Al Rose, *Storyville*, ix.

66. Coyle's and Long's research has revealed some of Rose's biases and errors. See Coyle's dissertation, "Intersection of Law and Desire," and Long, *Great Southern Babylon*.

67. Kasson, *Amusing the Million*, 6. See also Lears, "From Salvation to Self-Realization," 10–11.

68. Kasson, *Amusing the Million*, 8.

69. Ibid., 11.

70. Stokes, *Color of Sex*, 21.

71. Coyle interview. In her dissertation, Coyle bases her arguments in part on a meticulous reading of all available copies of the Blue Books.

72. Al Rose, *Storyville*, 152.

73. Crib women were prostitutes who worked out of small single rooms called cribs rather than houses; see ibid., 160. I have revised Rose's transliteration of her speech, replacing "heah" with "here," etc. Emphasis in original.

74. Ibid., 150.

75. Rosen, *Lost Sisterhood*, 41.

76. Ibid., xiii.

77. Connelly, *Response to Prostitution in the Progressive Era*, 102.

78. Leach, *Land of Desire*, 117.

79. Quoted in Rosen, *Lost Sisterhood*, 41.

80. Ibid.

81. Blue Book, 9th ed., Special Collections, Tilton Memorial Library.

82. Stange, *Personal Property*, 129.

83. Quoted in Leach, *Land of Desire*, 58.

84. See Connelly, *Response to Prostitution in the Progressive Era*, chap. 6, "Seventy Thousand Innocent Girls a Year: The White-Slavery Scare."

85. P. Gabrielle Foreman, " 'Reading Aright,' " 336.

86. Stange, *Personal Property*, 2.

87. P. Gabrielle Foreman, " 'Reading Aright,' " 336.

88. Cited in Gilfoyle, *City of Eros*, 283. Gilfoyle notes that "purity reformers [in the early 1900s] too often ignored the racial dimension of prostitution" (283).

89. Coyle and Van Dyke, "Sex, Smashing, and Storyville," 66–67.

90. Al Rose, "Storyville," n.p., Special Collections, Tilton Memorial Library. Emphasis in original.

91. Al Rose, *Storyville*, 165.

92. Quoted in Peiss, *Hope in a Jar*, 3.

93. Edward Anderson, "Uncovering the Vice Cesspool of New Orleans," 40.

94. Childs, "New Orleans Is a Wicked City," 62. For more on the quadroon balls, see Guillory, "Under One Roof."

95. Childs, "New Orleans Is a Wicked City," 72.

96. Basso, introduction, xi.

97. Faulkner, *New Orleans Sketches*, 49–50.

98. Grace King also wrote a remarkably detailed description of New Orleans as a woman: "New Orleans has been called the most feminine of cities. This difference from other cities is one of her charms. Her people, in imagination, love to picture her in the handsome old age of a grande dame of the old regime; sitting in her high back antique chair, dressed in flowing black satin, garnished at the neck and wrist with real lace" (quoted in Juncker, "Grace King," 216). Tour guides from the late twentieth century, however, echo the language of the Blue Books. For example: "Passionate, alluring, and intoxicating, New Orleans is like the fiery barmaid . . . in a dangerous and impossible romance. . . . New Orleans has long been recognized as a unique creature among American cities, and with good reason. It is bewitching and seductive, awash in indulgence and ripe with desire" (Fisher, *Best of New Orleans*, 1–2).

99. Armstrong grew up in the smaller part of the District located just uptown from Canal Street; see Long, *Great Southern Babylon*, 196.

100. "To see her at night, is like witnessing the . . . electrical display on the Cascade, at the late St. Louis Exposition" (Blue Book, Archive of Historic New Orleans Collection).

101. Sontag, introduction, 8.

102. Some research suggests that Bellocq actually intended to delete the unique backgrounds of these photos in order to create "unremarkable Victorian studio portraits" (see Malcolm, "Real Thing," 14). Glenda Skinner discusses the evidence of the photographs being defaced while the emulsion was still wet in her 1999 master's thesis, " 'Storyville Portraits.' " Pornographic images of a woman whom historians believe to be Lulu White provide a contrast to Bellocq's work. The subject of these explicit photos poses with a large, incongruously cheerful dog and an unidentified man. The woman looks distant and disengaged. See Special Collections, Long Library.

103. Malcolm, "Real Thing," 14.

104. For a discussion of the problems with valorizing the visible in twentieth-century U.S. culture, see Phelan, *Unmarked*.

## CHAPTER 2

1. Hale, *Making Whiteness*, 87–88.

2. West writes that the preservation of Mount Vernon, the first plantation as "house museum," was spearheaded by Ann Pamela Cunningham, who was "born in 1816 and raised at Rosemount, the Cunninghams' upcountry plantation" and "had ancestors close to the Washington family" (*Domesticating History*, 6).

3. Kammen, *Mystic Chords of Memory*, 532.

4. Ibid., 557. Emphasis in original. Kammen writes, "In the realm of actual historic preservation, efforts to revitalize Main Street in American communities during the later sixties and seventies owed much to Disney's fantasy creation of 1955," which was a "turn-of-the-century streetscape, scaled to three-quarter size, in which the daunting pace of twentieth-century social change was not permitted to intrude" (557).

5. See Yates, *Art of Memory*, 6–8, 22–23.

6. Yates discusses the sixteenth-century scholar Guilio Camillo's "theater of memory," a building in which memories could be called up through an elaborate system of classical references located at specific sites; see ibid., 129–72.

7. Geist, "Violence, Passion, and Sexual Racism," 70.

8. See Herbert, "Empty Apology."

9. Olmstead, *Journey to the Seaboard Slave States*, 40–41.

10. See Scott, *Domination and the Arts of Resistance*, xii–xiii.

11. Ripley, *Social Life in Old New Orleans*, 213. "I am sure he loved his mammy to death" was Sterling Brown's response to Thomas Nelson Page's paean: "Who may picture a mother? We may dab and dab at it, but when we have done our best we know that we have stuck on a little paint; and the eternal verity stands forth like the eternal verity of the Holy Mother, outside our conception, only to be apprehended in our highest moments. . . . So, no one can describe what the Mammy was, and only those can apprehend her who were rocked on her bed, fed at her table, were directed by her unsleeping eye, and led by her precept in the way of truth, justice, and humanity" (Sterling A. Brown, "Muted South," 768).

12. Quoted in Genovese, *Roll Jordan Roll*, 80.

13. Quoted in Blight, *Race and Reunion*, 40.

14. Quoted in Hale, *Making Whiteness*, 62.

15. The grandson Robert E. Lee made this comment in 1911. See Blight, *Race and Reunion*, 283.

16. Ibid., 291.

17. Eichstedt and Small, *Representations of Slavery*, 168–69.

18. Eichstedt and Small write, "As a white person, Eichstedt was invited to imagine herself as a guest at various plantations in ways that Small [who is Black British] was not. For instance, on tours Eichstedt attended that contained no people of color, white docents regularly said, 'If you came here to visit, this is the room you would have slept in,' or indicated the food 'you would have eaten.' On no tour that Professor Small attended was the inclusive language of 'you' used" (*Representations of Slavery*, 20).

19. Scott, *Domination and the Arts of Resistance*, 18.

20. Scott points out that the powerful are mostly engaged in auto-appreciation; see ibid., 49, 69.

21. Eichstedt and Small, *Representations of Slavery*, 109. Emphasis in original.

22. Samuel Sloan quoted in McAdams, *Building of "Longwood,"* 3.

23. Douglas, *Truth*, 32. Douglas's maternal grandmother was a close friend of Julia Nutt, the daughter of Haller Nutt, who built Longwood. "For me," Douglas says of Longwood, "there's nothing Faulknerian about it. I see that finished ground floor as a home, with my grandmother's furniture in it" (34).

24. Chappell, "Museums and American Slavery," 251.

25. Quoted in Eichstedt and Small, *Representations of Slavery*, 81.

26. I should note that the narratives do vary among guides.

27. LaFrance, "Unshackling the Truth."

28. Glassman, "Vodou and Colonial Louisiana," 119.

29. LaFrance, "Unshackling the Truth."

30. River Road African American Museum, <http://www.africanamericanmuseum.org/aboutmuseumpast.html>.

31. LaFrance, "Unshackling the Truth." Other often-repressed aspects of plantation life emerge in visual artist Kara Walker's detailed silhouettes in which she depicts rampant, utterly unpredictable, and often interracial sexuality. Walker explained in an interview published online by New York's Museum of Modern Art: "I knew that if I was going to make work that had to deal with race issues, they were going to be full of contradictions. Because I always felt that it's really a love affair that we've got going in this country, a love affair with the idea of it [race issues], with the notion of major conflict that needs to be overcome and maybe a fear of what happens

when that thing is overcome" (Museum of Modern Art, "Conversations with Contemporary Artists").

32. LaFrance, "Unshackling the Truth."

33. See Jameson, *Postmodernism*, 279. Jameson writes, "Historicity is, in fact, neither a representation of the past nor a representation of the future (although its various forms *use* such representations): it can first and foremost be defined as a perception of the present as history; that is, as a relationship to the present which somehow defamiliarizes it and allows us that distance from immediacy which is at length characterized as a historical perspective" (284).

34. See Benedict Anderson, *Imagined Communities*, 200.

35. Ellis, "Re: Living History," 22–24.

36. Associated Press, "Some Historic Sites Have Trouble Finding Black Reenactors."

37. See Association for the Preservation of Historic Natchitoches, <http://www.preservenatchitoches.org/?page_id=8>.

38. See Wilkie, *Creating Freedom*; Newton and Printon, "Behind the Façade"; and Dennis, "Seeing the Lowcountry Landscape." Newton and Printon write that textbooks in the field of landscape architecture "rarely examine in any depth the complex interplay of European, African, and Native American influences that shaped the early American landscape. The result has been a common misunderstanding that the American landscape grew from European roots only" ("Behind the Façade," 1).

39. Vlach, *Back of the Big House*, xi–xii.

40. Chappell, "Museums and American Slavery," 248–49.

41. Ball, *Slaves in the Family*, 211.

42. Goings writes, "Other scholars have asserted—and I agree—that 'a subconscious desire to "own" a slave or domestic was at the heart of the reasoning process behind the advertising and production of these items. . . .' In this domestic slave block that most people called a kitchen was found almost every item that could be used in personal service in a collectible motif. This buying of black servants could only reinforce the notion of the black servant/slave as deferential, quiet, and happy to be working for the 'massa'" (*Mammy and Uncle Mose*, 67). He cites Mercier's dissertation, "Evolution of the Black Image in White Consciousness."

43. Hale writes that during the Lost Cause era, "the mammy figure revealed, perhaps more than any other construction of the culture of segre-

gation, a desperate symbolic as well as physical dependence on the very people whose full humanity white southerners denied and the centrality of blackness to the making of whiteness" (*Making Whiteness*, 113).

44. Tucker, *Telling Memories among Southern Women*, examines relationships between black domestic workers and white employers during segregation.

45. In *Ar'n't I a Woman?*, 46–61, Deborah Gray White describes antebellum origins of the misleading myth of the mammy. See also Jacqueline Jones, *Labor of Love, Labor of Sorrow*; Clinton, *Plantation Mistress*; and Gutman, *Black Family in Slavery and Freedom*. For a discussion of the social functions of the mammy myth in the early twentieth century, see Hale, *Making Whiteness*, 97–119.

46. Saxon, *Old Louisiana*, 5.

47. Hurston, *Mules and Men* (Harper Perennial ed.), 234–36.

48. Saxon, *Old Louisiana*, 20.

49. Ibid., 366.

50. Yaeger, *Dirt and Desire*, describes the development of this theme in southern literature.

51. See Armour, "History Written in Jagged Lightning," 14, and Langman and Ebner, *Hollywood's Image of the South*, 89.

52. Clinton writes, "The embrace of Southern apologism by Northern audiences coincided with the flowering of cinema—as celluloid supplanted the printed page, the plantation, locus of literary and historical memory, became the perfect vehicle for exploring American dreams." Al Jolson's conversion of immigrant "otherness" into American identity by assuming a blackface persona—making Jewishness congruent with a whiteness that established itself through embodying "blackness"—created, Clinton argues, a "romantic attachment" between the immigrants who ran Hollywood's major studios and the plantation myth. See *Tara Revisited*, 204–5.

53. To inaugurate the shooting of the film, which was heavily hyped in advance, Selznick International Studios flew the Confederate flag over Hollywood—and as Tara McPherson notes, Confederate flags continue to wave over southern California; see *Reconstructing Dixie*, 35. McPherson writes that Selznick excised some explicitly racist aspects of the book, such as the "Klan sequence," from the film, but "in attempting to mitigate the novel's racism, Selznick failed to understand the complex history and powerful pull of the mise-en-scène of southernness he sculpted. Presenting

such a lush southern landscape while eliminating the novel's most overt racism helped soft-sell an image of the Grand Old South to those who might have reacted against Mitchell's more overt strategies" (63).

54. *Suntrust Bank v. Houghton Mifflin Co.*

55. Associated Press, "Wind Done Gone Injunction Lifted."

56. Hurston, *Mules and Men* (Indiana University Press ed.), 4–5.

57. Randall, *Wind Done Gone*, 52.

58. Ruppersburg, "Wind Done Gone."

59. White transgressions of white intellectual property have not been so carefully monitored. Responses to T. Coraghessan Boyle's story "Me Cago en la Leche (Robert Jordan in Nicaragua)," which "features the grandson of the main character in Ernest Hemingway's *For Whom the Bell Tolls*," and Raymond Carver's "The Train," which "continues the plot of John Cheever's classic 'The Five-Forty-Eight,'" have not included lawsuits. See Associated Press, "Frankly, My Dear, They All Give a Damn."

60. Tucker's column in the *Atlanta Journal-Constitution* quoted in Ruppersburg, "Wind Done Gone."

61. *Stewart v. Abend* cited in *Campbell v. Acuff-Rose Music, Inc.* Brackets added by judges writing the *Campbell* decision.

62. *Campbell v. Acuff-Rose Music, Inc.*

63. Ibid.

64. Associated Press, "Settlement Reached over Wind Done Gone."

65. "Morehouse College Gets $1.5 Million Gift."

66. Associated Press, "Settlement Reached over Wind Done Gone."

67. Campbell, *Celluloid South*, 74, 75, 99.

68. Ibid., 99.

69. Quoted in ibid., 110. Jan Herman writes that earlier in the decade, Davis and Warner "had been embroiled in a court battle over her contract. Every time she had refused what she considered an unsuitable role, Warner had forced her to take a suspension. So, objecting to her many contract extensions, she went to England to make pictures and tried unsuccessfully to break her ties with the studio. Warner not only won the suit, but out of spite he dropped his option on a soon-to-be-published novel, *Gone with the Wind*, which he had thought might be a good vehicle for Davis" (*Talent for Trouble*, 175).

70. In *Black Cinema Treasures*, 9, G. William Jones writes,

Well into the 1950s, it was a rare Hollywood film which presented black characters at all, and even rarer when the characters were not stereotyped as dumb-but-loyal servants or as entertainers. They were included in films as objects of derision or diversion, but hardly ever as having serious, fully formed lives with which audiences were invited to empathize. Such stereotyping and objectification possibly served to maintain a distance between whites and blacks which had been traditional since the days of slavery. But, sad to report, even the black-made films which had little or no interference from white backers had their share of stereotypes, too.

Jones goes on to discuss black filmmakers who were creating films for all-black audiences from 1910 to 1957 and provides details about a number of their films. In *Fire and Desire*, Jane M. Gaines provides further discussion of early "race movies." She writes that "by the second decade of race movies [the 1920s] the black press was expressing hostility to what it saw as reinforcement of the worst tendencies in color consciousness," such as a "persistent intraracial color fetishism," in the words of contemporary reviewer Theophilus Lewis, commenting on Oscar Micheaux's film *A Daughter of the Congo* (1926) in Harlem's *Amsterdam News*. Gaines goes on to point out that "while actors playing Negro characters in race movies had to be light-skinned, actors playing Negro characters in mainstream white cinema had to be dark-skinned. The same actor could not then play Negro roles in both cinemas, although in a few cases light-skinned actors were darkened for parts in white cinema" (148).

71. See Roach, *Cities of the Dead*, 211–17.

72. In the nineteenth century, Gallatin Street, a two-block street in the French Quarter, was the hangout of prostitutes, pimps, and drunken sailors. See Saxon, *Fabulous New Orleans*, 291–300.

73. According to Donald Bogle, *Toms, Coons, Mulattoes, Mammies, and Bucks*, 9, "One of the type's earliest appearances was in *The Debt* (1912), a two-reeler about the South. A white man's wife and his black mistress bear him children at the same time. Growing up together, the white son and the mulatto daughter fall in love and decide to marry, only to have their relationship revealed to them at the crucial moment. Their lives are thus ruined not only because they are brother and sister but also—and here was the catch—because the girl has a drop of black blood!"

74. See Campbell, *Celluloid South*, 109.

75. "Her eyes have changed color," remarks a white character as the octoroon, Zoë, expires. "Dat's what her soul's gwine to do," responds an old black slave. "It's going up dar, whar dere's no line atween folks" (Boucicault, *The Octoroon*, 39). In "*Jezebel* and the Emergence of the Hollywood Tradition of a Decadent South," Ida Jeter points out that while the play from which the film was taken ends with Pres declaring his love for Julie, rather than Julie's using his illness to "atone for her sins," this ending was impossible in the film because "the Production Code of the Motion Picture Producers and Distributors of America prohibited such adulterous relationships" (43). Jan Herman also notes that Julie's redemption was not convincing to some critics, who "would have preferred that the ruthless anti-heroine remain unregenerate to the bitter end," a stance Herman suggests was shared by the director; see *Talent for Trouble*, 182.

76. Campbell, *Celluloid South*, 112–15.

77. Jeter, "*Jezebel* and the Emergence of the Hollywood Tradition of a Decadent South," 32.

78. Tony Williams calls it "a dark Gothic version of a twentieth-century *Gone with the Wind*, revealing the toll on the human personality that property and patriarchal traditions demand" (*Body and Soul*, 220–21).

79. This popular film played to the appeal of the southern gothic, but just five years after its release, the well-preserved Houmas House would open to tourists.

80. Cracker Barrel Convenience Stores, <http://www.crackerbarrelc stores. com/travel.html>. Eichstedt and Small, *Representations of Slavery*, 92, attributes this passage to a 2001 website for Louisiana's Asphodel Plantation.

81. Quoted in Arnold and Miller, *Films and Career of Robert Aldrich*, 116. The original source is a 1973 interview with Aldrich by John Calendo, "Robert Aldrich Says, 'Life Is Worth Living.' "

CHAPTER 3

1. See MacCannell, *The Tourist*, 13. Emphasis in original.

2. See ibid., xiii.

3. *Georgia's Heartland of the Confederacy*. The slogan "Poultry Capital of the World" is emblazoned on a water tower in Gainesville.

4. Cash wrote, "So long as the Negro had been property, worth from five hundred dollars up, he had been taboo—safer from rope and faggot

than any common white man, and perhaps even safer than his master himself. But with the abolition of legal slavery, his immunity vanished. The economic interest of his former protectors, the master class, now stood the other way about—required that he should be promptly disabused of any illusion that his liberty was real, and confirmed in his ancient docility" (*Mind of the South*, 123).

5. Rice, *Witnessing Lynching*, 236; Allison Graham, *Framing the South*, 119.

6. Brundage, *Lynching in the New South*, 8.

7. Wood, "Lynching Photography and the 'Black Beast Rapist,'" 195.

8. Walter White, "I Investigate Lynchings," 255.

9. See, for example, Hale, *Making Whiteness*, 199–239; Hatt, "Race, Ritual, and Responsibility," 77; and Holloway, *Passed On*, chap. 2, "Mortifications: How *We* Die."

10. Wood discusses the role of photography in "Lynching Photography and the 'Black Beast Rapist.'" She argues that lynchers wanted their violence exposed only within certain circles: "Newspapers rarely published photographs of lynchings, although they often included extremely graphic details of the event," she writes. "There is also evidence that when outsiders, including journalists, attempted to photograph these killings, they were thwarted. A reporter for the St. Joseph, Missouri, *News-Press* had his camera ripped from him, and his film destroyed, when he tried to take pictures of a lynching in 1931. He had photographed the mob as it was dragging its victim to the lynching site to burn him, when the men angrily seized his camera. Once the burning had begun, however, several other photographers, not journalists, proceeded to take photographs" (196–97). She speculates that "for the image of the lynching to be presented in a wider context would have been to take the lynching and the purported heroism of the lynchers out of the community's domain" (206), and thus out of the community's control. Hatt argues that the production of these souvenirs, whether pieces of the body itself or photographs of it, was "not merely a separate citation of the act" but, rather, "part of the ritual itself" because souvenirs serve, in and of themselves, to authenticate the legitimacy of the subject's death. "Like the confession, the souvenir photograph is sufficient proof of black criminality and white justice done," he writes in "Race, Ritual, and Responsibility," 83.

11. Wood, "Lynching Photography and the 'Black Beast Rapist,'" 206–7.

12. "E. E. Brock, editor of the Waco (Texas) *Tribune*, told Elisabeth Freeman, a northern white woman who was in Waco in 1916 to investigate a lynching, only white southerners really understood African Americans: 'He told me he was raised with them, had a colored mammy, nursed at her breast, etc. "Then," I said, "you are part colored." At this he became very angry' " (Hale, *Making Whiteness*, 114).

13. See Lillian Smith, *Killers of the Dream*, 34–39.

14. As some of Susan Tucker's informants seemed to fear; see *Telling Memories among Southern Women*.

15. Stewart, *On Longing*, 133.

16. According to Kenneth Goings, collectible racist images experienced a resurgence in the 1970s and 1980s; see *Mammy and Uncle Mose*, xvii.

17. These postcards are reproduced in James Allen, *Without Sanctuary*, plates 26 and 55.

18. Hale argues that "spectacle lynchings became a southern way of enabling the spread of consumption as a white privilege. The violence both helped create a white consuming public and the structure of segregation where consumption could take place without threatening white supremacy" (*Making Whiteness*, 205–6; see also 203).

19. Goings, *Mammy and Uncle Mose*, xii, xxi.

20. Ibid., 1. Goings notes, "The period from the late 1880s to the 1930s has been termed by various scholars of black memorabilia one of 'symbolic slavery' or the 'freezing' of the sambo and Jemima slave images" (20).

21. Goings writes that Aunt Jemima and mammy "collectibles" and kitchen objects originated in the 1880s and 1890s, and many of these originals were reproduced in the 1940s and 1950s (ibid., 64). In *Passed On*, Holloway gives voice to the communities silenced in these kinds of white narratives as she examines, among other subjects, the black funeral home industry. She makes the point that "African Americans' particular vulnerability to an untimely death in the United States intimately affects how black culture both represents itself and is represented" (2).

22. Glissant, *Faulkner, Mississippi*, 30. All ellipses in original.

23. Morris, *Ghosts of Medgar Evers*, 72.

24. Schickel, *Intimate Strangers*, 23.

25. Schickel, quoted in Dyer, *Stars*, 9.

26. Wilson, *Judgment and Grace in Dixie*, 129.

27. Allison Graham, *Framing the South*, 128.

28. Ibid., 125.

29. In the film *King Creole*, as Allison Graham writes, "blackness is the central, defining context. . . . In the opening scene of the film, black characters fill the streets of the French Quarter melodically hawking their wares in the early morning. Foreboding music accompanies the tableau, complicated by a distinctive rock 'n' roll beat. Within this cultural mélange, Elvis appears, sitting in a window above the singers. He joins the voices below, sounding as if he, too, is peddling his wares, and is soon accompanied by black rhythm and blues singer Kitty White, who sings the song 'Crawfish' as a duet with Elvis" (ibid., 124–25).

30. This is the popular "Elvis flag." See Doss, *Elvis Culture*, 168–69. The process of conducting Elvis safely back to full whiteness began during his lifetime, as David Roediger notes; see "In Conclusion: Elvis, Wiggers, and Crossing Over to Nonwhiteness," in *Colored White*. According to Doss, many fans now "claim Elvis as a singer who emerged out of what they choose to remember as an essentially white culture, and as a star who appealed mostly to white audiences" (*Elvis Culture*, 169).

31. Roediger, *Colored White*, 219.

32. From "The Moores and the Presleys at Graceland." Quote from the *Commercial Appeal* cited in Marling, *Graceland*, 137.

33. Marling, *Graceland*, 143, 137.

34. Ibid., 146, 145.

35. As Sam Phillips said.

36. In 2005, billionaire Robert F. X. Sillerman bought the rights to Elvis's "name and likeness" for more than $100 million. Among other proposed changes, he plans to demolish the visitors' center and the Heartbreak Hotel across the street from Graceland and build "two 400-room hotels, convention space, an entertainment complex, restaurants, shops, an outdoor amphitheater and a spa." In what seems to be one of the more troubling possibilities in this change in ownership, Sillerman suggested that Elvis impersonators might need to be "authorized." See Bosman, "King's Legacy."

37. Marling, *Graceland*, 218.

38. Doss, *Elvis Culture*, 164–67.

39. Quoted in ibid., 164–65.

40. Fiedler, *Love and Death in the American Novel*, xii.

41. See Marling, *Graceland*, 11.

42. White working-class masculinity has been threatened by "changes in the ideologies of manhood, including the 1960s counterculture embrace

of androgyny, the encroaching obsolescence of anticommunist machismo, and the looming attractiveness of the 'sensitive man,' " as well as "a massive shift in political economy." This lessening of the social worth of white working-class men has been aided, Lott argues, by "multiculturalism," affirmative action, and globalization, perceived as forces of betrayal and marginalization. See Lott, "All the King's Men," 199–200.

43. See chap. 2, "The Prehistory of the White Worker: Settler Colonialism, Race, and Republicanism before 1800," and chap. 4, "White Slaves, Wage Slaves, and Free White Labor," in Roediger, *Wages of Whiteness*.

44. Chadwick, *In Search of Elvis*, 266–67, n. 3.

45. Marling, *Graceland*, 2, 5.

46. Manley, *Signs and Wonders*, 3. Manley explains that the exhibit's curators use the term "outsider art" as opposed to "folk art" to describe this work because traditionally, folklorists consider folk art as "something received from ancestors and passed down to descendants, with only slight individual creativity permitted during the process of transfer" (4). "Outsider art," by contrast, is improvisatory and individualized.

47. Paul MacLeod, "Why I'm the World's Number One Elvis Fan," 169.

48. Elvis MacLeod, "Generation E," 173.

49. Marling, *Graceland*, 28.

50. Joseph Roach notes that Elvis "inverted the doubling pattern of minstrelsy," as "black music pours from a white face" (*Cities of the Dead*, 69).

51. Wilson, *Judgment and Grace in Dixie*, 130.

52. Doss, *Elvis Culture*, 208; Lott, "All the King's Men," 209.

53. Paul MacLeod, "Why I'm the World's Number One Elvis Fan," 162.

54. Stewart argues that the souvenir "will not function without the supplementary narrative discourse that both attaches it to its origins and creates a myth with regard to those origins" (*On Longing*, 136).

55. Lott identifies a mixture of devotion and competition as common to Elvis impersonators: "Even as they recognize the uniqueness and special power of Elvis Presley," he writes, "these performers yearn in often unconscious ways to unseat the master" ("All the King's Men," 202–3).

56. Nora, "Between Memory and History," 13.

57. In Baudrillard's description of what he calls the "precession of simulacra," the reproduction is first "the reflection of a profound reality," which then "masks and denatures a profound reality," only to go on to "[mask] the *absence* of a profound reality" (*Simulacra and Simulation*, 1, 6).

58. *Visitor's Guide to Rowan Oak.*

59. See Cofield, *William Faulkner.*

60. Lawrence and Hise, *Faulkner's Rowan Oak*, 13.

61. Parini, *One Matchless Time*, 155.

62. Lawrence and Hise, *Faulkner's Rowan Oak*, 32.

63. According to Jay Parini's chronology, Faulkner was at Rowan Oak during the time he wrote this piece; see *One Matchless Time*, 385.

64. Faulkner, "If I Were a Negro," 71.

65. Ibid., 70.

66. See Sterling A. Brown, "Muted South," 768.

67. Faulkner, "If I Were a Negro," 74.

68. Glissant, *Faulkner, Mississippi*, 103.

69. Faulkner, "If I Were a Negro," 74.

70. Ibid., 75.

71. Baldwin, "Stranger in the Village," in *Notes of a Native Son*, 173. Baldwin actually writes that an unnamed "someone" made this "quite accurate observation."

72. Wright, *Black Power*, 62.

73. According to the back cover of the paperback edition of *Soul Sister*, John Howard Griffin proclaimed it "a magnificent book by a woman of great courage. To read it is to understand what it means to 'live black' in a white man's world." *Life* magazine declared, "It would be hard not to come away from such a journey of soul and body with a good book, and Miss Halsell's book is very good indeed. . . . This is a vital book. It must be read by white America."

74. Halsell, *Soul Sister*, 17.

75. Ibid., 28.

76. Ibid., 54.

77. Browder, *Slippery Characters*, 220. Browder shows how, for Halsell, "authentic" blacks are not (and cannot be) wealthy or even middle class.

78. Taylor, *In Search of the Racial Frontier*, 247.

79. Ibid., 64, 63, 71–73, 68, 69.

CHAPTER 4

1. Reprinted in Robert Murray Davis, *Owen Wister's West*, 56, 57. According to Davis, although the text is copyrighted 1896, it was published 8 November 1895; see ibid., 55.

2. Silber, *Romance of Reunion*, 188.

3. His maternal grandmother was the British actress Fanny Kemble.

4. Wister, *The Virginian*, 215–16.

5. Ibid., 158.

6. Wister, *Lady Baltimore*, 50.

7. Teddy Roosevelt hated the novel and told Wister in no uncertain terms that he found its negative portrayals of northerners and deified images of racist southerners utterly reprehensible. See Payne, *Owen Wister*, 241–43.

8. L. Ronald Foreman, *Audubon Institute Year End Letter*, 3.

9. Taylor, *In Search of the Racial Frontier*, 53, 80.

10. Ibid., 62.

11. Mihesuah, " 'Too Dark to Be Angels,' " 190, 187–88.

12. Durham and Jones, *Negro Cowboys*, 220. They conclude that "the trails end where fiction begins. As the records show, Negroes helped to open and hold the West. They explored the plains and mountains, fought Indians, dug gold and silver, and trapped wild horses and wolves. Some were outlaws and some were law officers. Thousands rode in the cavalry, and thousands more were cowboys. And for a while, at least, some performed in rodeos. . . . Yet Negroes rarely appear in Western fiction" (220).

13. Diffley, "Home on the Range," 199.

14. Turner, "The Significance of the Frontier in American History," in *Frontier in American History*, 23.

15. For a more extensive discussion of Turner's role in this process, see Brook Thomas, "Frederick Jackson Turner, José Martí, and Finding a Home on the Range."

16. Turner, "The Significance of the Frontier in American History," in *Frontier in American History*, 38.

17. Ibid., 24.

18. Douglass, "Frederick Douglass's Speech at Colored American Day," 193–94; Pokagon, "Red Man's Greeting," 31.

19. John Crowe Ransom and Allen Tate referenced southern culture as the equivalent, even the replacement, of European culture. In "Reconstructed but Unregenerate," Ransom asks, "Will the Southern establishment, the most substantial exhibit on this continent of a society of the European and historic order, be completely crumbled by the powerful acid of the Great Progressive Principle?" (20). Tate argues in "Remarks on the Southern Religion" that "if New England's break with Europe made her excessively interested in the European surface, the ignorance and simplic-

ity of the South's independence of Europe, in the cultural sense, witness a fact of great significance. The South could be ignorant of Europe because it *was* Europe" (171).

20. Quoted in Brinkmeyer, *Remapping Southern Literature*, 9-10.

21. Wright, *Black Power*, 191.

22. Meanwhile, in the newly independent state of Ghana the meaning of African freedom was being debated.

23. See Wrobel, *End of American Exceptionalism*, 105-6. In *West of Everything*, Jane Tompkins argues that this flood of stories was not the result of a nostalgia for lost wilderness; rather, scholarship that perceives such nostalgia has itself been shaped by the logic of the Western, which privileges male violence in wide open spaces as a primary means of identity formation.

24. In *Arc of Justice*, Kevin Boyle examines the 1925 case of Ossian and Gladys Sweet, who were surrounded by a mob that had been incited by white supremacists in Detroit when they attempted to move into a previously all-white neighborhood (their house had actually been sold to them by a man who was passing and his white wife). Sweet had brought a group of family and friends with him for protection; one of the members of his party fired into the crowd, killing a man.

25. See Ann Romines's introduction to *Willa Cather's Southern Connections* for a detailed description of the ways in which Cather's life in Nebraska was informed by southerners and southern history.

26. Welty, "House of Willa Cather," 47.

27. Merrill M. Skaggs argues that Cather influenced southern literature via Faulkner's work and, in particular, that *Death Comes for the Archbishop* provided inspiration for *The Sound and the Fury*; see "Willa Cather's *Death Comes for the Archbishop* and William Faulkner's *The Sound and the Fury*," 89-99, and "Thefts and Conversation," 115-36.

28. Cather, *Professor's House*, 16. Subsequent references to this title will appear parenthetically in the text.

29. John Hilgart writes,

> In her essays, interviews, and lectures of the twenties, Willa Cather repeatedly argued that mass culture had effaced the history, meaning, and very nature of art. Machine-made imitations, vehicles of dissemination such as the radio and film, and the homogenizing of cultural forms in an expanding middle-class all threatened art—for

Cather the measure of a society, a realm she valued for its artifactual uniqueness, craftsmanship, staying power, and discerning audience. Indeed, she rarely referred to contemporary culture as such— it was simply the negation of "human culture." ("Death Comes for the Aesthete," 377)

30. See ibid. Walter Benn Michaels's "Vanishing American" and *Our America* also analyze connections between Native Americans and the idea of culture in Cather.

31. Morrison, *Playing in the Dark*, 17.

32. Tom studies the *Aeneid* perched high above a valley in the Cliff City, and he sees "two pictures: the one on the page, and another behind that: blue and purple rocks and yellow-green piñons with flat tops, little clustered houses clinging together for protection, a rude tower rising in their midst, rising strong, with calmness and courage—behind it a dark grotto, in its depths a crystal spring" (Cather, *Professor's House*, 228).

33. Benjamin, *Reflections*, 151.

34. A ranch hand named Richard Wetherill was thirty when he stumbled upon the ruins in 1888, but Cather described him as a "young boy" at the time. Her informant, probably Richard's brother Clayton, was, according to Cather, "a very old man," although at the time Cather met him he would have been in his forties. (Richard Wetherill himself was dead by this time.) See Goldberg, *Willa Cather and Others*, 125–26. Cather insisted, however, that she "followed the real story very closely in Tom Outland's narrative" (*Willa Cather on Writing*, 32).

35. Hilgart, "Death Comes for the Aesthete," 349.

36. Roediger, *Wages of Whiteness*, 97.

37. See Rawick, *From Sundown to Sunup*, 132–33.

38. Marilee Lindemann argues that Tom's religious feeling and his patriotism conceal a "hypocritical" interest in ownership; see *Willa Cather*, 104.

39. Cather, *Willa Cather on Writing*, 7. Cather adopted many biographical details of both Lamy and his vicar, Joseph Machebeuf (as Joseph Vaillant), while calling other characters by the names of real people who bore little resemblance to their namesakes. She incorporated slanderous gossip into her portrait of the Mexican Padre Martínez; he figures as a lustful, corrupt charismatic with at least one illegitimate son. According to

Janis P. Stout, this description was so biased that some New Mexicans still hold a grievance; see *Willa Cather*, 245. Regardless of such liberties, Cather argued in an interview that it "won't hurt" if readers consider her novel "pure biography" and "I think I was accurate where accuracy was needed" (Bohlke, *Willa Cather in Person*, 109; reprinted from the *San Francisco Chronicle*, 23 March 1931).

40. Cather, *Willa Cather on Writing*, 9.

41. Cather, *Death Comes for the Archbishop*, 4. Subsequent references to this title will appear parenthetically in the text.

42. Cather, *Willa Cather on Writing*, 9.

43. Urgo, *Willa Cather and the Myth of American Migration*, 173.

44. Stout, *Willa Cather*, details the ways in which Cather's historical manipulations in this novel minimize the cruelty of the colonists' impact on Native peoples. Cather's statement regarding the pueblo of Santo Domingo that "the Spaniards had treated them very badly long ago" (56) misrepresents historical events through understatement, as Stout writes. In fact, "after the Spaniards destroyed the pueblo in 1599, with great loss of life, in retaliation for killing one of Oñate's aides, Oñate sentenced five hundred males of the pueblo to have one foot chopped off and to serve twenty years of hard labor. This sentence, so barbarous that some of the Spanish colonists found ways to help Acomas escape, was actually carried out on only twelve" (244).

45. Ibid., 244.

46. Reynolds, *Willa Cather in Context*, 168–69.

47. Elizabeth Sergeant remarked on Cather's unresponsiveness to the plight of contemporary Native Americans; Mabel Dodge Luhan, an heiress originally from Buffalo, New York, and wife of Taos Pueblo Indian Tony Luhan, whose home was a retreat of writers and artists in the Southwest, including Cather and D. H. Lawrence, "was pushing all her New York friends to . . . help defeat the politicians who were trying to destroy the Pueblo lands and ceremonies," Sergeant recalled, but "she made no headway with Willa Cather" (*Willa Cather*, 207).

48. Yaeger, "White Dirt," 140. Emphasis in original.

49. Peggy Phelan defines "queers [as] queer because we recognize that we have survived our own deaths" (*Mourning Sex*, 16). Stout views the cave as a "vaginal" space located within "a blatantly masculine landform" (*Willa Cather*, 242).

50. Goldberg, *Willa Cather and Others*, 178.

51. Renato Rosaldo defines the concept of imperialist nostalgia as a nostalgia for something one is helping to destroy; see *Culture and Truth*, 68.

52. Morrison, *Playing in the Dark*, 59.

53. Website for Bishop's Lodge Resort and Spa, <http://www.bishops lodge.com/>.

CHAPTER 5

1. According to the Myrtles Plantation "official website," <http://www. myrtlesplantation.com/>.

2. Robert Farris Thompson notes that "the meaning of 'Angola' broadened over the centuries. 'Ngola' once referred only to the ruler of the Ndongo part of the Kimbundu culture in what is now the northern part of Angola. According to historian Philip Curtin, '[Angola's] first European meaning referred quite precisely to the immediate hinterland of Luanda.' Then the term became the name of not only modern Angola but sometimes the whole west coast of Central Africa, from Cape Lopez in northwestern Gabon to Benguela on the coast of Angola proper" (*Flash of the Spirit*, 103).

3. Gudmestad, *Troublesome Commerce*, 206, 202.

4. Stack, Garbus, and Rideau, *The Farm*.

5. Baker, *Turning South Again*, 97. Most inmates in the United States are black. See Angela Y. Davis, "Race, Gender, and Prison History," 41.

6. According to Oshinsky, *"Worse Than Slavery,"* 6,

> [Mississippi] revised the state's criminal code in 1835, abandoning corporal punishment and restricting the death penalty to a handful of major crimes. In their place came "time sentences" in a penitentiary, a humanitarian and pragmatic change. Punishment would be less brutal, more precise, and far more certain than before. Juries could now convict the guilty without seeing them tortured or killed. This new code, however, was meant for white folk alone. Slaves "had no rights to respect," wrote one authority, "no civic virtue or character to restore, no freedom to abridge." Slaves were the property of their master, and the state did not normally intervene. In the words of one Natchez slaveholder, "Each plantation was a law unto itself."

See also Lichtenstein, *Twice the Work of Free Labor*, 23.

7. Du Bois, *Souls of Black Folk*, 129–30.

8. Lichtenstein, *Twice the Work of Free Labor*, 113. See also Mancini, *One Dies, Get Another*.

9. Lichtenstein, *Twice the Work of Free Labor*, 113.

10. Ibid., 20.

11. Wikberg and Rideau, *Life Sentences*, 35. As Oshinsky writes, in postbellum Mississippi, Edmund Richardson, originator of the convict leasing system there, became perhaps the richest man in the South as a result. Twelve years after initiating the state's convict lease system, Richardson "had built a mansion in New Orleans, another in Jackson, and a sprawling plantation house known as Refuge in the Yazoo Delta. His holdings included banks, steamboats, and railroads. He owned three dozen cotton plantations and a controlling interest in Mississippi Mills, the largest textile plant in the Lower South. His New Orleans–based brokerage house, Richardson and May, handled more than 250,000 bales of cotton each year" (*"Worse Than Slavery,"* 36).

12. Cable, *Silent South*, 168–69.

13. See Mancini, *One Dies, Get Another*, chap. 13, "The Abandonment of Convict Leasing."

14. Isay with Rideau and Wikberg, "Tossing Away the Keys."

15. Mancini, *One Dies, Get Another*, 150. Similarly, Wilbert Rideau suggests that the state bought the plantation because it wanted to turn a profit itself, not out of a genuine desire for reform; see Wikberg and Rideau, *Life Sentences*, 36.

16. See "History of Angola."

17. Wikberg and Rideau, *Life Sentences*, 41.

18. Office of the Deputy Warden, *Angola Story*, 9.

19. Stack, Garbus, and Rideau, *The Farm*.

20. Isay with Rideau and Wikberg, "Tossing Away the Keys."

21. Ibid.

22. Office of the Deputy Warden, *Angola Story*, 5.

23. On rodeo's myths of the West, see, for example, Burbick, *Rodeo Queens and the American Dream*.

24. Slotkin, *Regeneration through Violence*, 5.

25. Stoeltje, "Rodeo," 247.

26. Michael Allen, *Rodeo Cowboys in the North American Imagination*, 8. Emphasis in original. According to Kristine Fredricksson, "Even the most ambitious professional [rodeo] cowboy" spends only about an hour a

year performing activities in the ring that would never be part of a working cowboy's job (*American Rodeo*, 3).

27. Fredricksson writes that it was in the 1880s—"when the days of the open range were numbered and the 'cow-boys' fun' was beginning to be considered a curiosity, something that would disappear along with the cowboy himself and his work—that what was to become rodeo attracted . . . journalistic attention" (*American Rodeo*, 10).

28. See Patterson, *Slavery and Social Death*.

29. Stallybrass and White, *Politics and Poetics of Transgression*, 191.

30. Henderson was Angola's warden between 1968 and 1975.

31. He was later acquitted.

32. Quoted in Butler and Henderson, *Angola*, 97. In a 2002 Louisiana State Penitentiary Museum Foundation resolution, twelve employees, including Warden Henderson, and nine inmates, including Favor, received credit as rodeo "founders." See <http://www.angolarodeo.com/history.htm>. Another prison rodeo open to the public takes place at the Oklahoma State Penitentiary in McAlester. What seems to have been the first prison rodeo, at the Texas State Penitentiary at Huntsville, began in 1931 but was indefinitely suspended in 1986 due to safety issues with the stadium. The Cummins unit of the Arkansas State Penitentiary held a prison rodeo between 1972 and 1984, when the State Board of Corrections called a halt to it.

33. Bergner, "God of the Rodeo," 15. This citation refers to the manuscript copy in Tulane University's Special Collections; the final copy was published by Crown Press in 1998.

34. Johnson, *Soul by Soul*, 162.

35. Wilbert Rideau comments on this fear in Isay with Rideau and Wikberg, "Tossing Away the Keys," and the profile in Stack, Garbus, and Rideau, *The Farm*, of the prisoner who is eventually buried there includes his family's disbelief that he chose to stay behind bars.

36. See <www.dps.state.la.us/omv.2q2003.pdf>, "From the Commissioner's Dashboard," 1; Parenti, "Rehabilitating Prison Labor," 247.

37. Quoted in Bergner, "God of the Rodeo," 25.

38. Angela Y. Davis, "Racialized Punishment and Prison Abolition," 98.

39. Bergner also notes that in his experience, "whites made up about half the rodeo participants" ("God of the Rodeo," 10).

40. But in a sense, it now seems particularly American to *be* a prisoner.

Since the beginning of the "war on crime" in 1969, the U.S. prison population has grown exponentially. It doubled between 1994 and 1999, and at its current rate of increase, convicts might conceivably outnumber citizens within six decades, according to Lloyd C. Anderson, *Voices from a Southern Prison*, xii.

41. Announcers at other rodeos I attended were not quite so blatant.

42. Bragg, "Inmates Find Brief Escape in Rodeo Ring."

43. Ibid.

44. In "Exhibitionary Complex," an essay on the relationship between public spectacle and national identity, Tony Bennett elaborates on the concept of the "exhibitionary complex," which, like Foucault's theory of the carceral, is an attempt to understand social hierarchies. Based on an analysis of Great Exhibitions in the late nineteenth century, Bennett's model describes a national populace that sees from the perspective of power as well as being seen by it, and thereby develops a commitment to preserving the existing order of things.

45. Foucault, *Discipline and Punish*, 304.

46. Foucault, "Two Lectures," 105–8.

47. MacCannell asserted that the "work display"—the exhibition of work itself as a focal point for tourism—heralded the effective end of industrial society; see *The Tourist*, 36.

48. Elizabeth Atwood Lawrence comments on this event as part of the pro rodeo circuit; see *Rodeo*, 217.

49. Bergner writes that this event began in 1996; see "God of the Rodeo," 12.

50. Ibid., 25.

51. Jett interview.

52. The design of the new larger stadium does not allow for as dramatic an escape.

53. Dayan, "From the Plantation to the Penitentiary," 194–96.

54. Joseph Roach argues that a key aspect of cultural production lies in the performance of what is not the self—that groups articulate and define their identity by performing not only what they think they are but what they think they are not, thereby invoking the possible failure of difference; see *Cities of the Dead*, 5–6.

55. The reporter suggested that the prisoners might "dislike the markers," a suggestion Cain "brushe[d] off" (quoted in Dewan, "Golf Course Shaped by Prisoners' Hands").

56. Ibid.

57. Kirshenblatt-Gimblett, "Objects of Ethnography."

58. Angola State Penitentiary Museum.

59. Chris Rose, "Inside Story."

60. Personal conversation, Marie Campbell, 15 April 2001; see also "A Profile of the District Attorney's Office, East Baton Rouge, LA #1," <http://www/ldaa.org/roster/moreau.html>.

61. Wikberg and Rideau, *Life Sentences*, 4.

62. Ibid., 5.

### EPILOGUE

1. See, for example, Craton and Saunders, *Islanders in the Stream*, esp. chaps. 12–17.

2. See, among other texts, Dawsey and Dawsey, *Confederados*, and Harter, *Lost Colony of the Confederacy*.

# Bibliography

ARCHIVAL MATERIALS

Archive of the Historic New Orleans Collection, New Orleans, Louisiana
Blue Book. Accession no. 1969.19.6.
Special Collections, Howard Tilton Memorial Library, Tulane University,
New Orleans, Louisiana
Daniel Bergner, "God of the Rodeo: The Search for Hope, Faith, and
a Six-Second Ride in Louisiana's Angola Prison." Manuscript copy.
Blue Book. 9th ed.
Al Rose, "Storyville, New Orleans." Unpublished manuscript.
Special Collections, Earl K. Long Library, University of New Orleans,
New Orleans, Louisiana
Photographs of woman believed to be Lulu White

AUTHOR'S INTERVIEWS

Coyle, Katy. New Orleans, Louisiana, 6 July 2002.
Jett, Cathy. By telephone, 14 April 1997.

LEGAL CASES

*Campbell v. Acuff-Rose Music, Inc.*, 510 U.S. 569 (1994)
*Plessy v. Ferguson*, 163 U.S. 537 (1896)
*Slaughterhouse Cases* (83 U.S. 36)
83 U.S. (16 Wall.) 36, 71, 77–79 (1873)
*Stewart v. Abend*, 495 U.S. 207, 236 (1990)
*Suntrust Bank v. Houghton Mifflin Co.*, 252 F.3d 1165 (11th Cir. 2001)

BOOKS AND ARTICLES

Accilien, Cécile. "Survivance et importance de l'oralité dans les plantations:
Les Antilles et la Louisiane." *Revue française* 9 (2000): 43–53.
Alexander, Eleanor. *Lyrics of Sunshine and Shadow: The Tragic
Courtship and Marriage of Paul Laurence Dunbar and Alice Ruth
Moore.* New York: New York University Press, 2002.

Allen, James, ed. *Without Sanctuary: Lynching Photography in America*. Santa Fe: Twin Palms, 2000.

Allen, Michael. *Rodeo Cowboys in the North American Imagination*. Reno: University of Nevada Press, 1998.

Anderson, Benedict. *Imagined Communities*. London: Verso, 1991.

Anderson, Lloyd C. *Voices from a Southern Prison*. Athens: University of Georgia Press, 2000.

Armour, Robert A. "History Written in Jagged Lightning: Realistic South vs. Romantic South in *The Birth of a Nation*." In *The South and Film*, edited by Warren French, 14–22. Jackson: University Press of Mississippi, 1981.

Arnold, Edwin T., and Eugene L. Miller. *The Films and Career of Robert Aldrich*. Knoxville: University of Tennessee Press, 1986.

Bailey, Ronald. "The Slave(ry) Trade and the Development of Capitalism in the United States: The Textile Industry in New England." In *The Atlantic Slave Trade*, edited by Joseph E. Inikori and Stanley L. Engerman, 205–46. Durham, N.C.: Duke University Press, 1992.

Baker, Houston. *Modernism and the Harlem Renaissance*. Chicago: University of Chicago Press, 1987.

———. *Turning South Again: Re-thinking Modernism/Re-reading Booker T.* Durham, N.C.: Duke University Press, 2001.

Baldwin, James. *Notes of a Native Son*. 1955. Reprint, Boston: Beacon Press, 1963.

Ball, Edward. *Slaves in the Family*. New York: Ballantine, 1998.

Basso, Hamilton. Introduction to *The World from Jackson Square: A New Orleans Reader*, edited by Etoila S. Basso, i–xvii. New York: Farrar, Straus and Company, 1948.

Baudrillard, Jean. *Simulacra and Simulation*. Translated by Sheila Farr Glaser. Ann Arbor: University of Michigan Press, 1994.

Beard, Charles A., and Mary R. Beard. *The Rise of American Civilization*. Vols. 1 and 2. 1927. Reprint, New York: Macmillan, 1946.

Benítez-Rojo, Antonio. *The Repeating Island*. 1992. Reprint, Durham, N.C.: Duke University Press, 1996.

Benjamin, Walter. *Reflections*. Edited by Peter Demetz. New York: Schocken, 1978.

Bennett, Tony. "The Exhibitionary Complex." *New Formations* 4 (Spring 1988): 73–102.

Berendt, John. *Midnight in the Garden of Good and Evil*. New York: Random House, 1994.

Best, Stephen. *The Fugitive's Properties: Law and the Poetics of Possession*. Chicago: University of Chicago Press, 2004.

Birnbaum, Michele A. "Kate Chopin and the Colonization of Race." In *Subjects and Citizens: Nation, Race, and Gender from Oronooko to Anita Hill*, edited by Michael Moon and Cathy N. Davidson, 319–41. Durham, N.C.: Duke University Press, 1995.

Blight, David W. *Race and Reunion: The Civil War in American Memory*. Cambridge: Harvard University Press, 2001.

Bogle, Donald. *Toms, Coons, Mulattoes, Mammies, and Bucks: An Interpretive History of Blacks in American Films*. 3rd ed. New York: Continuum, 1994.

Bohlke, L. Brent, ed. *Willa Cather in Person: Interviews, Speeches, and Letters*. Lincoln: University of Nebraska Press, 1986.

Boucicault, Dion. *The Octoroon; or, Life in Louisiana*. 1861. Reprint, Salem, N.H.: Ayer, 1992.

Boyle, Kevin. *Arc of Justice: A Saga of Race, Civil Rights, and Murder in the Jazz Age*. New York: Henry Holt, 2004.

Brinkmeyer, Robert H., Jr. *Remapping Southern Literature*. Athens: University of Georgia Press, 2000.

Browder, Laura. *Slippery Characters: Ethnic Impersonators and American Identities*. Chapel Hill: University of North Carolina Press, 2000.

Brown, Gillian. *Domestic Individualism: Imagining Self in Nineteenth-Century America*. Berkeley: University of California Press, 1990.

Brown, Sterling A. "The Muted South." Originally published in *Phylon*, Winter 1945, 22–34. Reprinted in *Callaloo* 21, no. 4 (Fall 1998): 767–78.

Brundage, W. Fitzhugh. *Lynching in the New South: Georgia and Virginia, 1880–1930*. Urbana: University of Illinois Press, 1993.

Bryan, Violet Harrington. *The Myth of New Orleans in Literature: Dialogues of Race and Gender*. Knoxville: University of Tennessee Press, 1993.

Burbick, Joan. *Rodeo Queens and the American Dream*. New York: Public Affairs, 2002.

Bush, Robert. "The Patrician Voice: Grace King." In *Literary New Orleans: Essays and Meditations*, edited by Richard S. Kennedy, 8–15. Baton Rouge: Louisiana State University Press, 1992.

Butler, Anne, and C. Murray Henderson. *Angola: Louisiana State Penitentiary, a Half-Century of Rage and Reform*. Lafayette: Center for Louisiana Studies, University of Southern Louisiana, 1990.

Cable, George Washington. *The Silent South*. New York: Charles Scribner's Sons, 1885.

Campbell, Edward D. C., Jr. *The Celluloid South: Hollywood and the Southern Myth*. Knoxville: University of Tennessee Press, 1981.

Cash, W. J. *The Mind of the South*. Garden City, N.J.: Doubleday, 1941.

Cather, Willa. *Death Comes for the Archbishop*. 1927. Reprint, New York: Vintage, 1990.

———. *The Professor's House*. 1925. Reprint, New York: Vintage, 1990.

———. *Willa Cather on Writing: Critical Studies on Writing as an Art*. 1949. Reprint, Lincoln: University of Nebraska Press, 1988.

Chadwick, Vernon, ed. *In Search of Elvis: Music, Race, Art, Religion*. Boulder, Colo.: Westview Press, 1997.

Chappell, Edward. "Museums and American Slavery." In *"I, Too, Am America": Archaeological Studies of African-American Life*, edited by Theresa A. Singleton, 240–59. Charlottesville: University Press of Virginia, 1999.

Chopin, Kate. *The Awakening*. 1899. Reprint, New York: Norton, 1976.

Clinton, Catherine. *The Plantation Mistress*. New York: Pantheon, 1984.

———. *Tara Revisited: Women, War, and the Plantation Legend*. New York: Abbeville, 1995.

Cofield, Jack. *William Faulkner: The Cofield Collection*. Oxford: Yoknapatawpha Press, 1978.

Coleman, Linda S. "At Odds: Race and Gender in Grace King's Short Fiction." In *Louisiana Women Writers*, edited by Dorothy H. Brown and Barbara C. Ewell, 33–55. Baton Rouge: Louisiana State University Press, 1992.

Connelly, Mark Thomas. *The Response to Prostitution in the Progressive Era*. Chapel Hill: University of North Carolina Press, 1980.

Cooper, Frederick, Thomas C. Holt, and Rebecca J. Scott, eds. *Beyond Slavery: Explorations of Race, Labor, and Citizenship in Postemancipation Societies*. Chapel Hill: University of North Carolina Press, 2000.

Coyle, Katy, and Nadiene Van Dyke. "Sex, Smashing, and Storyville." In *Carryin' on in the Lesbian and Gay South*, edited by John Howard, 54–72. New York: New York University Press, 1997.

Craton, Michael, and Gail Saunders. *Islanders in the Stream: A History of the Bahamian People.* Vol. 1. Athens: University of Georgia Press, 1992.

Cross, Gary. *An All-Consuming Century: Why Commercialism Won in Modern America.* New York: Columbia University Press, 2000.

Curtis, Michael Kent. *No State Shall Abridge: The Fourteenth Amendment and the Bill of Rights.* Durham, N.C.: Duke University Press, 1986.

Davis, Angela Y. "Race, Gender, and Prison History: From the Convict Lease System to the Supermax Prison." In *Prison Masculinities,* edited by Don Sabo, Terry A. Kupers, and Willie London, 35–45. Philadelphia: Temple University Press, 2001.

———. "Racialized Punishment and Prison Abolition." In *The Angela Y. Davis Reader,* edited by Joy James, 96–109. Oxford: Blackwell Press, 1998.

Davis, Robert Murray, ed. *Owen Wister's West: Selected Articles.* Albuquerque: University of New Mexico Press, 1987.

Dawsey, Cyrus B., and James M. Dawsey. *The Confederados: Old South Immigrants in Brazil.* Tuscaloosa: University of Alabama Press, 1995.

Dayan, Joan. "From the Plantation to the Penitentiary: Chain, Classification, and Codes of Deterrence." In *Slavery in the Caribbean Francophone World: Distant Voices, Forgotten Acts, Forged Identities,* edited by Doris Y. Kadish, 191–210. Athens: University of Georgia Press, 2000.

———. *Haiti, History, and the Gods.* Berkeley: University of California Press, 1995.

D'Emilio, John, and Estelle B. Freedman. *Intimate Matters: A History of Sexuality in America.* 2nd ed. Chicago: University of Chicago Press, 1997.

Deyle, Stephen. *Carry Me Back: The Domestic Slave Trade in American Life.* Oxford: Oxford University Press, 2005.

Diffley, Kathleen. "Home on the Range: Turner, Slavery, and the Landscape Illustrations in *Harper's New Monthly Magazine,* 1861–1876." *Prospects* 14 (1989): 175–202.

Domínguez, Virginia. *White by Definition: Social Classification in Creole Louisiana.* New Brunswick, N.J.: Rutgers University Press, 1986.

Doss, Erika. *Elvis Culture: Fans, Faith, and Image.* Lawrence: University Press of Kansas, 1999.

Douglas, Ellen. *Truth: Four Stories I Am Finally Old Enough to Tell.* New York: Plume, 1999.

Douglass, Frederick. "Frederick Douglass's Speech at Colored American Day." In *All the World Is Here! The Black Presence at White City*, by Christopher Robert Reed, 193–94. Bloomington: Indiana University Press, 2000.

Du Bois, W. E. B. *Black Reconstruction*. Millwood, N.Y.: Kraus-Thompson Organization Ltd., 1935.

——. *The Souls of Black Folk*. 1903. Reprint, New York: Vintage, 1990.

Dunbar, Alice. *The Goodness of St. Rocque and Other Stories*. New York: Dodd, Mead, 1899.

Durham, Philip, and Everett L. Jones. *The Negro Cowboys*. Lincoln: University of Nebraska Press, 1965.

Dyer, Richard. *Stars*. London: British Film Institute, 1998.

Eichstedt, Jennifer L., and Stephen Small. *Representations of Slavery: Race and Ideology in Southern Plantation Museums*. Washington, D.C.: Smithsonian Institution Press, 2002.

Ellis, Rex. "Re: Living History: Bringing Slavery into Play." *American Visions*, December/January 1993, 22–24.

Ewell, Barbara, and Pamela Glenn Menke, eds. *Southern Local Color: Stories of Region, Race, and Gender*. Athens: University of Georgia Press, 2002.

Fabre, Michel. "New Orleans Creole Expatriates in France: Romance and Reality." In *Creole: The History and Legacy of Louisiana's Free People of Color*, edited by Sybil Kein, 179–95. Baton Rouge: Louisiana State University Press.

Fairman, Charles. *Reconstruction and Reunion, 1864–88*, pt. 2. Vol 7 of *History of the Supreme Court of the United States*. New York: Macmillan, 1987.

Faulkner, William. *Absalom, Absalom!* 1936. Reprint, New York: Vintage, 1990.

——. "If I Were a Negro." Reprinted in *White on Black: The Views of Twenty-Two White Americans on the Negro*, edited by Era Bell Thompson and Herbert Nipson, 68–75. Chicago: Johnson Publishing Company, 1963.

——. *New Orleans Sketches*. New Brunswick, N.J.: Rutgers University Press, 1958.

Fiedler, Leslie. *Love and Death in the American Novel*. New York: Stein and Day, 1966.

Fisher, Robert, ed. *The Best of New Orleans*. New York: Prentice Hall, 1991.

Foner, Eric. *Reconstruction: America's Unfinished Revolution, 1863–1877.* New York: Harper and Row, 1988.

Foreman, P. Gabrielle. " 'Reading Aright': White Slavery, Black Referents, and the Strategy of Histotextuality in *Iola Leroy.*" *Yale Journal of Criticism* 10, no. 2 (1997): 327–54.

Fortier, Alcée. *Louisiana Folk-tales, in French Dialect and English Translation.* Boston: Houghton Mifflin, 1895.

Foucault, Michel. *Discipline and Punish: The Birth of the Prison.* Translated by Alan Sheridan. New York: Vintage, 1979.

———. "Two Lectures." In *Power/Knowledge: Selected Interviews and Other Writings, 1972–1977,* edited by Colin Gordon, 78–108. New York: Pantheon, 1980.

Fredricksson, Kristine. *American Rodeo: From Buffalo Bill to Big Business.* College Station: Texas A&M Press, 1985.

Frow, John. *Time and Commodity Culture: Essays in Cultural Theory and Postmodernity.* Oxford: Clarendon Press, 1997.

Gaines, Jane M. *Fire and Desire: Mixed-Race Movies in the Silent Era.* Chicago: University of Chicago Press, 2001.

Geist, Christopher. "Violence, Passion, and Sexual Racism: The Plantation Novel in the 1970s." *Southern Quarterly,* 18, no. 2 (Winter 1980): 60–72.

Genovese, Eugene. *Roll Jordan Roll: The World the Slaves Made.* New York: Pantheon, 1974.

Gilfoyle, Timothy J. *City of Eros: New York City, Prostitution, and the Commercialization of Sex, 1790–1920.* New York: Norton, 1992.

Glassman, Sallie Ann. "Vodou and Colonial Louisiana." In *Revolutionary Freedoms: A History of Survival, Strength, and Imagination in Haiti,* edited by Cécile Accilien, Jessica Adams, and Elmide Méléance, 113–20. Deerfield Beach, Fla.: Caribbean Studies Press, 2006.

Glissant, Edouard. *Faulkner, Mississippi.* Translated by Barbara Lewis and Thomas C. Spear. New York: Farrar, Straus and Giroux, 1999.

Goings, Kenneth. *Mammy and Uncle Mose: Black Collectibles and American Stereotyping.* Bloomington: Indiana University Press, 1994.

Goldberg, Jonathan. *Willa Cather and Others.* Durham, N.C.: Duke University Press, 2001.

Gordon, Avery. *Ghostly Matters: Haunting and the Sociological Imagination.* Minneapolis: University of Minnesota Press, 1997.

Graham, Allison. *Framing the South: Hollywood, Television, and Race during the Civil Rights Struggle.* Baltimore: Johns Hopkins University Press, 2001.

Graham, Howard Jay. *Everyman's Constitution: Historical Essays on the Fourteenth Amendment, the "Conspiracy Theory," and American Constitutionalism.* Madison: State Historical Society of Wisconsin, 1968.

Gudmestad, Robert H. *A Troublesome Commerce: The Transformation of the Interstate Slave Trade.* Baton Rouge: Louisiana State University Press, 2003.

Guillory, Monique. "Under One Roof: The Sins and Sanctity of the New Orleans Quadroon Balls." In *Race Consciousness: African American Studies for the New Century*, edited by Judith Jackson Fosset and Jeffrey A. Tucker, 67–92. New York: New York University Press, 1997.

Gutman, Herbert G. *The Black Family in Slavery and Freedom, 1750–1925.* New York: Vintage, 1977.

Hale, Grace Elizabeth. *Making Whiteness: The Culture of Segregation in the South, 1890–1940.* New York: Pantheon, 1998.

Hall, Gwendolyn Midlo. "The Formation of Afro-Creole Culture." In *Creole New Orleans: Race and Americanization*, edited by Arnold R. Hirsch and Joseph Logsdon, 58–87. Baton Rouge: Louisiana State University Press, 1992.

Hall, Joan Wylie. "Louisiana Writers of the Postbellum South." In *The History of Southern Women's Literature*, ed. Carolyn Perry and Mary Louise Weaks, 201–9. Baton Rouge: Louisiana State University Press, 2002.

Halsell, Grace. *Soul Sister.* New York: Fawcett Crest, 1969.

Harris, Cheryl I. "Whiteness as Property." In *Critical Race Theory: The Key Writings That Formed the Movement*, edited by Kimberlé Crenshaw, Neil Gotanda, Gary Peller, and Kendall Thomas, 276–91. New York: New Press, 1995.

Harter, Eugene C. *The Lost Colony of the Confederacy.* Jackson: University Press of Mississippi, 1985.

Hartman, Saidiya V. *Scenes of Subjection: Terror, Slavery, and Self-Making in Nineteenth-Century America.* Oxford: Oxford University Press, 1997.

Hatt, Michael. "Race, Ritual, and Responsibility: Performativity and Southern Lynching." In *Performing the Body/Performing the Text,* edited by Amelia Jones and Andrew Stephenson, 76–88. London: Routledge, 1999.

Hawkins, Harriet. "Shared Dreams: Reproducing Gone with the Wind." In *Novel Images: Literature in Performance*, edited by Peter Reynolds, 122–38. London: Routledge, 1993.

Herman, Jan. *A Talent for Trouble: The Life of Hollywood's Most Acclaimed Director, William Wyler*. New York: G. P. Putnam's Sons, 1995.

Hilgart, John. "Death Comes for the Aesthete: Commodity Culture and the Artifact in Cather's *The Professor's House*." *Studies in the Novel* 30, no. 3 (Fall 1998): 377–404.

Holloway, Karla F. C. *Passed On: African American Mourning Stories*. Durham, N.C.: Duke University Press, 2002.

Hurston, Zora Neale. *Mules and Men*. 1935. Reprint, New York: Harper Perennial, 1990.

——. *Mules and Men*. Bloomington: Indiana University Press, 1978.

——. *Tell My Horse: Voodoo and Life in Haiti and Jamaica*. 1938. Reprint, New York: Harper and Row, 1990.

Jackson, Joy J. *New Orleans in the Gilded Age: Politics and Urban Progress, 1880–1896*. Baton Rouge: Louisiana State University Press, 1969.

Jameson, Fredric. *Postmodernism; or, the Logic of Late Capitalism*. Durham, N.C.: Duke University Press, 1991.

Jeter, Ida. "*Jezebel* and the Emergence of the Hollywood Tradition of a Decadent South." In *The South and Film*, edited by Warren French, 31–46. Jackson: University Press of Mississippi, 1981.

Johnson, Walter. *Soul by Soul: Life inside the Antebellum Slave Market*. Cambridge: Harvard University Press, 1999.

Jones, G. William. *Black Cinema Treasures: Lost and Found*. Denton: University of North Texas Press, 1991.

Jones, Jacqueline. *Labor of Love, Labor of Sorrow*. New York: Vintage, 1986.

Juncker, Clara. "Grace King." In *The History of Southern Women's Literature*, edited by Carolyn Perry and Mary Louise Weaks, 216–19. Baton Rouge: Louisiana State University Press, 2002.

Kammen, Michael. *Mystic Chords of Memory*. New York: Vintage, 1991.

Kasson, John F. *Amusing the Million: Coney Island at the Turn of the Century*. New York: Hill and Wang, 1978.

Kern-Foxworth, Marilyn. *Aunt Jemima, Uncle Ben, and Rastus: Blacks in Advertising Yesterday, Today, and Tomorrow*. Westport, Conn.: Praeger, 1994.

King, Grace. *Tales of a Time and Place*. New York: Harper and Brothers, 1892.

Kirshenblatt-Gimblett, Barbara. "Objects of Ethnography." In *Exhibiting Cultures: The Poetics and Politics of Museum Display*, edited by Ivan Karp and Stephen D. Lavine, 386–443. Washington, D.C.: Smithsonian Institution Press, 1991.

Langman, Larry, and David Ebner. *Hollywood's Image of the South: A Century of Southern Films*. Westport, Conn.: Greenwood Press, 2001.

Lawrence, Elizabeth Atwood. *Rodeo: An Anthropologist Looks at the Wild and the Tame*. Knoxville: University of Tennessee Press, 1982.

Lawrence, John, and Dan Hise. *Faulkner's Rowan Oak*. Jackson: University of Mississippi Press, 1993.

Leach, William. *Land of Desire: Merchants, Power, and the Rise of a New American Culture*. New York: Pantheon, 1993.

Lears, T. J. Jackson. "From Salvation to Self-Realization: Advertising and the Therapeutic Roots of the Consumer Culture, 1880–1930." In *The Culture of Consumption: Critical Essays in American History, 1880–1980*, edited by Richard Wightman Fox and T. J. Jackson Lears, 3–38. New York: Pantheon, 1983.

LeCompte, Mary Lou. "Hispanic Roots of American Rodeo." *Studies in Latin American Popular Culture* 13 (1994): 57–75.

Lichtenstein, Alex. *Twice the Work of Free Labor: The Political Economy of Convict Labor in the New South*. London: Verso, 1996.

Lindemann, Marilee. *Willa Cather: Queering America*. New York: Columbia University Press, 1999.

Lipsitz, George. *The Possessive Investment in Whiteness*. Philadelphia: Temple University Press, 1998.

———. *Time Passages: Collective Memory and Popular Culture*. Minneapolis: University of Minnesota Press, 1990.

Locke, John. *Two Treatises of Government and A Letter Concerning Toleration*, ed. Ian Shapiro. 1680. Reprint, New Haven: Yale University Press, 2003.

Logsdon, Joseph, and Carolyn Cossé Bell. "The Americanization of Black New Orleans." In *Creole New Orleans: Race and*

*Americanization*, edited by Arnold R. Hirsch and Joseph Logsdon, 201–61. Baton Rouge: Louisiana State University Press, 1992.

Long, Alecia P. *The Great Southern Babylon: Sex, Race, and Respectability in New Orleans, 1865–1920*. Baton Rouge: Louisiana State University Press, 2004.

Lott, Eric. "All the King's Men: Elvis Impersonators and White Working-Class Masculinity." In *Race and the Subject of Masculinities*, edited by Harry Stecopoulos and Michael Vebel, 196–227. Durham, N.C.: Duke University Press, 1997.

MacCannell, Dean. *The Tourist: A New Theory of the Leisure Class*. New York: Schocken, 1976.

MacLeod, Elvis. "Generation E." In *In Search of Elvis: Music, Race, Art, Religion*, edited by Vernon Chadwick, 171–78. Boulder, Colo.: Westview Press, 1997.

MacLeod, Paul. "Why I'm the World's Number One Elvis Fan." In *In Search of Elvis: Music, Race, Art, Religion*, edited by Vernon Chadwick, 161–70. Boulder, Colo.: Westview Press, 1997.

MacPherson, C. B. *The Political Theory of Possessive Individualism, Hobbes to Locke*. Oxford: Oxford University Press, 1962.

McAdams, Ina May Ogletree. *The Building of "Longwood."* Natchez, Miss.: Pilgrimage Historical Association, 1972.

McCurry, Stephanie. *Masters of Small Worlds: Yeoman Households, Gender Relations, and the Political Culture of the Antebellum South Carolina Low Country*. New York: Oxford University Press, 1995.

McPherson, Tara. *Reconstructing Dixie: Race, Gender, and Nostalgia in the Imagined South*. Durham, N.C.: Duke University Press, 2003.

Mancini, Matthew J. *One Dies, Get Another: Convict Leasing in the American South, 1866–1928*. Columbia: University of South Carolina Press, 1996.

Manley, Roger. *Signs and Wonders: Outsider Art inside North Carolina*. Raleigh: North Carolina Museum of Art, 1989.

Manring, M. M. *Slave in a Box: The Strange Career of Aunt Jemima*. Charlottesville: University Press of Virginia, 1998.

Marling, Karal Ann. *Graceland: Going Home with Elvis*. Cambridge: Harvard University Press, 1996.

Martin, Joan M. "*Plaçage* and the Louisiana *Gens de Couleur Libre*: How Race and Sex Defined the Lifestyles of Free Women of Color." In

Creole: The History and Legacy of Louisiana's Free People of Color,
edited by Sybil Kein, 57–70. Baton Rouge: Louisiana State University
Press, 2000.

Marx, Karl. *Capital*. Vol. 1. Translated by Ben Fowkes. New York:
Vintage, 1977.

Massey, Sara R., ed. *Black Cowboys of Texas*. College Station: Texas A&M
Press, 2000.

Medley, Keith Weldon. *We as Freemen: Plessy v. Ferguson*. Gretna, La.:
Pelican, 2003.

Meltzer, Milton. *Langston Hughes: A Biography*. New York: Thomas Y.
Crowell, 1968.

Michaels, Walter Benn. *Our America: Nativism, Modernism, and
Pluralism*. Durham, N.C.: Duke University Press, 1995.

———. "The Vanishing American." *American Literary History* 2, no. 2
(Summer 1990): 220–41.

Mihesuah, Devon H. " 'Too Dark to Be Angels': The Class System
among the Cherokees at the Female Seminary." In *Unequal Sisters: A
Multicultural Reader in U.S. Women's History*, 3rd ed., edited by
Vicki L. Ruiz and Ellen Carol DuBois, 183–96. New York: Routledge,
2000.

Morris, Willie. *The Ghosts of Medgar Evers*. New York: Random House,
1998.

Morrison, Toni. *Playing in the Dark: Whiteness and the Literary
Imagination*. New York: Vintage, 1993.

Mullen, Edward J., ed. *Langston Hughes in the Hispanic World and
Haiti*. Hamden, Conn.: Archon Books, 1977.

Nora, Pierre. "Between Memory and History: Les Lieux de Memoire."
Translated by Marc Roudebush. *Representations*, no. 26 (Spring
1989): 7–24.

Olmstead, Frederick Law. *A Journey to the Seaboard Slave States*. 1865.
Reprint, New York: G. P. Putnam's Sons, 1959.

Olsen, Otto H., ed. *The Thin Disguise: Turning Point in Negro History*.
New York: Humanities Press, 1967.

Oshinsky, David. *"Worse Than Slavery": Parchman Farm and the Ordeal
of Jim Crow Justice*. New York: Free Press, 1996.

Parenti, Christian. "Rehabilitating Prison Labor: The Uses of Imprisoned
Masculinity." In *Prison Masculinities*, edited by Don Sabo, Terry A.

Kupers, and Willie London, 247–54. Philadelphia: Temple University Press, 2001.

Parini, Jay. *One Matchless Time: A Life of William Faulkner*. New York: HarperCollins, 2004.

Pattee, Fred Lewis. *A History of American Literature since 1870*. New York: Century, 1915.

Patterson, Orlando. *Slavery and Social Death: A Comparative Study*. Cambridge: Harvard University Press, 1982.

Payne, Darwin. *Owen Wister: Chronicler of the West, Gentleman of the East*. Dallas: Southern Methodist University Press, 1985.

Peiss, Kathy. *Hope in a Jar: The Making of America's Beauty Culture*. New York: Henry Holt, 1998.

Phelan, Peggy. *Mourning Sex: Performing Public Memories*. London: Routledge, 1997.

———. *Unmarked*. New York: Routledge, 1994.

Pokagon, Simon. "The Red Man's Greeting." Reprinted in *Talking Back to Civilization: Indian Voices from the Progressive Era*, edited by Frederick Hoxie, 31–35. Boston: Bedford/St. Martin's, 2001.

Rampersad, Arnold. *The Life of Langston Hughes*. Vol. 2. New York: Oxford University Press, 1988.

Randall, Alice. *The Wind Done Gone*. Boston: Houghton Mifflin, 2001.

Ransom, John Crowe. "Reconstructed but Unregenerate." In *I'll Take My Stand*, by Twelve Southerners, 1–27. New York: Harper and Brothers, 1930.

Rawick, George. *From Sundown to Sunup: The Making of the Black Community*. Westport, Conn.: Greenwood Press, 1972.

Rehder, John B. *Delta Sugar: Louisiana's Vanishing Plantation Landscape*. Baltimore: Johns Hopkins University Press, 1999.

Reinhardt, Catherine A. *Claims to Memory: Beyond Slavery and Emancipation in the French Caribbean*. Oxford: Berghahn Books, 2006.

Renda, Mary. *Taking Haiti: Military Occupation and the Culture of U.S. Imperialism, 1915–1940*. Chapel Hill: University of North Carolina Press, 2001.

Reynolds, Guy. *Willa Cather in Context: Progress, Race, Empire*. London: Macmillan, 1996.

Rice, Anne P., ed. *Witnessing Lynching: American Writers Respond*. New Brunswick, N.J.: Rutgers University Press, 2003.

Ripley, Eliza. *Social Life in Old New Orleans: Being Recollections of My Girlhood*. New York: D. Appleton and Company, 1912.

Roach, Joseph. *Cities of the Dead: Circum-Atlantic Performance*. New York: Columbia University Press, 1996.

Roberts, Diane. *The Myth of Aunt Jemima: Representations of Race and Region*. London: Routledge, 1994.

Robinson, Amy. "Forms of Appearance of Value: Homer Plessy and the Politics of Privacy." In *Performance and Cultural Politics*, edited by Elin Diamond, 237–61. London: Routledge, 1996.

Roediger, David. *Colored White: Transcending the Racial Past*. Berkeley: University of California Press, 2002.

———. *The Wages of Whiteness: Race and the Making of the American Working Class*. London: Verso, 1991.

Romines, Ann. Introduction to *Willa Cather's Southern Connections: New Essays on Cather and the South*, edited by Ann Romines, 1–7. Charlottesville: University Press of Virginia, 2000.

Rosaldo, Renato. *Culture and Truth: The Remaking of Social Analysis*. Boston: Beacon, 1989.

Rose, Al. *Storyville, New Orleans: Being an Authentic, Illustrated Account of the Notorious Red Light District*. Tuscaloosa: University of Alabama Press, 1974.

Rosen, Ruth. *The Lost Sisterhood: Prostitution in America, 1900–1918*. Baltimore: Johns Hopkins University Press, 1982.

Rothman, Adam. *Slave Country: American Expansion and the Origins of the Deep South*. Cambridge: Harvard University Press, 2005.

Saxon, Lyle. *Fabulous New Orleans*. 1928. Reprint, Gretna, La.: Pelican, 1995.

———. *Old Louisiana*. New York: Century, 1929.

Schickel, Richard. *Intimate Strangers: The Culture of Celebrity*. Garden City, N.J.: Doubleday, 1985.

Scott, James C. *Domination and the Arts of Resistance: Hidden Transcripts*. New Haven: Yale University Press, 1990.

Sergeant, Elizabeth Shepley. *Willa Cather: A Memoir*. Lincoln: University of Nebraska Press, 1963.

Silber, Nina. *The Romance of Reunion: Northerners and the South, 1865–1900*. Chapel Hill: University of North Carolina Press, 1993.

Skaggs, Merrill M. "Thefts and Conversation: Cather and Faulkner." *Cather Studies* 3 (1996), 115–36.

———. "Willa Cather's *Death Comes for the Archbishop* and William Faulkner's *The Sound and the Fury*." *Faulkner Journal* 13, no. 1/2 (Fall 1997): 89–99.

Slotkin, Richard. *Regeneration through Violence*. Middletown, Conn.: Wesleyan University Press, 1973.

Smith, Felipe. "The Economics of Enchantment: Two Montego Bay, Jamaica Great House Tours." In *Cultural (Con)fusion?: TransCaribbean Performance and Performers*, edited by Lowell Fiet and Janette Becera, 21–33. Río Piedras: Sargasso/Caribbean 2000, 2001.

Smith, Jon, and Deborah Cohn, eds. *Look Away! The U.S. South in New World Studies*. Durham, N.C.: Duke University Press, 2004.

Smith, Lillian. *Killers of the Dream*. 1940. Rev. and enl. ed., New York: Norton, 1961.

Sontag, Susan. Introduction to *Bellocq: Photographs from Storyville, the Red-Light District of New Orleans*, 7–8. Reproduced from prints made by Lee Friedlander, interviews edited by John Szarkowski. New York: Random House, 1996.

Stallybrass, Peter, and Allon White. *The Politics and Poetics of Transgression*. Ithaca: Cornell University Press, 1986.

Stange, Margit. *Personal Property: Wives, White Slaves, and the Market in Women*. Baltimore: Johns Hopkins University Press, 1998.

Stewart, Susan. *On Longing: Narratives of the Miniature, the Gigantic, the Souvenir, the Collection*. Baltimore: Johns Hopkins University Press, 1984.

Stoeltje, Beverly. "Rodeo: From Custom to Ritual." *Western Folklore* 48 (1989): 244–60.

Stokes, Mason. *The Color of Sex: Whiteness, Heterosexuality, and the Fictions of White Supremacy*. Durham, N.C.: Duke University Press, 2001.

Stout, Janis P. *Willa Cather: The Writer and Her World*. Charlottesville: University Press of Virginia, 2000.

Strachan, Ian. *Paradise and Plantation: Tourism and Culture in the Anglophone Caribbean*. Charlottesville: University Press of Virginia, 2002.

Sundquist, Eric. "Mark Twain and Homer Plessy." *Representations*, no. 28 (Fall 1988): 102–28.

Tate, Allen. "Remarks on the Southern Religion." In *I'll Take My Stand*, by Twelve Southerners, 155–75. New York: Harper and Brothers, 1930.

Taussig, Michael. *The Magic of the State*. London: Routledge, 1997.

Taylor, Quintard. *In Search of the Racial Frontier: African Americans in the American West, 1528–1990*. New York: Norton, 1998.

Thomas, Brook. "Frederick Jackson Turner, José Martí, and Finding a Home on the Range." In *José Martí's "Our America": From National to Hemispheric Cultural Studies*, edited by Jeffrey Belknap and Raul Fernandez, 275–92. Durham, N.C.: Duke University Press, 1998.

Thompson, Robert Farris. *Flash of the Spirit: African and Afro-American Philosophy*. New York: Vintage, 1984.

Tolnay, Stewart, and E. M. Beck. *A Festival of Violence: An Analysis of Southern Lynchings, 1882–1930*. Urbana: University of Illinois Press, 1995.

Tompkins, Jane. *West of Everything: The Inner Life of Westerns*. New York: Oxford University Press, 1992.

Tregle, Joseph G., Jr. "Creoles and Americans." In *Creole New Orleans: Race and Americanization*, edited by Arnold R. Hirsch and Joseph Logsdon, 131–85. Baton Rouge: Louisiana State University Press, 1992.

Tucker, Susan. *Telling Memories among Southern Women*. New York: Schocken, 1988.

Turner, Frederick Jackson. *The Frontier in American History*. New York: Henry Holt, 1920.

Urgo, Joseph. *Willa Cather and the Myth of American Migration*. Urbana: University of Illinois Press, 1995.

Veblen, Thorstein. *The Theory of the Leisure Class*. 1899. Reprint, New York: Modern Library, 1934.

Vlach, John Michael. *Back of the Big House: The Architecture of Plantation Slavery*. Chapel Hill: University of North Carolina Press, 1993.

——. *The Planter's Prospect: Privilege and Slavery in Plantation Paintings*. Chapel Hill: University of North Carolina Press, 2002.

Welty, Eudora. "The House of Willa Cather." In *The Eye of the Story: Selected Essays and Reviews*, 41–60. New York: Random House, 1977.

West, Patricia. *Domesticating History: The Political Origins of America's House Museums*. Washington, D.C.: Smithsonian Institution Press, 1999.

White, Deborah Gray. *Ar'n't I a Woman?: Female Slaves in the Plantation South*. 1985. Rev. ed., New York: Norton, 1995.

White, Walter. "I Investigate Lynchings." Originally published in *American Mercury*, January 1929, 77–84. Reprinted in *Witnessing Lynching: American Writers Respond*, edited by Anne P. Rice, 252–60. New Brunswick, N.J.: Rutgers University Press, 2003.

Wikberg, Ron, and Wilbert Rideau, eds. *Life Sentences: Rage and Survival behind Bars*. New York: Times Books, 1992.

Wilkie, Laurie A. *Creating Freedom: Material Culture and African American Identity at Oakley Plantation, Louisiana, 1840–1950*. Baton Rouge: Louisiana State University Press, 2000.

Williams, David. *The Georgia Gold Rush: Twenty-Niners, Cherokees, and Gold Fever*. Columbia: University of South Carolina Press, 1993.

Williams, Tony. *Body and Soul: The Cinematic Vision of Robert Aldrich*. Lanham, Md.: Scarecrow Press, 2004.

Wilson, Charles Reagan. *Judgment and Grace in Dixie: Southern Faiths from Faulkner to Elvis*. Athens: University of Georgia Press, 1995.

Wister, Owen. *Lady Baltimore*. New York: Macmillan, 1906.

———. Preface to *Red Men and White*. Reprinted in *Owen Wister's West: Selected Articles*, edited by Robert Murray Davis, 55–64. Albuquerque: University of New Mexico Press, 1987.

———. *The Virginian*. New York: Grosset and Dunlap, 1902.

Wood, Amy Louise. "Lynching Photography and the 'Black Beast Rapist' in the Southern White Masculine Imagination." In *Masculinity: Bodies, Movies, Culture*, edited by Peter Lehman, 193–212. New York: Routledge, 2001.

Wright, Richard. *Black Power: A Record of Reactions in a Land of Pathos*. 1954. Reprint, New York: Harper Perennial, 1995.

Wrobel, David M. *The End of American Exceptionalism: Frontier Anxiety from the Old West to the New Deal*. Lawrence: University of Kansas Press, 1993.

Yaeger, Patricia. *Dirt and Desire*. Chicago: University of Chicago Press, 2000.

———. "White Dirt: The Surreal Landscapes of Willa Cather's South." In *Willa Cather's Southern Connections: New Essays on Cather and the South*, edited by Ann Romines, 138–55. Charlottesville: University Press of Virginia, 2000.

Yates, Frances A. *The Art of Memory*. Chicago: University of Chicago Press, 1966.

DISSERTATIONS AND THESES

Caddell, John. "White Flight and the Desegregation of the New Orleans Public Schools, 1965–1975." Honors thesis, Tulane University, 2005.

Coyle, Katy. "The Intersection of Law and Desire: Sex, Storyville, and Prostitution in Turn-of-Century New Orleans." Ph.D. diss., Tulane University, in progress.

Dennis, Samuel F., Jr. "Seeing the Lowcountry Landscape: 'Race,' Gender, and Nature in Lowcountry South Carolina and Georgia, 1750–2000." Ph.D. diss., Pennsylvania State University, 2000.

Guillory, Monique. "Some Enchanted Evening on the Auction Block: The Cultural Legacy of the New Orleans Quadroon Balls." Ph.D. diss., New York University, 1999.

Mercier, John Denis. "The Evolution of the Black Image in White Consciousness, 1876–1954: A Popular Culture Perspective." Ph.D. diss., University of Pennsylvania, 1984.

Newton, James, and Stacy Printon. "Behind the Façade: African Influences in the Design of the South Carolina Lowcountry Rice Plantation Landscape." Master's thesis, University of Michigan, 2000.

Skinner, Glenda D. "The 'Storyville Portraits': A Collaborative History." Master's thesis, Virginia Commonwealth University, 1999.

MATERIAL IN POPULAR MEDIA

Anderson, Edward. "Uncovering the Vice Cesspool of New Orleans." *Real Detective*, March 1935, 40–68.

Associated Press. "Frankly, My Dear, They All Give a Damn," 5 April 2001, <http://www.freedomforum.org/templates/document.asp?documentID=13607>. 24 June 2005.

———. "Settlement Reached over Wind Done Gone," 10 May 2002, <http://www.freedomforum.org/templates/document.asp?documentID=16230>. 23 June 2005.

———. "Some Historic Sites Have Trouble Finding Black Reenactors." *Hornell (New York) Spectator*, 19 May 2002, 8A.

———. "Wind Done Gone Injunction Lifted," 25 May 2001, <http://

www.freedomforum.org/templates/document.asp?documentID=
14009>. 22 June 2005.

"Beyond Face Value: Depictions of Slavery in Confederate Currency." A
project of the U.S. Civil War Center. Online exhibition,. 26 May 2006.

Bosman, Julie. "The King's Legacy, All Shook Up." *New York Times*, 5
March 2006, C1.

Bragg, Rick. "Inmates Find Brief Escape in Rodeo Ring." *New York
Times*, 25 October 1996, A1, A13.

Calendo, John. "Robert Aldrich Says, 'Life Is Worth Living.'" *Andy
Warhol's Interview*, August 1973, 30–33.

Childs, Marquis. "New Orleans Is a Wicked City." *Vanity Fair*,
November 1934, 62–72.

Dejoie, Kathy Taylor. "Buffalo Soldiers: The Pride of New Orleans,"
<http://www.imdiversity.com/villages/african/history_heritage/
buffalo_0605.asp> . . . 2006, IMDiversity Inc. 28 May 2006.

Dewan, Shaila K. "Golf Course Shaped by Prisoners' Hands; Greens
Open to the Public but Not to Their Keepers." *New York Times*,
15 August 2004, A20.

Dobbin, Ben. "Future of Historic Home Unclear." *New Orleans Times-
Picayune*, 13 June 2005, A8.

Elliot, Debbie. "Jury Selection Begins in Killen Trial." *NPR Morning
Edition*. 13 June 2005.

Etheridge, Frank. "Derailing Plessy Park: Students, Developers, Activists,
and Politicians Are at Odds on How to Best Commemorate Civil
Rights Pioneer Homer Plessy." *New Orleans Gambit*, 5 July 2005,
<http://www.bestofneworleans.com/dispatch/2005-07-05/news_
feat.php>. 10 July 2005.

Foreman, L. Ronald. *Audubon Institute Year End Letter*, 3 January 2005.

"From the Commissioner's Dashboard," <www.dps.state.la.us/omv.
2q2003.pdf>. 8 October 2006.

Henderson, Skip. "Plessy Park Now Endangered." Greater New Orleans
Louis A. Martinet Legal Society website, 25 March 2005, <http://
www.martinetsociety.org/martinet_web5/_disc11/00000004.htm>.
5 November 2005.

Herbert, Bob. "An Empty Apology." *New York Times*, 18 July 2005, A19.

Indians of All Nations, "Alcatraz Proclamation to the Great White Father and His People," 1969, <ftp://ftp.halcyon.com/pub/FWDP/Americas/alcatraz.txt>. 10 August 2005.

Isay, David, with Wilbert Rideau and Ron Wikberg. "Tossing Away the Keys." *NPR Weekend All Things Considered*, 29 April 1990, <http://www.soundportraits.org/on-air/tossing_away_the_keys/transcript.php3>. 10 August 2005.

LaFrance, Siona. "Unshackling the Truth." *New Orleans Times-Picayune*, 2 February 2003, E1, E5–6.

Malcolm, Janet. "The Real Thing." *New York Review of Books*, 9 January 1997, 12–15.

"Morehouse College Gets $1.5 Million Gift in the Name of Pulitzer Prize Winning Author Margaret Mitchell," 18 March 2002, <http://www.morehouse.edu/News_Releases/2002/March/mitchellgift0318.html>. 30 June 2005.

Museum of Modern Art, New York. "Conversations with Contemporary Artists: Kara Walker," <http://www.moma.org/onlineprojects/conversations/kw_f.html> . . . 1999, The Museum of Modern Art, New York. 20 May 2006.

*New Orleans Daily Picayune*, 4 March 1898, 1.

"A Profile of the District Attorney's Office, East Baton Rouge, LA #1." <http://www/ldaa.org/roster/moreau.html>. 15 June 2002.

Rose, Chris. "Inside Story." *New Orleans Times-Picayune*, 19 May 1998, F1.

Ruppersburg, Hugh. "The Wind Done Gone." *New Georgia Encyclopedia*, 23 December 2002, . . . 2004–2005 the Georgia Humanities Council and the University of Georgia, <http://www.georgiaencyclopedia.org/nge/Article.jsp?id=h-776>. 15 July 2005.

Russell, Gordon. "An 1878 Map Reveals That Maybe Our Ancestors Were Right to Build on Higher Ground. Almost Every Place That Was Uninhabited in 1878 Flooded in 2005 after Katrina." *New Orleans Times-Picayune*, 3 November 2005, A1.

Starr, S. Frederick. "Bywater Neighborhood Boasts City's Last Plantation." *Preservation in Print*, April 2005, 16–19.

Thevenot, Brian. "The McDonogh Three." *New Orleans Times-Picayune*, 16 May 2004, A19.

———. "Unintended Consequences." *New Orleans Times-Picayune*, 17 May 2004, A1.

Trotta, Geri. "Visiting Plantation Houses—I." *Gourmet*, April 1982, 25–27, 144–54.

FILM

Stack, Jonathan, Liz Garbus, and Wilbert Rideau, dirs. *The Farm: Life inside Angola Prison*, 1998.


TOURIST INFORMATION AND PROMOTIONAL MATERIAL

Angola State Penitentiary Museum, <http://www.angolamuseum.org>. 7 February 2006.

Association for the Preservation of Historic Natchitoches, <http://www.preservenatchitoches.org/?page_id=8>. 11 February 2006.

Bishop's Lodge Resort and Spa, <http://www.bishopslodge.com/>. 18 August 2005.

Carnival Cruise Lines. <http://www.carnival.com/Default.aspx>. 30 November 2005.

Cracker Barrel Convenience Stores.<www.crackerbarrelcstores.com/travel.html>. 17 July 2005.

"Elvis Presley's Graceland Visitor's Guide."

"Elvis Presley's Graceland, Memphis Tennessee."

*Georgia's Heartland of the Confederacy: Leaders, Life, Legacy*. Tourist brochure published by the Athens Convention and Visitors Bureau. Athens: Georgia Press, n.d.

"History of Angola." <http://www.corrections.state.la.us/lsp/history.htm>. 26 August 2005.

"The Moores and the Presleys at Graceland," © 2000, Elvis Presley Enterprises. <www.elvisfacts.btinternet.co.uk/grace.htm>. 15 June 2003.

The Myrtles Plantation. <http://www.myrtlesplantation.com/>. 22 May 2006.

Office of the Deputy Warden for Administrative Services and the Classification Department. *The Angola Story*. Angola: Louisiana State Penitentiary, 1995, 1999.

Quaker Oats, <http://quakeroats.com/qfb_PressRoom/brandinfo/BrandDetail.cfm?BrandID=22&section=brandhistory>. 3 December 2005.

River Road African American Museum, <http://www.africanamerican museum.org/aboutmuseumpast.html>. 15 August 2005.

*A Visitor's Guide to Rowan Oak*. Oxford: University Publishing Center, University of Mississippi, ca. 2001.

# Index

(film): relationship of to earlier films about U.S. South, 81, 82; depiction of plantation house in, 81–83; depiction of whiteness in, 83

*Interview with the Vampire* (film): depiction of whites in, 83–85; depiction of people of color in, 84

Integration, 103–4, 187 (n. 24)

Jackson, Michael, 94

*Jezebel* (film): and film of *Gone with the Wind*, 76–77; depiction of racialized sexuality in, 77–80; depiction of black characters in, 78, 79–80; symbolism of slavery in, 80–81; relationship of to *Hush . . . Hush Sweet Charlotte*, 81

Johnson, Walter, 6–7, 144

Kammen, Michael, 55

Killen, Edgar Ray, 5

King, Grace, 25; origins of as writer, 26; relationship of with Charles Gayarré, 29, 169 (n. 16); and depiction of New Orleans, 173 (n. 98). *See also* "Bonne Maman"

Kirshenblatt-Gimblett, Barbara, 155–56

Ku Klux Klan, 6, 87

*Lady Baltimore* (Wister). *See* Wister, Owen

Laura Plantation, 62–63

Lee, General Robert E., 58

Leisure, changing concepts of, 42. *See also* Plantation tourism; Tourism

Lipsitz, George, 8

"Little Miss Sophie" (Dunbar), 33; interracial relationship in, 34; property in, 35–36

Local color, literature of, 6, 23–24. See also *Awakening, The*; "Bonne Maman"; "Little Miss Sophie"

Locke, John, 3

Long, Alecia P., 23, 36–37

Longwood Plantation, 60–62

Lost Cause, 29, 54

Lott, Eric, 95

Louisiana, 16; connections to Caribbean, 13, 14. *See also* Angola Plantation; Angola Rodeo; Creole; Creoles, of color; Creoles, white; Destrehan Plantation; Evergreen Plantation; Houmas House; Laura Plantation; Louisiana State Penitentiary at Angola; Melrose Plantation; New Orleans; Nottoway Plantation; Oak Alley Plantation; River Road African American Museum; San Francisco Plantation

Louisiana State Penitentiary at Angola, 135; history of as plantation, 135–36, 190 (n. 2); origins of as prison, 138; and "natural-life" sentences, 139–40; inmate labor at, 145; and normalization, 149–50, 157–58;

and possession, 154; tours of, 154–55; golf course at, 155; museum at, 156–57. *See also* Angola Rodeo

Lulu White's Octoroon Club. *See* Mahogany Hall

Lynching: increase in, 87; as tourist spectacle, 87–88, 108–9; souvenirs of, 88–89; and consumer culture, 89; and photography, 181 (n. 10)

MacCannell, Dean, 86

MacLeod, Paul, 96, 97, 100. *See also* Graceland Too

Mahogany Hall, 39–40, 52, 171 (n. 60). *See also* White, Lulu

"Mammy" icon, 57, 70–71, 174 (n. 11). *See also* Aunt Jemima

Marx, Karl, 8, 9–10

Mass culture, 6, 91. *See also* Consumer culture

Mays, Dr. Benjamin E., 76

McDaniel, Hattie, 106–7

McPherson, Tara, 17, 177–78 (n. 53)

Melrose Plantation, 69

Memory, black, 15, 32–33, 68; and plantation tourism, 55–56, 67–68; in *Wind Done Gone*, 74; and "whitewashed" plantations, 85; body as site of, 87, 88–89; at Graceland Too, 100, 101–2. *See also* Nostalgia; Souvenirs

Midlo Hall, Gwendolyn, 26–27

Minstrelsy, 109–10, 131. *See also* Blackface

Mississippi, 16, 90, 105; Natchez, 60; Holly Springs, 96. *See also* Graceland Too; Longwood Plantation; Rowan Oak.

Mitchell, Margaret, 76

Monticello, 4, 62, 69, 92

Morehouse College, 76

Morton, Jelly Roll, 39

Mount Vernon, 4, 54–55, 92

Native Americans: as slaveholders, 18, 107, 112, 167 (n. 59); and blackface, 112; Agrarian view of, 114–15; as represented in U.S. popular culture, 116, 120; Willa Cather's view of, 128. See also *Death Comes for the Archbishop*; Pokagon, Simon; *Professor's House, The*

New Orleans: landscape of, 1–2, 38; and hurricane Katrina, 19; history of sexuality in, 23; in work of William Faulkner, 23, 51; in work of Grace King, 25–26, 173 (n. 98); Creoles in, 27–28; in work of Alice Dunbar, 33; prostitution in after Storyville, 48–50; in national imaginary, 50–51; and Buffalo Soldiers, 111; slave pens in, 144. *See also* Storyville

Nora, Pierre, 101–2

Normalization, 149–50, 158

Nostalgia: history of term, 5; for Old South, 5–6, 33, 57, 86, 111; and black body as object of consumption, 10, 89; and sexuality, 17; as violent, 17, 140; "nostalgia for the present," 67;

"imperialist nostalgia," 131; and prison rodeo, 141; and western frontier, 187 (n. 23). *See also* Memory; Plantation tourism

Nottoway Plantation, 71

Oak Alley Plantation, 59, 60, 62, 67, 70, 83
O'Connor, Flannery, 56
Octoroons, 38, 39–40, 50, 51, 52, 80. *See also* Tragic octoroon
*Octoroon, The* (Boucicault), 81
*Old Louisiana* (Saxon), 72–73
Olmstead, Frederick Law, 57

Page, Thomas Nelson, 174 (n. 11)
Passing. *See* Racial passing
Performance: in *Plessy* case, 2; of slavery, 31–33, 68; in Storyville, 39–40; and plantation tourism, 70, 71; trans-Atlantic, 105, 115; at Angola Rodeo, 147–53
Pickett, Bill, 109, 150
Plaçage, 23, 34
Plantation: in U.S. South, 4; postslavery evolution of, 5, 10–11, 17–18, 20; and western frontier, 18; depicted in *The Awakening*, 25; depicted in "Bonne Maman," 25–26, 28–29; pulp fiction about, 56; and industrialism, 60; depicted in *Wind Done Gone*, 74; William Faulkner's, 103; and the Louisiana State Penitentiary at Angola, 135, 146, 158; and disciplinarity, 136; larger American plantation region, 159–60; in

work of Kara Walker, 175–76 (n. 31). *See also* Plantation tourism
Plantation tourism, 53; souvenirs of, 54, 70; origins of, 54–55; and memory, 55–56, 85; and nostalgia, 57, 60–61, 67; depiction of whites in, 58–59, 89; depiction of chattel slavery in, 59–67, 69–70, 71; and responses to tourists of color, 63, 175 (n. 18); African American responses to, 66–67. *See also* Graceland; Graceland Too
Plessy, Homer, 2, 3, 19, 38
*Plessy v. Ferguson*, 2–4
Pokagon, Simon, 114
Possession: definition of, 11; in *Absalom, Absalom!*, 11–13; and racial identity, 14–15; and race, 68; in *Jezebel*, 80; in *Professor's House, The*, 123–24; in *Death Comes for the Archbishop*, 133; and Louisiana State Penitentiary at Angola, 154
Presley, Elvis: dead body of, 90, 94; souvenirs of, 91, 98–99; racial ambiguity of, 91–92; impersonation of, 95–95, 99–100. *See also* Graceland; Graceland Too
Presley, Lisa Marie, 94
*Professor's House, The* (Cather), 116; property in, 117–18, 123–24; depiction of Native Americans in, 118–22, 123; origins of, 120; depiction of slavery in, 122–23, 133; possession in, 123, 124
Property: and personhood, 3–4, 7–

8, 35–36; human body as, 11, 12–13, 24–25, 30–31, 40, 43–44, 87, 117, 123–24, 131–33; and racial identity, 34–35, 94; intellectual, 74–75. *See also* Chattel slavery

Prostitution: relationship of to race, 28; opposed to slavery, 30; and consumer culture, 44–45; in New Orleans after Storyville, 48–50. *See also* Storyville; White slavery

Quadroons, 25, 29–30, 49, 171 (n. 61)

Queer. *See* Sexuality

Race: relationship of to chattel slavery, 6–8; as mobile signifier, 14–15, 68, 105–6; relationship of to gender, 22–23, 24–25, 77–78; and property rights, 34–35; and heterosexuality, 42–43; and origins of *Death Comes for the Archbishop*, 125

Racial impersonation, 103–6

Racial passing, 2, 40, 171 (n. 61)

Randall, Alice, 73–75

Ransom, John Crowe, 115

Rastus, 6

"Red Man's Greeting, The" (Pokagon). *See* Pokagon, Simon

*Red Men and White* (Wister). *See* Wister, Owen

Renan, Ernest, 67–68

Rideau, Wilbert, 138–39

River Road African American Museum, 66

Rodeo, origins and development of, 140–41. *See also* Angola Rodeo

Roediger, David, 122

Rose, Al, 41–42, 48, 171 (n. 60)

Rowan Oak, 103

Rutherford, Mildred, 58

San Francisco Plantation, 54, 63–64

*Sapphira and the Slave Girl* (Cather), 116, 133

Saxon, Lyle, 69. See also *Old Louisiana*

Scott, James C., 59

Segregation: and interracial sexuality, 21, 23, 42–43; in Indian Territory, 112; and Louisiana State Penitentiary at Angola, 139–40

Sexuality, interracial, 21, 23, 36–37; in *The Awakening*, 24–25; and Civil War, 37; heterosexual, 42–43; in pulp fiction about southern plantations, 56; in *Jezebel*, 77–78, 80; queer, 130–31. *See also* Plaçage; Prostitution; Storyville

"Significance of the Frontier in American History" (Turner). *See* Turner, Frederick Jackson

Slavery. *See* Chattel slavery

Slotkin, Richard, 140

Smith, Bessie, 90

Social death, 141, 144

Sontag, Susan, 52

*Soul Sister* (Halsell). *See* Halsell, Grace